DEC
Recommended Practices

A Comprehensive Guide for Practical Application

in Early Intervention/Early Childhood Special Education

Susan Sandall • Mary Louise Hemmeter • Barbara J. Smith • Mary E. McLean

Disclaimer

Funding for this publication came in part from grants from the U.S. Department of Education (grant nos. H324M.000051 and H324D.980033). The contents of this book do not necessarily reflect the views or policies of the U.S. Department of Education or the University of Colorado at Denver.

Office of Special
Education Programs

The Division for Early Childhood assumes no liability or risk that may be incurred as a consequence, directly or indirectly, of the use and application of any of the contents of this publication. DEC does not perform due diligence on advertisers or their products or services and cannot endorse or guarantee that their offerings are suitable or accurate.

Published and Distrbuted by

SOPRIS
WEST
EDUCATIONAL SERVICES

4093 Specialty Place
Longmont, CO 80504
(303) 651-2829
www.sopriswest.com

634 Eddy Avenue
Missoula, MT 59812-6696
(406) 243-5898
www.dec-sped.org

The Division for Early Childhood (DEC) a division of the Council for Exceptional Children, is an international membership organization for individuals who work with or on behalf of young children with disabilities and other special needs. Founded in 1973, DEC's mission is to promote policies and advance evidence-based practices that support families and enhance the optimal development of young children who have or are at risk for developmental delays and disabilities. Information about membership and other resources available can be found at www.dec-sped.org.

Contributors

. . . .

Linda Askew, M.A.
University of Colorado–Denver
Center for Collaborative Educational
   Leadership
1380 Lawrence Street, Suite 650
Denver, CO 80204

Stephen J. Bagnato, Ed.D.
Children's Hospital of Pittsburgh
The UCLID Center at the University of
   Pittsburgh
3705 5th Avenue
Pittsburgh, PA 15213

Alison Broudy Ramsey, M.A.
Orelena Hawks Puckett Institute
18A Regent Park Boulevard
Asheville, NC 28806

Camille Catlett, M.A.
CB #8185
University of North Carolina
Chapel Hill, NC 27599-8185

Carl J. Dunst, Ph.D.
Orelena Hawks Puckett Institute
18A Regent Park Boulevard
Asheville, NC 28806

Linda Frederick, B.A.
124 West 5th Avenue
Denver, CO 80204

Gloria Harbin, Ph.D.
University of North Carolina
FPG Child Development Center
137 East Franklin Street
Chapel Hill, NC 27514

Heidi Heissenbuttel, M.A.
Sewall Child Development Center
1360 Vine
Denver, CO 80206

Mary Louise Hemmeter, Ph.D.
University of Illinois–Urbana-Champaign
61 Children's Research Center
51 Gerty Drive
Champaign, IL 61820

Mary E. McLean, Ph.D.
University of Wisconsin–Milwaukee
Department of Exceptional Education
P.O. Box 413
Milwaukee, WI 53201

Robin A. McWilliam, Ph.D.
Department of Pediatrics
Vanderbilt University Medical Center
Suite 426, Medical Center South
2100 Pierce Avenue
Nashville, TN 37232-3573

Patricia S. Miller, Ph.D.
Department of Special Education
School of Education, Cecil Street
North Carolina Central University
Durham, NC 27707

John T. Neisworth, Ph.D.
Penn State University
Special Education Program
207 Cedar
University Park, PA 16802

Christine Salisbury, Ph.D.
UIC Child and Family Development
    Center (MC 628)
1640 West Roosevelt Road, Room 336
University of Illinois–Chicago
Chicago, IL 60608

Patricia S. Salcedo, M.A.
Supporting Early Education Delivery
    Systems (SEEDS Project)
Sacramento County Office of Education
P.O. Box 269003
Sacramento, CA 95826

Susan Sandall, Ph.D.
University of Washington
College of Education
Box 353600
Seattle, WA 98195

Rosa Milagros (Amy) Santos, Ph.D.
University of Illinois–Urbana
    Champaign
Department of Special Education
61 Children's Research Center
51 Gerty Drive
Champaign, IL 61820

Barbara J. Smith, Ph.D.
University of Colorado–Denver, School
    of Education
Center for Collaborative Educational
    Leadership
1380 Lawrence Street, Suite 650
Denver, CO 80204

Patricia Snyder, Ph.D.
Louisiana State University Health
    Sciences Center
School of Allied Health Professions
1900 Gravier Street
New Orleans, LA 70112

Vicki D. Stayton, Ph.D.
Western Kentucky University
College of Education and Behavioral
    Sciences
#1 Big Red Way
Bowling Green, KY 42101

Kathleen Stremel, M.A.
Western Oregon University
Teaching Research
345 North Monmouth Avenue
Monmouth, OR 97361

Carol M. Trivette, Ph.D.
Orelena Hawks Puckett Institute
128 South Sterling Street
Morganton, NC 28655

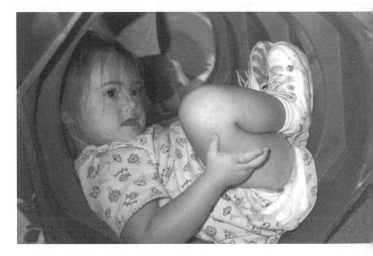

Gail Whitman, M.S.
Douglas County School District
8218 Carder Court
Littleton, CO 80125

Mark Wolery, Ph.D.
Vanderbilt University
Department of Special Education
Box 328
Peabody College
Nashville, TN 37203

Acknowledgments

· · · · · · · · · ·

DEC wishes to recognize those who have given of their expertise, time, and resources to help identify Recommended Practices and to produce this book. First, we wish to acknowledge the vision, leadership, and hard work of the late Dr. David Sexton. As DEC Vice President, President Elect, and President, Dr. Sexton encouraged DEC to expand our products and training efforts in order to impact the quality of services and outcomes for young children with special needs and their families. In June 1998 he joined Drs. Barbara Smith, Susan Sandall, and Mary McLean at the DEC Executive Offices to write a grant proposal to the U.S. Department of Education that resulted in funding for the research efforts that led to the Recommended Practices and this book. In addition to serving on the Management Team of the project, Dr. Sexton also directed the project's extensive literature review activities associated with determining the scientific support for early intervention/early childhood special education practice. This book and the associated other products and training that are available to the field are a result of Dr. Sexton's vision, and will contribute to the improvement of services to and outcomes for young children with special needs and their families for years to come.

Eight individuals managed the overall initiative, serving as investigators and methodology consultants: Dr. Barbara J. Smith, Principal Investigator; Drs. Mary McLean, Susan Sandall, and David Sexton served as Co-Investigators; Dr. Sam Odom coordinated the Strand Chairs and served as a methodology consultant; and Drs. Pat Snyder, Phil Strain, and Bruce Thompson served as methodology consultants. Thirteen experts in the field served as Strand Chairs and coordinated the work of the Recommended Practices strands: Drs. Stephen J. Bagnato, Mary Beth Bruder, Carl J. Dunst, Gloria Harbin, Robin A. McWilliam, Patricia S. Miller, John T. Neisworth, Christine Salisbury, Rosa Milagros (Amy) Santos, Vicki D. Stayton, Kathleen Stremel, Carol M. Trivette, and Mark Wolery. Dr. Mary Louise Hemmeter joined the project as it moved into outreach and dissemination activities.

Dedicated staff on the first edition included those at the University of Colorado at Denver—Alison Broudy Ramsey, Linda Frederick, and Carl Sumi; those at the University of Washington—Joan Ronk and Kari Moe; the University of Wisconsin at Milwaukee—Becky Reimbold and Ali Faber; and Louisiana State University Health Sciences Center—Marcia Lobman, Jeff Oremland, and Sally Fussell.

Members of the DEC Executive Board, Committee Chairs, and Editors who served over the two-year period of the project supported and, in some cases, directly assisted the effort. They were Lucinda Bernheimer, Patricia Blasco, Linda Brault, Jerry Christensen,

Laurie Dinnebeil, Lourdes Gonzalez, Sarah Hadden, Mary Louise Hemmeter, Gail Joseph, Jennifer Kilgo, John Killoran, Maggie LaMontagne, Diana LaRocco, Rich Lewis, Susan McBride, Mary McEvoy, Mary McLean, Robin A. McWilliam, Billie Navojosky, Micki Ostrosky, Philip Printz, Maurine Ballard-Rosa, Sharon Rosenkoetter, Beth Rous, Gwen Wheeler Russell, Susan Sandall, Rosa Milagros (Amy) Santos, David Sexton, Vicki D. Stayton, Judy Swett, Vicki Turbiville, Laura Vagianos, and Amy Whitehead.

The list of individuals and organizations who provided thoughtful advice and assistance to this project is expansive. All of the strand leaders made valuable contributions to the second edition. Sarah Mulligan, DEC Executive Director, participated in many of the planning meetings for this edition. Her perspective and help were greatly appreciated. Hazel Jones, Chair of DEC's Publications Committee, contributed mightily to this effort. Hazel and members of the editorial boards of DEC publications read drafts of the new edition and offered useful suggestions. The reviewers were Drs. Mary Jane Brotherson, William H. Brown, Ilene Schwartz, Scott Snyder, Phillipa Campbell, Katherine McCormick, Margaret Werts, D. Michael Malone, Vicki Stayton, Michaelene M. Ostrosky, Harriet Able-Boone, and Jennifer Kilgo.

We also thank Camille Catlett, Linzy Abraham, Patsy Pierce, and Libby Simmons. Camille spearheaded our effort to add resources to this edition of the book. Based on feedback from readers of the first edition, we realized that practitioners, family members, and teacher trainers often are looking for additional materials to help them adopt and use the Recommended Practices in their own programs. Thank you Camille.

The team in Denver continued to provide the support and encouragement to get the job done. Linda Askew, Project Coordinator for the Bridging the Gap Project, managed the people, paper, e-mails, and schedules that were involved in bringing the second edition to completion. Linda did a tremendous job. Andrea Nelson, Jill Giacomini, and Julie Walden added their considerable support. We thank you all.

Sopris West publishing helped our vision become a reality with an incredibly talented team of individuals who provided us with their expertise, support, and deadlines. Thank you for your help, patience, and keeping us on track.

Thanks, also, to the more than 370 individuals who completed the field validation survey that contained 125 items!

Finally, approximately 150 other individuals participated and assisted in the project as focus group participants and literature review coders or validators. We want to also thank all the people at the Sewall Child Development Center and Douglas County School District who worked with us for three years on the Bridging the Gap Project in order to learn the lessons presented throughout this new edition. Their hands-on experiences with the Recommended Practices and this book contributed to what we hope are helpful suggestions for using the Recommended Practices. *All these individuals and groups are listed in Appendix A.*

Thank you to all the people who have taken time from their busy schedules to help DEC serve the early childhood community by recommending practices that should lead to better outcomes for young children with special needs and their families.

Contents

· · · · · · · · · ·

Contents

Indirect Supports

Part III: Using the DEC Recommended Practices

Part IV: Concluding Thoughts and Appendicies

Part I:

Identifying the DEC Recommended Practices

Images of Early Intervention/Early Childhood Special Education

Teacher

Steve pulls into a parking space at Walters School. He reaches in the back seat of his car for a plastic crate filled with file folders. As he walks through the door of the school he remembers that he once taught preschoolers in this building. Now he has a desk and file cabinets. He spends his days with children at many different schools, centers, and homes. Once or twice a day he stops in to exchange file folders, grab toys, and check his messages.

Today he spent most of the day at Green Tree, a child care center in a small town about 10 miles away. There are four children with disabilities enrolled at the center, and Steve is their itinerant early childhood special education teacher from the school district. Steve spent time watching the children, leading a couple of small group activities, reviewing notes, and talking with the teachers. He introduced one little boy to a picture schedule to help him participate in daily activities. It seemed like the schedule would help him so Steve demonstrated for the teacher, watched the teacher try it, and told her that he would check in with her in a few days.

During the children's naptime, Steve and one of the teachers phoned Jason's mother, Ms. Thomas, to see if they could arrange a meeting to review his IEP. They arrived at a few tentative times that Steve will confirm with the speech therapist and the school district's special education director. They also got to spend a few minutes comparing notes and delighting in Jason's growing vocabulary. Ms. Thomas said that she thinks that Jason's improving language has made a big difference in his behavior. Steve makes a note to himself and asks Ms. Thomas if she will share that information with the whole team at the IEP meeting.

Steve's caseload includes some children under the age of 3 whose early intervention program is administered by the county school district's office. Now Steve replaces file folders in his cabinet and retrieves a folder for one of those children, Emma. He will stop to see Emma and her family on his way home from work. Emma is 2 years old and has Down syndrome. She stays at home with her mother during the day. Emma's mother speaks primarily Vietnamese, and the family has requested that home visits be

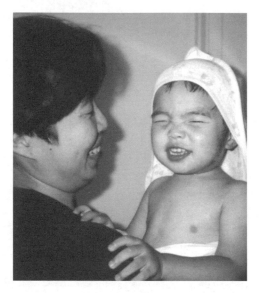

scheduled for the end of the work day so that Emma's father, who is bilingual, can participate. Steve looks forward to this visit. Emma recently began to walk, and home visits usually begin with a cheerful show of her new talent. Last week Emma's grandmother was at the home visit for the first time. Emma took turns taking steps to her mother, father, grandmother, and big sister. What a fun visit. This week Steve will bring the video camera and make a video that can be shared with the consulting physical therapist.

Steve often thinks about how much his job has changed. Sometimes, he misses his classroom. But working at child care centers and visiting homes has opened his eyes. He's glad his supervisor understands the time and energy this new job requires.

Family Member

Teri gives Anthony just one more kiss on the forehead; says good-bye to her sister, Kim; and then turns and opens the door. Cathy Johnson, the early intervention service coordinator, is sitting in her parked car waiting for Teri to come out of the house. Cathy is taking Teri to the IEP meeting at Prescott School. Long before Anthony's third birthday,

Teri had begun to worry about this day. This IEP meeting signaled the end of early intervention for Anthony and the beginning of services from the public schools. School! How could Anthony be going to school?

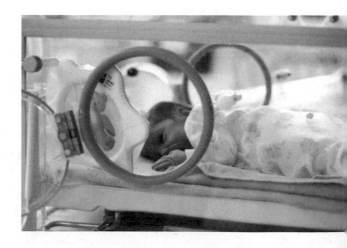

It is hard to believe that Anthony is almost 3 years old. Teri thought back to the night of his birth. The premature arrival of her little boy had changed everything in Teri's life. Not only did he arrive early, but also he was in the hospital for a long time.

When he finally did come home from the hospital, he was so little and fragile. He was still on a monitor, and Teri was afraid to go to sleep, thinking that the monitor would go off and she wouldn't wake up. Her sister and mother had helped her a lot during that time. That's also the time she first met Cathy, who works for the county's early intervention program. Cathy has been there almost from the beginning. Teri cannot imagine what it will be like when Cathy no longer comes to help her with Anthony.

That isn't the only change that Teri is facing. She has been accepted into a training program to become a nurse's aide. She will be in the next class to begin the program. Anthony isn't the only member of the family who is going to school! That's another reason that the IEP meeting is so important. Teri has to be certain that Anthony is happy and is getting everything he needs. Only then will she be able to concentrate on becoming a nurse's aide.

This IEP meeting is really important. Last week, Cathy told Teri that a lady from the school district wanted her to be on a special team that the school was putting together. Cathy said the school wanted to have the best early childhood services they could, and Teri was being asked to be one of the parents on this team that would learn about good programs and make suggestions for Anthony's school. Well, there won't be a lot of extra time in Teri's life once she starts the nurse's aide program. But how could she say no? This would give her the opportunity to see that Anthony, and other children too, would have the best possible services. Teri was going to find out more information about this team today.

Teri closes the door behind her and walks toward Cathy's car. She smiles to herself. It actually feels like more than an end to something. It feels like a beginning too. . . .

Administrator

As the new Director of Special Education for the Green Valley School District, Janice Logan is responsible for ensuring that all eligible children with disabilities receive a free appropriate public education (FAPE) as defined by federal and state laws and regulations. Until 5 years ago, none of the elementary schools served children under the age of five. Today they all do, using a variety of models including school-based segregated classrooms and community-based itinerant services.

Janice has little previous experience or training in early childhood. Like all administrators, Janice has more work to do than time or resources. When she was learning about her new job, she often faced a series of crises. However, since she didn't know much about early childhood services, she decided to focus for 4 months on learning more about how to appropriately serve the young children with disabilities and their families in her district. What Janice did know about early childhood was that high quality early experiences lead to better school outcomes.

During those months Janice did three things: (1) created a supervisory position in early childhood special education; (2) learned about early childhood practices that promote positive outcomes; and (3) identified early childhood/early childhood special education leaders, stakeholders, and resources either in the education system or in the community.

First, she talked with principals and learned that the National Association for Elementary School Principals as well as several other national organizations had position statements encouraging school districts to have a separate unit and supervisor to oversee educational programs for young children. Following that recommendation, the district had recently designed an early childhood unit and hired a supervisor who was

responsible for programs for children under the age of 8 including Title I; Even Start, the state funded preschool program; kindergarten; and 1st and 2nd grade. However, no one had thought to include special education services. Janice decided to hire an early childhood special educator (ECSE) to work with the early childhood education (ECE) supervisor and decided that the special education and related services needed by young children would be a collaborative effort of the special education and early childhood units.

Second, Janice improved her knowledge of effective practices for young children with disabilities and their families by hiring and learning from the ECSE supervisor. As she learned more, Janice encouraged and supported the purchase of materials and training related to implementing recommended practices in ECSE and ECE.

Third, Janice knew that in order to create new and improved services the district would need to make some changes. She knew about systems change since she had been involved in the restructuring of special education in her previous job. She knew that she had to bring individuals together to share in making systems change decisions. A team of individuals could share ideas, resources, and vision and create commitment to a new way of doing things. Janice invited the early childhood supervisor to co-sponsor the development of an early childhood recommended practices team of parents, teachers, related services personnel, and community administrators from Head Start and child care. She invited several parents including Teri, a new parent coming into the preschool program from the county's Part C program. She also invited Steve, an ECSE teacher who had been through the transition from classroom teacher to itinerant teacher. She invited Rena from the University. This team will begin meeting monthly to create a vision of including all children with disabilities in all early childhood services and programs. Janice also hopes that this team will begin to identify the key issues for the district and help identify some solutions.

Now, at the end of the 4 months, Janice knows more about high quality practices for improving outcomes for young children with disabilities and their families. She turns her attention to other areas of need knowing that the ECE and ECSE supervisors and the recommended practices team will monitor progress and let her know when they need her support.

Higher Education Faculty Member

Over the course of a week, Rena receives calls from a child care provider, a public school administrator, an early interventionist, and a Head Start director. They are all calling to inquire about the University's teacher education program in early childhood special education. The child care provider has suddenly found her center serving several children with disabilities, and there is no one on staff who has any experience working with these children or with their itinerant teachers. The early interventionist has just been hired and does not have the appropriate certification. The program has given her 1 year to complete the requirements. The Head Start Director is calling because of the new mandate requiring more advanced training for lead teachers. And Janice, the public school administrator, wants to talk about some ideas she has for retooling her current teachers.

While the early interventionist is calling about the teacher education program for herself, the Head Start Director and child care provider are inquiring about training opportunities for their staff. Rena describes the early childhood special education certification program including the entrance requirements, courses and field experiences, and the student teaching requirement. While the certification program meets the needs of some of the people who have called, it does not work for all of them.

In fact, Rena and Janice, the public school administrator, have a long conversation about the curriculum itself and whether or not it addresses the needs of teachers who will spend a great deal of time working with other adults. Janice tells her that several of the district's preschool teachers are reluctant to leave their classrooms for itinerant positions.

In addition, the callers tell her that the schedule and location of the courses often conflict with work schedules. Sometimes the entrance requirements and/or prerequisites prevent individuals from enrolling, and the program is too lengthy to meet the immediate needs of some individuals. Rena tries her best to help the callers identify alternative options.

At the next early childhood faculty meeting, Rena discusses the issues that have been raised in her conversations with these and other early childhood professionals. The faculty has grown increasingly aware of the diverse needs of individuals pursuing educational opportunities in the field of early childhood special education. They are committed to working with the various early childhood systems that provide services to young children with disabilities and their families. They realize that they are going to have to look at a variety of options including distance learning, evening and weekend courses, on-site training and technical assistance, and alternative routes to certification. They have a big job ahead of them.

Rena, Janice, Teri, and Steve all find themselves in the midst of the changing field of Early Intervention/Early Childhood Special Education. They have a wealth of knowledge and skills, but they find themselves searching for new ways to meet today's challenges. Our hope is that DEC Recommended Practices: A Comprehensive Guide for Practical Application will provide information and direction for meeting these challenges.

An Introduction to the DEC Recommended Practices

· · · · · · · · · ·

Susan Sandall and Barbara J. Smith

The vignettes in the previous sections provide glimpses of the challenges, complexities, and rewards of living and working with young children with disabilities. Families and educators share the goal of improved development and learning outcomes for these children. The meanings we attach to such outcomes—improved social competence, independence, problem solving, and enhanced family functioning—may differ. Similarly, the practices we select and use may differ based on our knowledge and beliefs. However, some practices are more likely to yield positive outcomes than other practices. The purpose of this book is to provide guidance on effective practices for attaining our shared goal of improved development and learning outcomes for young children with disabilities and their families.

Evidence from a variety of sources supports the connection between early learning experiences and later school and work performance. In this book we bring together those guiding, Recommended Practices—based on research evidence and shared beliefs—to help educators, other practitioners, families, and administrators provide high-quality, productive learning experiences.

At the beginning of the 1990s, several members of DEC undertook a project to identify Recommended Practices in early intervention/early childhood special education. The Practices were compiled in two products: a DEC document first published in 1993 (DEC Task Force on Recommended Practices, 1993), and a later book that extended the underlying concepts (Odom & McLean, 1996). As the 20th Century drew to a close, we asked several questions including, "Are the Practices current?" "What else have we learned?" and "Are the Practices being used?" We realized that widespread adoption of the Practices had not occurred. We wondered why and arrived at three possible challenges to widespread adoption. First, the Practices were not based on a systematic and thorough synthesis of the knowledge base. Second, we had not done an adequate job of translating and disseminating the information to those individuals who have the actual responsibility for educating young children. Third, we had not fully appreciated the administrative and systems change supports that are necessary for the sustained delivery of high-quality services to children and their families.

Inspired by the goal of improved outcomes for young children with disabilities and their families, we designed a new project to review the research literature, integrate the literature with those practices identified as critical by our various stakeholders, develop and disseminate user-friendly products, and address the administrative and systems change foundations necessary for long-term adoption and use of quality practices.

Photo by David Naylor

This book is part of a series of materials and activities aimed at bridging the gap between research and practice. Our primary goal was to identify practices that are related to better outcomes for young children with disabilities, their families, and the personnel who serve them. We identified the practices through focus groups of key stakeholders: practitioners, researchers, administrators, and family members. These practices were integrated with those found during our extensive review of the scientific literature. The resulting Recommended Practices underwent a field validation. (More information about the process is found in Chapter 2.)

Organization of This Book

The number and organization of the strands as they appear in this book reflect changes in the project from its original conceptualization through identification and validation of the Practices. We began the project with a view of the field of early intervention/early childhood special education as comprised of *direct services* as well as *indirect supports* that are necessary for the direct services to occur.

Direct Services

We began the project with six categories, or strands, of direct service practices: child-focused interventions, family-based practices, cultural/linguistic sensitivity, interdisciplinary models, technology applications, and learning environments. It soon became apparent that we needed to add the category of assessment.

Cultural/linguistic sensitivity crossed all other categories. It also represented a fundamental value. In collaboration with the strand participants, it was decided that the practices identified by this focus group would be embedded within the other categories rather than have this category stand apart from the others.

Learning environments are the places where children experience learning opportunities that promote and enhance behavioral and developmental competencies.

Members of this focus group identified many critical practices. At the synthesis phase of the project, we recognized the consistency of practices in this strand with those in other strands. Consequently, in collaboration with the strand participants it was decided that practices related to learning environments would be embedded throughout the other categories of practices.

Thus, we now have five *direct services* strands:
1. Assessment
2. Child-Focused Practices
3. Family-Based Practices
4. Interdisciplinary Models
5. Technology Applications

Indirect Supports

At the beginning of the project we adopted the concept of indirect supports to be those fundamentals that are necessary for high-quality direct services to occur. We organized the concept of indirect supports into three groupings: policy and procedures; personnel preparation; and systems change, maintenance, and leadership climate. The scientific focus groups generated many important practices. It became clear, however, that two of our original groupings were not necessarily distinct. Thus we combined two of the strands to form the strand of policies, procedures, and systems change.

The third original indirect support strand, personnel preparation, also presented us with an interesting challenge. In 1995, DEC, in collaboration with the National Association for the Education of Young Children (NAEYC) and the Association of Teacher Educators (ATE), developed and validated personnel standards for the early childhood special educator (DEC, NAEYC & ATE, 2000). These standards represent the necessary *content or competencies* (i.e., *knowledge and skills*) needed by EI/ECSE personnel. These standards are found on the DEC Web site (www.dec-sped.org). Chapter 9 contains the Recommended Practices for the *design and delivery* of preservice and inservice training programs for EI/ECSE personnel. These two sets of personnel practices (i.e., knowledge and skills, and design and delivery) should be used as companion pieces.

Thus, we arrived at two strands of *indirect supports:*
1. Policies, Procedures, and Systems Change
2. Personnel Preparation

Our model of professional practices needed for effective and successful EI/ECSE is illustrated in Figure 1. The outer ring represents practices related to indirect supports. These practices are the infrastructure that must be in place to support and sustain the direct services. Thus, inside the model are those direct services practices that impact children and families on a daily basis.

Figure 1.

DEC'S Recommended Practices

Direct Services Strands: Assessment, Child-Focused Practices, Family-Based Practices, Interdisciplinary Models, Technology Applications

Indirect Supports Strands: Policies, Procedures, Systems Change, and Personnel Preparation

Policies, Procedures,
and Systems Change

Assessment
Child-Focused Practices
Family-Based Practices
Interdisciplinary Models
Technology Applications

Personnel Preparation

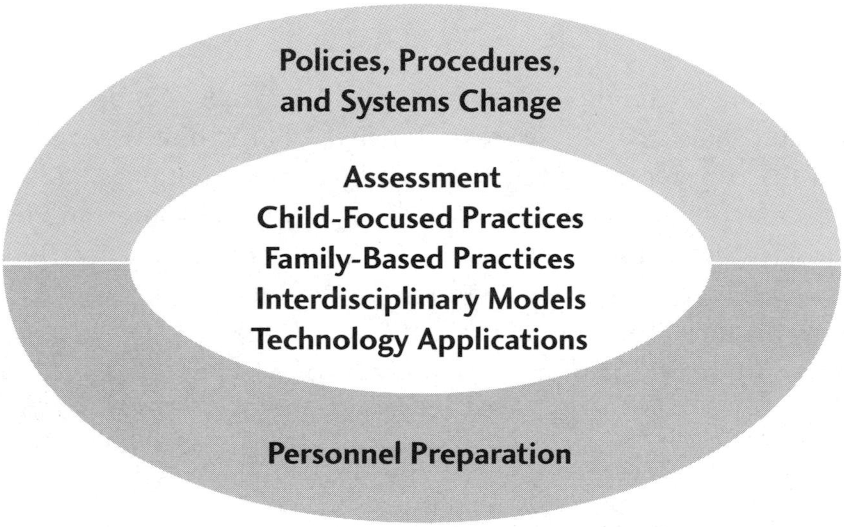

Age Grouping

At the outset of the project, we expected that age range (i.e., birth to 3 and 3 through 5) would be an important characteristic by which to group the practices. However, this did not occur. Our focus groups discussed the issue of age and whether or not birth to 3 and preschool practices should be separated. Participants noted the similarities as well as the differences between services for infants and toddlers as compared to preschool-age children. More often than not, participants concluded that the Recommended Practices spanned the full age range. Thus, in this book we have not separated the age groups. However, the examples after the Practices include both age groups.

Format of Chapters

The first two chapters describe: (1) the contexts for the DEC Recommended Practices, and (2) the methods we used to identify the Recommended Practices. The next seven chapters describe the specific Recommended Practices, beginning with an introduction written by the research Strand Chairs. Their introductions include the organizing principles or key features that serve as the foundation for each strand. A list of the Recommended Practices follows the introduction in each chapter. The Practices are grouped under unifying statements. This list of practices is followed by a glossary of terms and an annotated list of resources. Following most of the Practices there are examples of the Practice. These are provided to help clarify the meaning of the Practice.

We and our colleagues have produced a number of products and materials designed to bridge the gap that too often exists between research evidence and everyday practice. The products include a program assessment guide (Hemmeter, Joseph, Smith, & Sandall, 2001), a videotape that illustrates some of the child-focused practices (DEC, 2001), and a guide for applying the Recommended Practices in personnel preparation programs (Stayton, Miller, & Dinnebeil, 2002). A collection of articles describing the research basis of the Practices appeared in the *Journal of Early Intervention* in 2002 (McLean, Snyder, Smith, & Sandall, 2002; Odom & Strain, 2002; Sandall, Smith, McLean, & Broudy Ramsey, 2002; Smith et al., 2002; Snyder, Thompson, McLean, & Smith, 2002). The list of research articles that were reviewed for this project are now found on the DEC Web site (www.dec-sped.org). The *Young Exceptional Children Monograph Series* (Horn & Jones, in press; Horn, Ostrosky, & Jones, 2003; Ostrosky & Horn, 2002; Ostrosky & Sandall, 2001; Sandall & Ostrosky, 1999; Sandall & Ostrosky, 2000) links the Recommended Practices with research-based, practitioner-oriented articles. Accompanying this book will be a workbook for assessing a program's current use of the DEC Recommended Practices and improving the program's services to young children with disabilities (Hemmeter, Smith, Sandall, & Askew, in press).

In this book, we provide a number of tools that we hope will further assist teachers, therapists, family members, administrators, and others. First, the Practices are enhanced with examples. These *examples* are meant to clarify the Practices. Be aware that the examples represent *some* of the ways that practices are enacted. These examples are *not* the *only* way.

Second, the Practices are followed by an annotated list of *resources* compiled by Camille Catlett and her colleagues. Several sources informed the selection of resources. Some were identified by contributing authors and others were suggested by knowledgeable administrators, faculty members, community partners, and family members throughout the country. Many selections came from Systems Change in Personnel Preparation archives at the FPG Child Development Institute in Chapel Hill, North Carolina, a working collection that has been reviewed by early intervention colleagues from more than 30 states.

Guiding principles used in the review and selection of resources include reflection of family-centered practices, support for family and consumer participation, and responsiveness to cultural and linguistic diversity. Also, many resources incorporate the latest technology applications and offer great promise. We recognize that many other resources are available or are "in the works." And, we were not able to include single articles. We encourage you to review journals such as *Young Exceptional Children, Young Children*, and *Teaching Exceptional Children* for practical applications.

Part III of this book is designed to provide the reader with information on how to use the DEC Recommended Practices. It includes lessons we have learned, strategies for assessing one's own practice as well as program-wide practices, and two checklists. Learning from school and agency personnel, we found that adoption of the DEC Recommended Practices can assume many forms and must be tied to self-assessment and action planning. The information in Part III is intended to assist in improving practices and outcomes for children and families and the personnel who work with them. This section includes three chapters:

- **Chapter 10**
  Real-Life Experiences: Tips for Using the DEC Recommended Practices
- **Chapter 11**
  Using the DEC Recommended Practices for Program Assessment and Improvement
- **Chapter 12**
  Checklists for Family Members and Administrators
    - *Administrator's Essentials*
    - *Parent Checklist*

Chapter 10 provides an overview of our work with two programs in the Denver, Colorado, area. Our work with these two programs was designed to serve two purposes. First, we wanted to understand how programs might go about implementing the Recommended Practices. Specifically, we wanted to know what types of supports programs might need and the steps they might take to fully implement the Practices. Our second purpose was to get input and feedback from local programs about the materials we developed to support the DEC Recommended Practices. Many of the revisions of this book are a direct result of the input and feedback we received from these programs. Chapter 10 provides an overview of our work with the programs, the results of that work, and most important, the lessons we learned from our work with them.

Chapter 11, "Using the DEC Recommended Practices for Program Assessment and Improvement," provides a framework for using the Practices for the purposes of program improvement. This chapter builds on and expands an earlier publication, *DEC Recommended Practices Program Assessment: Improving Practices for Young Children With Special Needs and Their Families* (Hemmeter, Joseph, Smith, & Sandall, 2001). We build on the lessons learned in community-based programs about how programs can assess themselves on the Recommended Practices and use that assessment information to develop a program improvement or action plan. We provide some examples of ways to conduct assessments and planning. (A complete set of forms and instructions is provided in Hemmeter, Smith, Sandall, & Askew, in preparation. This new workbook will be available from the Division for Early Childhood.)

The final chapter of this section, Chapter 12, provides specific tools for administrators and families. "The Administrator's Essentials" checklist is designed to be used by program administrators, policy makers, and others in leadership positions to ensure that policies and procedures are in place that will support the implementation of high-quality practices at the local level. The "Parent Checklist" is designed to be used by parents and other caregivers as they observe their child's existing program or visit programs as part of the enrollment process. In addition, this checklist provides parents with important issues that they can address in talking with professionals about their child's current or future program.

Summary

The Recommended Practices listed and described in this book are the result of an effort that integrated the best available research evidence with knowledge gained through experience. It is our aim that teachers, therapists, family members, administrators, researchers, and those in personnel preparation will take these practices, learn about them, and put them into practice.

References

Division for Early Childhood (DEC). (2001). *DEC recommended practices video: Selected strategies for teaching young children with special needs.* Longmont, CO: Sopris West.

Division for Early Childhood (DEC), National Association for the Education of Young Children (NAEYC), & the Association of Teacher Educators (ATE). (2000). *Personnel standards for early education and early intervention: Guidelines for licensure in early childhood special education.* http://www.dec-sped.org.

Division for Early Childhood (DEC) Task Force on Recommended Practices. (Eds.). (1993). *DEC recommended practices: Indicators of quality in programs for infants and young children with special needs and their families.* Reston, VA: Council for Exceptional Children (CEC).

Hemmeter, M. L., Smith, B. J., Sandall, S., & Askew, L. R. (in preparation). *DEC recommended practices: A program assessment workbook.*

Hemmeter, M. L, Joseph, G., Smith, B. J., & Sandall, S. R. (2001). *DEC recommended practices program assessment: Improving practices for young children with special needs and their families.* Longmont, CO: Sopris West.

Horn, E., & Jones, H. A. (Eds.). (in press). *The Young Exceptional Children Monograph Series No. 6: Interdisciplinary Teams.* Longmont, CO: Sopris West.

Horn, E., Ostrosky, M. M., & Jones, H. (Eds.). (2003). *The Young Exceptional Children Monograph Series No. 5: Family-based practices.* Longmont, CO: Sopris West.

McLean, M. E., Snyder, P., Smith, B. J., & Sandall, S. R. (2002). The DEC recommended practices in early intervention/early childhood special education: Social validation. *Journal of Early Intervention, 25,* 120-128.

Odom, S. L., & McLean, M. E. (1996). *Early intervention/early childhood special education: Recommended practices.* Austin, TX: Pro-Ed.

Odom, S. L., & Strain, P. S. (2002). Evidence-based practice in early intervention/early childhood special education: Single-subject design research. *Journal of Early Intervention, 25,* 151-160.

Ostrosky, M. M., & Horn, E. (Eds.). (2002). *The Young Exceptional Children Monograph Series No. 4: Assessment: Gathering meaningful information.* Longmont, CO: Sopris West.

Ostrosky, M. M., & Sandall, S. (Eds.). (2001). *The Young Exceptional Children Monograph Series No. 3: Teaching strategies: What to do to support young children's development.* Longmont, CO: Sopris West.

Sandall, S., McLean, M., & Smith, B. (Eds.). (2000). *DEC recommended practices in early intervention/early childhood special education.* Longmont, CO: Sopris West.

Sandall, S., & Ostrosky, M. M. (Eds.). (1999). *The Young Exceptional Children Monograph Series No. 1: Practical ideas for addressing challenging behavior.* Longmont, CO: Sopris West.

Sandall, S., & Ostrosky, M. M. (Eds.). (2000). *The Young Exceptional Children Monograph Series No. 2: Natural environments and inclusion.* Longmont, CO: Sopris West.

Sandall, S. R., Smith, B. J., McLean, M. E., & Broudy Ramsey, A. (2002). Qualitative research in early intervention/early childhood special education. *Journal of Early Intervention, 25,* 129-136.

Smith, B. J., Strain, P. S., Snyder, P., Sandall, S. R., McLean, M. E., Broudy Ramsey, A., & Sumi, W. C. (2002). DEC recommended practices: A review of nine years of EI/ECSE research literature. *Journal of Early Intervention, 25,* 108-119.

Snyder, P., Thompson, B., McLean, M. E., & Smith, B. J. (2002). Examination of quantitative methods used in early intervention research: Linkages with recommended practices. *Journal of Early Intervention, 25,* 137-150.

Stayton, V. D., Miller, P. S., & Dinnebeil, L. A. (Eds.). (2002). *Personnel preparation in early childhood special education: Implementing the DEC recommended practices.* Longmont, CO: Sopris West.

Chapter 1

DEC's Recommended Practices: The Context for Change

. . . .

Susan Sandall, Mary E. McLean, Rosa Milagros (Amy) Santos, and Barbara J. Smith

DEC's Recommended Practices are based on two key sources. One source is the scientific literature on effective practices for young children with disabilities, their families, and the personnel who work with them. The second source is the knowledge and experience of researchers and other stakeholders. That is, the Practices are based on a current synthesis of scientific *and* experiential knowledge. Still, there are other contextual variables that influence the Practices. In this chapter we examine some of those influences.

A basic premise underlying the definition and dissemination of Recommended Practices is recognition of the relationship between early experiences and later outcomes. There is a clear link between the quality of an early childhood program and child outcomes (Bowman, Donovan, & Burns, 2000; Shonkoff & Phillips, 2000). Defining Recommended Practices for the field of early intervention/early childhood special education (EI/ECSE) is guided by an intention to identify practices that result in quality programs and thus have a positive impact on both child and family outcomes.

DEC's Recommended Practices involve the integration of the best available research with knowledge gained through experience. Research evidence and experience are both guided by and interpreted through the context of history and values. Our aim is to provide a synthesis of Recommended Practices that informs everyday practices.

The Changing Nature of Early Intervention and Education

. . . .

Early intervention and early childhood special education have been shaped by history, legislation, and by society's changing views about young children with or without disabilities and other special needs and their families. We often trace our historical roots to the early nonprofit efforts in communities as well as to the establishment of federally-funded model demonstration programs for young children. The model programs, first funded by the Bureau of Education for the Handicapped of the U.S. Office of Education in the 1960s, were created to demonstrate the feasibility of various models for serving young children with disabilities. Over the past 40 years, these programs have exerted a strong influence on the *look* of EI/ECSE. However, model programs reached only some children. Federal law extended services to *all* eligible children with disabilities in 1986 (Hebbeler, Smith, & Black, 1991).

The legislative history dates back to a few state laws passed in the 1970s: the passage in 1975 of a federal law, Public Law 94-142, now known as Part B of the Individuals with Disabilities Education Act (IDEA); and the 1986 amendments to IDEA. Though

Photo by David Naylor

PL 94-142 was focused primarily on special education and related services for school-age children, the Law was designed to apply to children ages 3 through 5 if state laws included this group. The basic tenets of this landmark legislation were free and appropriate public education (FAPE); zero reject; individualized education; nondiscriminatory testing, classification, and placement; least restrictive environment; rights to procedural due process; and shared decision making. In 1986, Congress amended IDEA and insured these important rights to young children and their families. This law (PL 99-457) extended all of the rights and protections of the earlier law to children with disabilities ages 3 through 5 regardless of state age limits. In addition, the Law included important incentives to states to provide services for infants and toddlers (birth through age 2) with disabilities and their families. IDEA, along with other legislation and state and local policies, has had a significant impact on the services and supports young children with disabilities and their families receive.

Societal views also influence early intervention/early childhood special education. Knowledge and perspectives about children and families change, and our programs and practices reflect this change. First, there is heightened awareness of the importance of the child's early years on development and learning. Due, in part, to the remarkable findings of brain researchers (see Diamond & Hopson, 1999; Shore, 1997) we know that during the early years brain cells form most of the connections that will be maintained throughout a child's lifetime. During this same period, brain cells maintain their greatest malleability. Healthy early brain development is central to establishing developmental trajectories that are conducive to children's optimal learning and development. Research from behavioral and social science as well as neuroscience adds to our understanding of the conditions that

Knowledge and perspectives about children and families change, and our programs and practices reflect this change.

influence child development. An explosion of research has had a vast impact on policy and practice (Shonkoff & Phillips, 2000).

Second, there is increased attention to the need for quality care for young children. We know that there is a critical link between early experiences and later performance in school and in the community. Recent studies show that the quality of children's early experiences in child care matters more than experts had previously thought (Child Care Action Campaign, 2000). Unfortunately, quality early care is not assured, and yet the demand for care is increasing (Cost, Quality, & Child Outcomes Study Team, 1995; Smolensky & Gootman, 2003).

Third, there is knowledge of the rights of children with disabilities to have access to child care, education, and recreational activities. There is growing awareness of the importance of participation and membership for a full and meaningful life. Within families and communities, young children with disabilities are increasingly included in the same settings and activities where we find their brothers, sisters, and typical peers. Young children with disabilities have a right to be included and to be supported in their families and communities.

Thus, any attempt to define and share guidance about the practices that should be in place for young children with disabilities is influenced by our history, legislation, and the societal context and values in which the practices are identified. Early intervention/early childhood special education is an ever-changing field. The guidance offered in these Recommended Practices incorporates current knowledge from the research literature and integrates that knowledge with important values.

Our Values and Beliefs

Grounded in the empirical research, DEC's Recommended Practices also embrace some fundamental values that are described in this section. For additional discussion of these values and beliefs see "DEC Positions and Concept Papers" at the DEC Web site (www.dec-sped.org).

Respect for All Children and Families

Respect for all children and families is a fundamental value supported by DEC. All children and families means *all*—including children with disabilities, children at risk for school failure, children who live in poverty, children who speak languages other than English, children with gifts and talents, and all of their families.

Respect for all children and families is a fundamental value supported by DEC.

In addition, the concept of respect for all children and families was articulated in one of our focus groups, the Cultural and Linguistic Sensitivity group. The group amplified the understanding that cultures are not static but rather are dynamic and fluid. Everyone is diverse, and we are all members of several different cultural groups. The term *culture* is broadly defined to include shared and learned beliefs, values, and traditions associated with race, ethnicity, language, and social and economic status (DEC, 2002).

Culture and language are integrated within each of us and within each child and family. We must honor and acknowledge each individual's culture and language in ways that do not make them seem unusual or exotic. We must recognize that each individual's culture and language are one of many, enabling us to be more open and accepting of various cultures and languages and to view other cultures and languages as equally valid as our own.

Differences exist among members of cultural and linguistic groups. That is, there are intragroup as well as intergroup differences. Individuals affiliate themselves with various cultural and linguistic groups. Behavior or attitude based on group affiliation should not be predicted. Barrera (2000) wrote that, "The purpose of recognizing culture and cultural dynamics is not to predict or anticipate. It is, rather, to become open and respectful to diverse behaviors even when these are outside of our areas of familiarity" (p. 18).

Photo by David Naylor

A power differential too often exists between families and service providers. Language, race, ethnicity, educational attainment, and social and economic status influence knowledge about and access to EI/ECSE services and supports. These factors also have an impact on the way services are received.

Each child and family's dignity and their right to privacy must be respected. It is important that we ensure that children and their families maintain their dignity and identity as they cross the bridge between the family's culture and the culture of early intervention/early childhood special education.

Finally, we must recognize that we view individuals and the world around us through "culturally-tinted lenses" (Barrera, 2000, p. 17). Though professionals may share some characteristics and experiences with the children and families they serve, each of us has our own views and behaviors. Kalyanpur and Harry (1999) wrote:

> There is no evidence that professionals who do belong to the same culture as their clients are any more successful at accomplishing collaborative relationships than those who do not; on the contrary, as studies [Harry, 1992; Ladson-Billings, 1994] indicated, the best examples of collaborative relationships can occur with professionals who have little or no affiliation with the culture of families. (p. 131)

Rather, the important factor is that individualized, appropriate services for children and families truly reflect mutual respect and appreciation. Teachers and others who work with and on behalf of children and families must respect, value, and support the culture, values, and languages of each home and promote the active participation of all families (DEC, 2002; NAEYC, 1995).

High-Quality, Comprehensive, Coordinated, and Family-Centered Services and Supports

DEC supports the identification and delivery of high-quality, comprehensive, coordinated, and family-centered services and supports that help children reach their full potential. This value is based on the belief that high-quality EI/ECSE services and supports make a positive difference in the lives of young children and their families. EI/ECSE can help ensure that children attain meaningful and functional skills and that their families are supported in their role of nurturing and guiding their children.

Services and supports are individualized based on the child's strengths and needs, and the family's priorities and concerns. Thus EI/ECSE encompasses a variety of services and supports that range in intensity, specificity, and frequency based on the child's needs rather than what is available from the program. Inasmuch as services and supports can be diverse and complex, collaboration and coordination are required to ensure that the individuals and agencies who work with or on behalf of the child and family come to agreement on goals and strategies and share sometimes scarce resources.

DEC acknowledges that the family is the constant in the child's life. This belief recognizes that practices should honor and facilitate the family's caregiving and decision-making roles. Services and supports must be delivered in a manner that conforms to the family's lifestyle, priorities, and concerns.

Recognizing the central role of the family, providers, agencies, and family members must work together as a team rather than as individuals. Collaboration requires shared goals, open and effective communication, and a willingness to discuss and solve problems as a team. Collaborative skills must be taught and practiced in personnel preparation programs. Further, service delivery structures must be in place that provide the time, resources, and other supports to provide EI/ECSE in a collaborative and integrated way.

Rights of All Children to Participate Actively and Meaningfully Within Their Families and Communities

DEC believes in the rights of all children, regardless of their diverse abilities, to participate actively and meaningfully within their families and communities. The principle of *normalization* continues to be a useful guide. Normalization has been defined as " ... making available to all persons with disabilities patterns of life and conditions of everyday living [that] are as close as possible to the regular circumstances and ways of life of society" (Nirje, 1985, p. 67). For young children, these "patterns of life and conditions of everyday living" also present prime opportunities for learning. Traditionally, intervention was delivered in a clinic or special setting with little or no interface with the family's life at home or within their community. Valuing the child's meaningful participation in family and community environments has significant implications for practice.

Young children with disabilities do not have to be in a particular place with particular materials or people in order to learn. Learning opportunities abound for children in their home and community environments. Opportunities for learning in the child's natural settings must be identified. A natural setting is one in which the child would spend time if he or she did not have a disability. Yet just being in such settings is not enough. The individual learning needs of the child must be identified, and the learning opportunities that occur in those settings must also be identified. Effective, well-matched intervention strategies and supports must be identified. Families and caregivers can then use these strategies and supports to enhance natural settings as environments for learning.

Recommended Practices for All Children

Children with disabilities and other special needs are, first of all, children. When we think about practices that will help to optimize young children's development we need to look beyond the orientation of children with special needs to include a number of other guides and standards to help us provide quality services for young children and their families. The National Association for the Education of Young Children (NAEYC) and Head Start provide us with important guidance and resources in this regard.

Children with disabilities and other special needs are, first of all, children.

It is NAEYC's aim to promote high-quality programs for all children and their families. To this end, NAEYC publishes position statements on developmentally appropriate practices for the education and care of young children (Bredekamp & Copple, 1997). Developmentally appropriate practices are defined as " ... those that result from the process of professionals making decisions about the well-being and education of children based on at least three important kinds of information or knowledge: [1] what is known about child development and learning ...; [2] what is known about the strengths, interests, and needs of each individual child ...; [3] and knowledge of the social and cultural contexts in which children live" (Bredekamp & Copple, 1997, pp. 8-9). NAEYC also offers a system of program accreditation. This system sets a standard of practice for programs and provides a process through which the care and education of young children can be improved through accreditation. NAEYC's developmentally appropriate practice guidelines and accreditation system serve as necessary foundations for quality programs for all young children.

Another important resource for informing practices for young children is the Head Start Program Performance Standards (ACYF, 1999). In addition, the Child Outcomes Framework (Head Start Bureau, 2001) provides expectations for children as they leave Head Start programs and enter school. Head Start serves young children, pregnant women, and their families. Their goal is to improve outcomes for young children in low income families. By law, at least ten percent of enrollment opportunities in Head Start must be available to children with disabilities. Thus Head Start represents a significant inclusion opportunity for the early education of young children with disabilities. The standards and guidance provide Head Start programs and those who collaborate with them with valuable information and support for serving children in integrated, developmentally appropriate programs.

The DEC Recommended Practices build on and extend this foundation of quality programs for all children in order to meet the specific needs of children with disabilities. We return to this concept in Part III of this book. Program assessment is a powerful tool for improving the quality of programs and services for young children with disabilities and other special needs. These programs and services must be built on practices that are essential for all children. The DEC Recommended Practices are intended to help meet the individual and unique needs of young children with disabilities and their families who may also be served by programs serving typically developing children.

References

Administration on Children, Youth, and Families (ACYF). (1999). *Head Start program performance standards and other regulations.* Washington, DC: Author.

Barrera, I. (2000). Honoring differences: Essential features of appropriate ECSE services for young children from diverse sociocultural environments. *Young Exceptional Children 3*(4), 17-24.

Bowman, B. T., Donovan, M. S., & Burns, M. S. (Eds.). (2000). *Educating our preschoolers.* Washington, DC: National Academy Press.

Bredekamp, S., & Copple, C. (Eds.). (1997). *Developmentally appropriate practice in early childhood programs.* Washington, DC: National Association for the Education of Young Children (NAEYC).

Child Care Action Campaign. (2000, August). High-quality child care can improve children's school readiness by 50%. *Child Care Action News, 17*(4), 1, 8.

Cost, Quality, & Child Outcomes Study Team. (1995). *Cost, quality, and child outcomes in child care centers public report.* Denver, CO : University of Colorado at Denver, Economics Department.

Diamond, M., & Hopson, J. (1999). *Magic trees of the mind: How to nurture your child's intelligence, creativity, and healthy emotions from birth through adolescence.* New York: Plume.

Division for Early Childhood (DEC). (2002). *DEC position statement on responsiveness to family cultures, values, and languages.* http://www.dec-sped.org.

Harry, B. (1992). Developing cultural self-awareness: The first step in values clarification for early interventionists. *Topics in Early Childhood Special Education, 12,* 333-350.

Head Start Bureau. (2001). Head Start child outcomes framework. *Head Start Bulletin, 70,* 44-50.

Hebbeler, K. M., Smith, B. J., & Black, T. L. (1991). Federal early childhood special education policy: A model for the improvement of services for children with disabilities. *Exceptional Children, 58,* 104-112.

Kalyanpur, M., & Harry, B. (1999). *Culture in special education.* Baltimore: Paul H. Brookes.

National Association for the Education of Young Children (NAEYC). (1995). *NAEYC's position statement on responding to linguistic and cultural diversity.* http//www.naeyc.org.

Nirje, B. (1985). The basis and logic of the normalization principle. *Australia and New Zealand Journal of Developmental Disabilities, 11*(2), 65-68.

Shonkoff, J. P., & Phillips, D. A. (Eds.). (2000). *From neurons to neighborhoods: The science of early childhood development.* Washington, DC: National Academy Press.

Shore, R. (1997). *Rethinking the brain: New insights into early development.* New York: Families and Work Institute.

Smolensky E., & Gootman, J. A. (Eds.). (2003). *Working families and growing kids: Caring for children and adolescents.* Washington, DC: National Academy Press.

Chapter 2

DEC Recommended Practices: The Procedures and Evidence Base Used to Establish Them

. . . .

Barbara J. Smith, Mary E. McLean, Susan Sandall, Patricia Snyder, and Alison Broudy Ramsey

To update and improve the 1993 version of the DEC Recommended Practices (DEC Task Force on Recommended Practices, 1993; Odom & McLean, 1996), a grant proposal was submitted to the U.S. Office of Special Education Programs (OSEP). OSEP funded the grant in the fall of 1998, which provided resources for an expanded effort to produce a set of evidence-based Recommended Practices.

DEC leaders recognized the need to expand the methods used to: (1) produce a set of Recommended Practices; and (2) increase the likelihood of their adoption and implementation at the program, child, and family levels. These expanded methods included: (1) reviewing the research literature for practices that have scientific evidence that the practice is related to improved outcomes; (2) conducting focus groups of parents, practitioners, administrators, and researchers to ascertain their beliefs and values about practices that result in improved outcomes; (3) synthesizing these sources of information; (4) producing recommendations for "indirect" practices or supports, such as personnel preparation and policy and systems change activities necessary for the implementation of Recommended Practices with children and families; and (5) increasing the awareness and use of the Recommended Practices by disseminating the Practices through user-friendly products, engaging in training activities, and collaborating with partner national organizations for dissemination to key stakeholder groups such as families and administrators.

Two primary goals guided the revision of the Recommended Practices:

1. To produce an empirically supported set of recommendations for practice with young children with disabilities birth through age 5, their families, and those who work with them.

2. To increase the likelihood of the use and adoption of the Recommended Practices by identifying "indirect supports" necessary for improving direct

service practice, and by formatting and disseminating the Practices to increase their use by stakeholder groups such as families, personnel trainers, practitioners, and administrators.

These goals required a multimethod, multisource approach to identifying the Practices, and involved many individuals. As noted in the "Acknowledgements" section, the project was conducted by a Management Team consisting of four investigators (Drs. Barbara J. Smith, Mary McLean, Susan Sandall, and David Sexton); a strand coordinator (Dr. Sam Odom); three methodology consultants (Drs. Pat Snyder, Phil Strain, and Bruce Thompson); 13 Strand Chairs (Drs. Stephen J. Bagnato, Mary Beth Bruder, Carl J. Dunst, Gloria Harbin, Robin A. McWilliam, Patricia S. Miller, John T. Neisworth, Christine Salisbury, Rosa Milagro (Amy) Santos, Vicki D. Stayton, Kathleen Stremel, Carol M. Trivette, and Mark Wolery); more than 100 focus group participants; more than 50 literature review coders; and nearly 400 field validators. As David Sexton, past DEC President, stated, "In short, this extremely important endeavor could not [have been] possible without the ongoing support and participation of such a large percentage of our membership" (Sexton, 1999, p. 1).

Goal 1: To produce an empirically supported set of recommendations for practice with young children with disabilities birth through age 5, their families, and those who work with them.

This goal was accomplished by identifying practices that were supported by: (1) research evidence; (2) experiences and values of stakeholders such as parents, practitioners, and administrators; and (3) field validation. The process involved the integration of the best available research evidence combined with knowledge gained through experience and the perspectives of stakeholders (Sackett, Strauss, Richardson, Rosenberg, & Haynes, 2000). The Recommended Practices also were subjected to review and validation by the field. The process was guided by questions promulgated by Peters and Heron (1993), and discussed in the *Journal of Early Intervention* (Snyder, Thompson, McLean, & Smith, 2002), related to confirming Recommended Practices: (1) Does the Practice have a sound theoretical base? (2) Is the methodological integrity of the research convincing and compelling? (3) Is there consensus within the existing literature? (4) Is there evidence that desired outcomes are consistently produced? and (5) Is there evidence of social validity? The DEC process involved collecting experience-based perspectives about practices by conducting focus groups of stakeholders and collecting research-based evidence from a review of the research literature. After integrating the empirical and experiential recommendations, the social validity of the Practices was established by conducting a national field validation study of the Recommended Practices. Each of the procedures is described following.

Experience-Based Knowledge: Focus Groups

In 1998-99, focus groups were conducted to gather recommendations for practices based on experiences and values. Four categories of focus groups were created to determine the Recommended Practices that stakeholders believed were important for improved outcomes for children and families. Focus groups were organized by role, including (1) research experts (by strand); (2) families; (3) administrators; and (4) practitioners.

The research expert focus groups were organized by nine strands and were conducted during the 1998 DEC conference by Strand Chairs selected for their extensive and recognized expertise in a particular area. The nine strands were determined by the project's Management Team and categorized according to whether they reflected "direct services" or "indirect supports." The six direct service strands and Strand Chairs were:

l   Child-Focused Practices—Mark Wolery

l   Cultural/Linguistic Sensitivity—Rosa Milagros (Amy) Santos

l   Family-Based Practices—Carol M. Trivette and Carl J. Dunst

l   Interdisciplinary Models—Robin A. McWilliam

l   Learning Environments—Mary Beth Bruder

l   Technology Applications—Kathleen Stremel

The three indirect supports strands and Strand Chairs were:

l   Personnel Preparation—Patricia S. Miller and Vicki D. Stayton

l   Policy/Procedures—Gloria Harbin

l   Systems Change/Leadership—Christine Salisbury

The Strand Chairs each selected up to ten individuals with research expertise in topics relevant to the strand to participate in focus groups. These focus group participants are noted in each of the Recommended Practices chapters in this book (Chapters 3–9). The Strand Chairs met with the project Management Team prior to the focus groups to review the purpose of and general procedures for conducting the focus groups. Definitions were discussed and agreement reached on the format for writing the Practices. Finally, follow-up procedures and timelines were developed. The focus groups each lasted approximately two hours and were audiotaped. The practices generated by the focus groups were subsequently compiled by the Strand Chairs and mailed to each member of the focus group for review and verification within eight weeks. When finalized, the lists of practices were sent to the investigators.

Subsequently, based on advice from the Strand Chairs and Management Team, a strand on Assessment was added (chaired by John T. Neisworth and Stephen J.

Bagnato), the Policy/Procedures strand was combined with the Systems Change/Leadership strand, and the Learning Environments and Cultural/Linguistic Sensitivity practices were integrated across all the other strands. These steps resulted in the final seven strands of Recommended Practices included in this book. The seven strands are five "direct services" strands (assessment, child-focused, family-based, interdisciplinary, and technology) and two "indirect supports" strands (policies, procedures, and systems change, and personnel preparation). The practices generated by the research focus groups formed the corpus of information that was ultimately integrated with the practices generated from both the research literature and the stakeholder focus groups.

The practices generated by the research focus groups formed the corpus of information that was ultimately integrated with the practices generated from both the research literature and the stakeholder focus groups.

Three additional focus groups were held with families, practitioners, and administrators. These focus groups were conducted by the investigators during 1998-1999. The focus groups were conducted using the same procedures described above. Following each focus group, one investigator summarized the recommended practices generated by the group. This summary was sent to each focus group member for review and verification within eight weeks. The practices from each focus group were subsequently organized by strand. All recommendations from the focus groups were categorized by the investigators into the same seven strands of practice (e.g., child-focused, personnel preparation) depending on their topic. Table 1 lists the number of Recommended Practices by strand that each of the stakeholder and research groups produced.

Table 1. Total Number of Practices Generated by Each Stakeholder Group Across Strands

	Stakeholder Group			
	Family Members	Practitioners	Administrators	Researchers
Strands	Number of Practices Generated			
Assessment	4	10	0	46
Child-Focused	2	7	2	27
Family-Based	13	15	6	16
Interdisciplinary	0	6	0	19
Technology	2	0	2	22
Policies, Procedures, and Systems Change	16	25	28	43
Personnel Preparation	5	13	2	66
Total	**42**	**76**	**40**	**239**

Research-Based Knowledge: Literature Review

The growing emphasis on evidence-based practice has produced varying approaches to defining the term "evidence-based" and to evaluating the strength of empirical evidence for practices, including determining whether the evidence is convincing, compelling, and consistently produced (Snyder et al., 2002). Guidelines proposed for measuring the strength or level of evidence in support of interventions or practices have included those that promote randomized controlled trials as the most convincing and compelling evidence (e.g., What Works Clearinghouse, 2003) to those that acknowledge the value of other methods such as single-subject experimental and qualitative designs (Dunst, Trivette, & Cutspec, 2002; Odom et al., in press; Shavelson & Towne, 2002; Snyder et al., 2002). These latter approaches suggest alternative criteria for evaluating the strength or rigor of a study or a body of evidence. In the DEC

Recommended Practices project, the decision was made to evaluate evidence using criteria that related specifically to the type of design employed by developing methodology coding sheets. For example, Odom and Strain (2002) suggested criteria for measuring the scientific rigor of studies using single-subject experimental designs including: (1) assessment of fidelity of intervention; (2) evidence of improvement over time; (3) evidence of intervention maintenance and generalization; (4) the number of replications; and (5) assessment of social validity of the intervention.

Empirical research published in peer-reviewed professional journals between 1990 and 1998 was included in the literature review. Forty-eight journals across disciplines were selected by the Management Team and Strand Chairs and reviewed (see Table 2). First, the article abstract was reviewed by project staff to determine if the article was a research report involving children with disabilities, birth through age 5 or their families; personnel who work with them; or policies, procedures, or systems that support services to them. Second, if an article met this criterion, the article was read by coders who were either project staff or volunteers with relevant expertise who were recruited by the Management Team and/or Strand Chairs. The coders completed coding sheets on each article.

Coding sheets were developed by the methodology consultants to ensure that each article was appropriately reviewed according to the type of research methodology used (e.g., qualitative, single-subject, etc.). A "generic" coding sheet (Form A) was used uniformly across all articles, which included information such as article title, authors, journal, study participant characteristics, and the setting in which the study was conducted. Then, coders completed a specialized coding sheet (Form B) by methodology

chapter

2

Table 2. Peer-Reviewed Journals Included in DEC Research Synthesis

American Journal on Mental Retardation	Journal of Communication Disorders
Archives of Physical Medicine and Rehabilitation	Journal of Early Intervention
Augmentative and Alternative Communication	Journal of Emotional and Behavioral Disorders
Behavior Modification	Journal of Marriage and Family
Behavior Therapy	Journal of Pediatric Nursing
Behavioral Disorders	Journal of Pediatric Psychology
Child: Care, Health, & Development	Journal of Special Education Technology
Child Development	Journal of Speech, Language, and Hearing Research
Developmental Medicine and Child Neurology	Journal of Visual Impairment and Blindness
Developmental Psychology	Language, Speech, & Hearing Services in Schools
Diagnostique	Mental Retardation
Early Childhood Research Quarterly	Merrill-Palmer Quarterly
Early Education and Development	Neonatal Network: Journal of Neonatal Nursing
Education and Training in Mental Retardation and Developmental Disabilities	Pediatric Physical Therapy
	Pediatrics
Education and Treatment of Children	Physical & Occupational Therapy in Pediatrics
Exceptional Children	Physical Therapy
Exceptionality	Teacher Education and Special Education
Family Relations	The American Journal of Occupational Therapy
Infant-Toddler Intervention	The Journal of Special Education
Infants & Young Children	The Journal of the Association for Persons With Severe Handicaps
Journal of Abnormal Child Psychology	
Journal of Applied Behavior Analysis	The Occupational Therapy Journal of Research
Journal of Applied Developmental Psychology	The Volta Review
Journal of Behavioral Education	Topics in Early Childhood Special Education

---

type: group quantitative design, single-subject experimental design, descriptive design, qualitative design, and mixed method design. The information on the specialized coding sheets included article identification, research design features, sample, setting, outcome measures, duration of intervention, findings, Recommended Practices supported by the study, and the strand category with which the Practice would be associated.

Forty-two coders were trained to code Form A and a version of Form B relating to one type of methodology, and intercoder reliability was established with the methodology consultant who developed the form. These coders were assigned articles; they read each article and completed generic and specialized coding sheets for each. Twenty-nine additional coders read approximately one third of the articles that had been coded by a first stage coder and validated the Recommended Practice and strand placement generated by the first coder. If discrepancies occurred, the article was reviewed and agreement reached by the investigators. Discrepancies occurred with less than five percent of the articles. The Practices and strand placement were also verified by the investigators.

The number of articles derived from the initial screening was 1,018.* Coders excluded articles if there was not a clear Recommended Practice, the article did not meet the criteria for inclusion in the process, or the standard of scientific rigor was not met. The percentage of articles using each research design was:

- Group Quantitative—54%
- Single Subject—22%
- Descriptive—15%
- Qualitative—9%
- Mixed Method—1%

This entire process generated literature support 977 times across all seven strands. This number is higher than the actual number of articles (n=835) because some articles supported more than one practice according to the judgment of the coders. Table 3 shows the number of empirical literature supports for practices by strand. For further analyses of the literature review see Odom & Strain, 2002; Sandall, Smith, McLean, & Broudy Ramsey, 2002; Smith et al., 2002; and Snyder, Thompson, McLean, & Smith, 2002.

Table 3. Empirical Literature Supports by Strand

	Assessment	Child-Focused	Family-Based	Inter-disciplinary	Technology	Policies, Procedures, and Systems Change	Personnel Preparation
Number of Articles	104	399	223	30	32	106	83

Note: Articles could support practices in more than one strand.

Source: Reprinted with permission from *Journal of Early Intervention.*

Smith, B. J., Strain, P. S., Snyder, P., Sandall, S., McLean, M. E., Ramsey, A. B., & Sumi, W. C. (2002). DEC recommended practices: A review of nine years of EI/ECSE research literature. *Journal of Early Intervention, 25*(2), 108-119.

---

* In the original publication of this book, it was reported that 1,022 articles resulted from the screening, which was an error. The correction involving four fewer articles than originally reported is reflected in all other data reported in this chapter.

Synthesizing the Recommendations

The Recommended Practices from the focus groups and literature reviews were combined (synthesized) within each strand (see Figure 1) by the investigators. This synthesis combined similar practices, deleted duplications, and added new practices when several similar practices could be subsumed under a larger practice statement. These lists of practices by strand were submitted to participants attending the 1999

Figure 1. Data Collection, Analysis, and Synthesis of Recommendations From Data

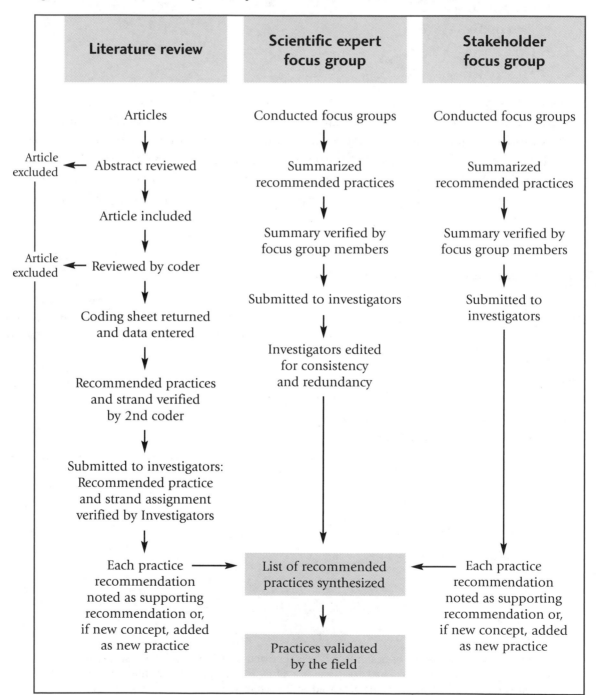

DEC conference in several sessions for review and comment and were subsequently submitted to the Strand Chairs and Management Team for final verification. The final number of Recommended Practices after this synthesis was 250.

Field Validation

The validation stage included two steps: (1) verification among experts (Strand Chairs, Management Team, participants in selected DEC conference sessions, NAEYC personnel); and (2) validation by a national sample of the field (McLean, Snyder, Smith, & Sandall, 2002).

For the field validation, the list of 250 Recommended Practices was formatted into a questionnaire. Due to the large number of Practices, two forms of the questionnaire were created by assigning odd-numbered items to Questionnaire A and even-numbered items to Questionnaire B. Respondents, therefore, only had to validate 125 Practices each. They used a Likert-type scale to rate each item (*strongly agree* [SA], *agree* [A], *disagree* [D], *strongly disagree* [SD], or *undecided* [?]) as to whether it was a Recommended Practice in early intervention/early childhood special education. Respondents also were asked to rate how often the practice was used (*frequently* [F], *sometimes* [S], *rarely* [R], *never* [N], or *undecided* [?]) in programs with which they were familiar. (See Figure 2 for an example of an item from a field validation questionnaire.) A space for comments was also provided.

Figure 2: Field Validation Questionnaire Example

	This is a recommended practice	Extent to which you see this in practice
A1. Professionals provide families with easy access by phone or other means for arranging initial screening and other activities.	SA A D SD ?	F S R N ?
Code: SA = strongly agree; **A** = agree; **D** = disagree; **SD** = strongly disagree; **?** = undecided **F** = frequently; **S** = sometimes; **R** = rarely; **N** = never; **?** = undecided		

The groups comprising the validation sample of 800 people represented families, practitioners, higher education, and administrators. All groups included individuals who responded to requests for survey participants at the annual DEC conference, from the DEC Family Consortium Committee, and a notice in the *Young Exceptional Children* (YEC) magazine. These recruitment efforts resulted in 211 volunteers: 78 practitioners, 62 professionals from higher education, 46 administrators, and 25 parents. The practitioner sample was then expanded to a sample of 400 by adding 322 individuals randomly selected from the DEC membership, which is comprised primarily of practitioners but could include some higher education faculty and students, administrators, and family members. A second group consisted of the volunteer parents (25) and 175 names randomly selected from the mailing list of members of the Federation for Children With Special Needs, totaling a sample of 200 parents. The third and fourth groups were comprised of the 62 higher education and 46 administrator volunteers and 92 randomly selected names from currently funded OSEP personnel preparation projects and a list of Part C, and 619 Coordinators from the states and territories.

The initial mailing of questionnaires to respondents was followed one month later by a postcard reminder. A second postcard reminder was mailed approximately one month after the first. A return rate for the questionnaires of 51% was obtained.

The criterion used to determine whether a practice should be considered a validated Recommended Practice was that more than 50% of the respondents to a particular item indicated *strongly agree* or *agree* in response to the statement: "This is a Recommended Practice." In fact, 90% of the respondents rated each practice as *strongly agree* or *agree*. All of the 250 practices included in Questionnaires A and B passed the criterion and were validated as Recommended Practices.

Relative to the question of how often a practice is used, 50% of all responses to the question were answered by *frequently* or *sometimes*, with *sometimes* being the most common response and *frequently* the second. However, for the technology and policy/system change practices, *rarely* was the second most common response. For further analyses of the validation data, see McLean et al., 2002.

Following field validation, ten practices that were duplicative of others were synthesized into other Recommended Practices statements. This final synthesis resulted in 240 DEC Recommended Practices in early intervention/early childhood special education.

Goal 2: To increase the likelihood of the use and adoption of the Recommended Practices by identifying "indirect supports" necessary for improving direct service practice, and by formatting and disseminating the Practices to increase their use by stakeholder groups such as families, personnel trainers, practitioners, and administrators.

Based on evaluation of the first set of DEC Recommended Practices generated in 1993, the subsequent effort was improved by including practices related to "indirect supports" for the Practices more closely associated with direct services such as assessment and child-focused practices. These "indirect" practices related to administrative and policy support for direct service and personnel preparation.

To improve dissemination and use of the Practices, four focus groups were held in 1999 to determine what formats stakeholder groups preferred for the Practices. The focus groups were comprised of families, practitioners, administrators, and personnel trainers. We hypothesized that producing products in styles and formats preferred by these groups would likely increase the adoption of the Practices and impact the likelihood that services would be improved. Focus groups recommended development and dissemination of products that would not be overly technical, would be reader-friendly, and easy to use. All focus group participants recommended using a variety of media to illustrate practices including print, video, and Web-based. All focus groups stressed the need for multiple formats ranging from short, awareness-type products to more skill-based products. They also suggested that products provide examples for use.

As a result of these recommendations, DEC has produced a line of products and trainings including checklists, overviews, training modules, videos, and Web-based materials and workshops. The series of products that have been disseminated thus far includes:

- *DEC Recommended Practices in Early Intervention/Early Childhood Special Education* (1st ed.) (Sandall, McLean, & Smith, 2000), a text describing the Practices and explaining the purpose and methods used to produce the Practices along with some related resources.
- *DEC Recommended Practices Program Assessment: Improving Practices for Young Children With Special Needs and Their Families* (Hemmeter, Joseph, Smith, & Sandall, 2001), a guide for self-assessing and improving the quality of services by using the DEC Recommended Practices.

- *DEC Recommended Practices Video: Selected Strategies for Teaching Young Children With Special Needs* (DEC, 2001), a demonstration of several teaching strategies from the child-focused practices strand.
- *Personnel Preparation in Early Childhood Special Education: Implementing the DEC Recommended Practices* (Stayton, Miller, & Dinnebeil, 2002), a resource for applying the DEC personnel preparation Recommended Practices.

DEC also offers regional workshops on DEC Recommended Practices as well as targeted sessions at the annual DEC conference. Additional planned offerings include guides for implementing the Practices in local programs, "tool kits" related to applying the Practices to specific issues such as challenging behavior or embedding instruction, and additional Web-based applications. The second edition of this book is a further step toward attaining Goal 2 by including many practical strategies and lessons we and others have learned from using the DEC Recommended Practices (see "An Introduction to the DEC Recommended Practices" and Chapters 10 and 11). Finally, a workbook for program assessment to be used in conjunction with this book has been produced and is described in Chapter 11.

References

Division for Early Childhood (DEC). (2001). *DEC recommended practices video: Selected strategies for teaching young children with special needs.* Longmont, CO: Sopris West.

Division for Early Childhood (DEC) Task Force on Recommended Practices. (Eds.). (1993). *DEC recommended practices: Indicators of quality in programs for infants and young children with special needs and their families.* Reston, VA: Council for Exceptional Children (CEC).

Dunst, C. J., Trivette, C. M., & Cutspec, P. A. (2002, September). Toward an operational definition of evidence-based practices. *Centerscope, 1,* 1-10.

Hemmeter, M. L., Joseph, G. E., Smith, B. J., & Sandall, S. (2001). *DEC recommended practices program assessment: Improving practices for young children with special needs and their families.* Longmont, CO: Sopris West.

McLean, M., Snyder, P., Smith, B. J., & Sandall, S. (2002). The DEC recommended practices in early intervention/early childhood special education: Social validation. *Journal of Early Intervention, 25*(2), 120-128.

Odom, S. L., Brantlinger, E., Gersten, R., Horner, R. H., Thompson, B., & Harris, K. R. (in press). Research in special education: Scientific methods and evidence-based practices. *Exceptional Children.*

Odom, S. L., & McLean, M. E. (1996). *Early intervention/early childhood special education: Recommended practices.* Austin, TX: Pro-Ed.

Odom, S. L., & Strain, P. S. (2002). Evidence-based practice in early intervention/early childhood special education: Single-subject design research. *Journal of Early Intervention, 25*(2), 137-150.

Peters, M. T., & Heron, T. E. (1993). When the best is not good enough: An examination of best practice. *The Journal of Special Education, 26,* 371-385.

Sackett, D. L., Strauss, S. E., Richardson, W. S., Rosenberg, W., & Haynes, R. B. (2000). *Evidence-based medicine: How to practice and teach EBM* (2nd ed.). New York: Churchill Livingstone.

Sandall, S., McLean, M. E. & Smith, B. J. (Eds.). (2000). *DEC recommended practices in early intervention/early childhood special education* (1st ed.). Longmont, CO: Sopris West.

Sandall, S. R., Smith, B. J., McLean, M. E., & Broudy Ramsey, A. B. (2002). Qualitative research in early intervention/early childhood special education. *Journal of Early Intervention, 25*(2), 129-136.

Sexton, D. (1999). President's message. *Young Exceptional Children, 3*(4), 1.

Shavelson, R. J., & Towne, L. (Eds.). (2002). *Scientific research in education.* Washington, DC: National Academy Press.

Smith, B. J., Strain, P. S., Snyder, P., Sandall, S., McLean, M. E., Ramsey, A. B., & Sumi, W. C. (2002). DEC recommended practices: A review of nine years of EI/ECSE research literature. *Journal of Early Intervention, 25*(2), 108-119.

Stayton, V. D., Miller, P. S., & Dinnebeil, L. A. (Eds.). (2002). *Personnel preparation in early childhood special education: Implementing the DEC recommended practices.* Longmont, CO: Sopris West.

Snyder, P., Thompson, B., McLean, M. E., & Smith, B. J. (2002). Examination of quantitative methods used in early intervention research: Linkages with recommended practices. *Journal of Early Intervention, 25*(2), 137-150.

What Works Clearinghouse. (2003, July). *Introduction to the What Works Clearinghouse report process and the role of scientific standards.* Retrieved April 26, 2004 from the Internet: http://w-w-c.org/july2003.html

chapter

2

Notes

Part II:

The DEC Recommended Practices

Direct Services

• • • • • •

Chapter 3

DEC Recommended Practices: Assessment

· · · · · · · · · ·

Introduction

· · · · · · · · · · · · ·

John T. Neisworth and Stephen J. Bagnato

Professionals and families have promoted some notable changes in assessment for young children with disabilities since the early 1980s. Yet, these changes are meager in comparison to fundamental transformations witnessed in early intervention/early childhood special education (EI/ECSE): use of natural settings, developmentally appropriate practices, and family-centered methods. In this respect, assessment for early intervention has been *delayed* in its own development. Materials that are family-friendly and that link assessment and teaching seem critical to early intervention; however, few changes have occurred in the process, style, and methods of assessment to complement inclusion or developmentally appropriate and family-centered practices (Neisworth & Bagnato, 2004).

Assessment is a pivotal event for families and their children; assessment results are used to include or exclude children from specialized interventions that can change their developmental destinies. Beyond the eligibility determination or *gate keeping* purpose, assessment also is critical for program planning, monitoring (formative) progress, and for program (summative) evaluation. Given the importance of assessment, it is understandable that the materials and procedures for early childhood assessment are contentious. The professional literature, newsletters of parent organizations—and, indeed, the pages read by hearing officers—illustrate the assessment struggle.

The Recommended Practices included in this chapter emerged from focus groups and are supported by the literature. In addition, they reflect the ideas and experiences of many professionals and families with whom we have collaborated over several years. The Practices also echo many of the suggestions and concerns of other professional standards, including the National Association for the Education of Young Children (NAEYC) and the National Association of Early Childhood Specialists in State

Departments of Education (NAEYC/NAECSSDE, 2003), the National Association of School Psychologists (NASP) (Thomas & Grimes, 2002), the American Speech-Language-Hearing Association (ASHA) (1990), and the Association for Childhood Education International (ACEI) (Perrone, 1991). Previously, we proposed a definition for early childhood assessment that is consistent with the recommendations reported in this chapter:

> *Early childhood assessment is a flexible, collaborative decision-making process in which teams of parents and professionals repeatedly revise their judgments and reach consensus about the changing developmental, educational, medical, and mental health service needs of young children and their families. (Bagnato & Neisworth, 1991, p. xi)*

Early childhood assessment is a flexible, collaborative decision-making process. . . .

Guiding Principles

The professionals and parents who participated in this effort repeatedly expressed two concerns. First, as principle stakeholders, parents and family members must play a vital and indispensable role in assessment from beginning to end. Second, assessment methods and materials must accommodate children's developmental and disability-specific characteristics. Because of the importance of these concerns, they are presented separately.

Parents as Partners

As professionals, we are committed to working with parents and others who know and care about the child. It is true, of course, that there can be obstacles to effective family participation. Families may be overwhelmed by their child's possible diagnosis and may be intimidated by jargon and differences in educational levels. Cultural differences; language barriers; and work, health, schedule, and transportation difficulties also can make collaboration difficult.

In addition to our legal and ethical responsibilities to partner with parents, there are sound professional and practical reasons for doing so. First, families provide valuable authentic and longitudinal information about their child not otherwise available (Diamond & Squires, 1993). Because of differing perspectives and contexts, professionals and families should be considered independent rather than interchangeable raters (Suen, Lu, & Neisworth, 1993). Further, family members provide needed information about their circumstances and the possible impact on the child. More active involvement of parents in their child's program appears to be related to greater developmental progress (Ramey & Ramey, 1998). Not an isolated or perfunctory recommendation, parents as partners is a dominant theme that runs across all phases of the assessment and intervention sequence.

Developmental Appropriateness

Organizations representing young children (e.g., NAEYC, ACEI) have for some time advocated approaches and materials that match children's interests and developmental status. Early childhood professionals oppose the use of school-age demands and practices with children who are neither developmentally prepared for nor benefit from such imposition. Conventional standardized norm-referenced assessment materials and tasks are very often seen as entirely wrong even for use with children of typical development (Perrone, 1991). The *inappropriateness* of such materials and demands becomes greatly exacerbated when considering young children with special needs (Bagnato, Neisworth, & Munson, 1997):

> *Assessment of infants and preschoolers remains dominated by restrictive methods and styles that place a premium on inauthentic, contrived developmental tasks; that are administered by various professionals in separate sessions using small, unmotivating toys from boxes or test kits; staged at a table or on the floor in an unnatural setting; observed passively by parents; interpreted by norms based solely on typical children; and used for narrow purposes of classification and eligibility determination. (p. 69)*

Photo by David Naylor

The styles, methods, and content of assessment must become compatible with, rather than at odds with, the behavior and interests of young children. A fundamental precept of developmentally appropriate practice is that teaching and assessment must take place in the child's *natural context* rather than being decontextualized (Bagnato & Neisworth, 2000):

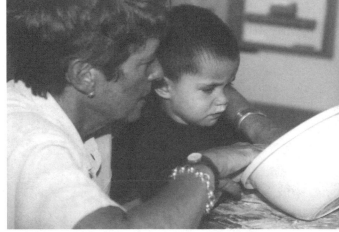

> *A developmental approach presumes a more whole-child view. Many developmental areas are sampled and child differences, from time to time, are highlighted so that the child's previous performance serves as the baseline for monitoring progress.*
>
> *Professionals use a flexible approach in choosing toys that are motivating for the child and are often the child's own. They are responsive to the fact that young children rarely sit still at tables or respond on command to typical structured tasks. A developmental approach acknowledges that professionals must adjust their own language, behavior, and expectations to the young child's level of developmental maturity. A more familiar play-based approach is used that does not force conformance to standardized procedures that are at odds with the typical behavior of young children. (p. 1)*

New directions and professional standards for early childhood assessment must reflect eight critical qualities: assessment must be useful, acceptable, authentic, collaborative, convergent, equitable, sensitive, and congruent (Bagnato & Neisworth,

1999). These eight qualities operationalize the concept of developmentally appropriate practice and parents as partners in assessment for early intervention.

Utility. Assessment must be useful to accomplish the multiple and interrelated purposes of early care and education and early intervention. Assessment is critical for detecting possible problems and, through intervention, averting later more intractable and complex difficulties. Children must be able to access programs through flexible eligibility determination processes; assessment is crucial for planning individualized interventions, for monitoring progress through regular repeated assessments, and for documenting the impact of quality programs. Above all, assessment must have treatment validity—there must be an essential similarity or linkage among program goals, individual child objectives, and the developmental competencies that are assessed. Materials and methods of assessment must help families and professionals to identify instructional objectives and methods for helping.

Acceptability. The methods, styles, and materials for assessment must be mutually agreed upon by families and professionals. The objectives and methods suggested by assessment must be considered worthwhile and acceptable. Further, assessment should detect changes in behavior that are noticeable to caregivers in the home and early childhood environments. This standard of acceptability is an aspect of the wider construct usually referred to as social validity.

Authenticity. Contrived tasks and materials as well as unfamiliar people and circumstances are not optimal for true appraisals of what children really know and do. Tabletop testing with tiny little toys is often a task dreaded by the child, parents, and, indeed, the professional!

Photo by David Naylor

Psychometric items typically do not sample useful curricular content that could guide intervention. Observing children perform in their natural settings offers authentic information that is much more descriptive of the child. Rating scales, direct observation, curriculum-based checklists, and caregiver interview inventories are useful in helping professionals obtain a realistic appraisal of the child's strengths and intervention priorities.

Collaboration. Assessment methods and styles should promote teamwork among families and professionals. Parents and other family members are central partners in the assessment of their children; assessment materials should be chosen and used because they are written in understandable, family-friendly, jargon-free language to which anyone can respond. Assessment must promote the concept of parent-professional decision making in which *tests do not make decisions—people do.* Curriculum-based assessment can be used as a unifying approach that invites input from multiple team members, including family members.

Convergence. Functional, reliable, and valid information on the status and progress of children can be obtained when typical behavior in everyday routines is observed repeatedly by several individuals—teachers, other professionals, and parents. Differences in such data are important to highlight so that areas of needed change or special emphasis in programming can be underscored. The pooling (convergence) of several perspectives (family, professional) provides a better information base.

When materials and procedures accommodate a child's sensory, response, affective, and cultural characteristics, they are equitable.

Equity. Assessment must accommodate individual differences. The principle of equity is recognized (and mandated) as essential for instructional materials. For example, one would not use the same standard print material with children of low vision. Materials can be chosen that allow the child to demonstrate capabilities through several different response modes by using materials that can be changed in a flexible manner. When materials and procedures accommodate a child's sensory, response, affective, and cultural characteristics, they are equitable. Conventional materials have been standardized with children of typical development; to force fit these materials on atypical children violates not only the standard of equity and developmental appropriateness, but common sense.

Sensitivity. Professionals and families must be given the opportunity to use assessment materials that sample evidence of progressively more complex skill development so that even the smallest increment of change can be detected and celebrated. Children with more severe delays and impairments especially need assessment that is sensitive to small increments of progress. Many conventional instruments do not include a sufficient number of items to make possible sensitive measurement of progress.

Congruence. Materials must be designed for, and field validated with, the very children who will be assessed, including those with typical development and those with varying degrees of mild to severe disabilities. Early intervention, specifically, and early childhood education, generally, require specialized materials that address the emerging talents of young children at play in various home- and center-based educational settings. Early childhood assessment materials and methods must be developed specifically for infants, toddlers, and preschool children and match the style and interests typical of young children.

Organization of the Practices

The Recommended Practices in assessment are organized around five statements. They reflect the issues just discussed and include: (1) professionals and familes collaborate in planning and implementing assessment; (2) assessment is individualized and appropriate for the child and family; (3) assessment provides useful information for intervention; (4) professionals share information in respectful and useful ways; and (5) professionals meet legal and procedural requirements and Recommended Practices guidelines. Two central themes or dimensions inform all of the Practices: (1) family members are partners in assessment; and (2) materials and practices must be developmentally appropriate.

References

American Speech-Language-Hearing Association. (1990). *Guidelines for practices in early intervention.* Rockville, MD: Author.

Bagnato, S. J., & Neisworth, J. T. (1991). *Assessment for early intervention: Best practices for professionals.* New York: Guilford.

Bagnato, S. J., & Neisworth, J. T. (1999). Collaboration and teamwork in assessment for early intervention. *Child and Adolescent Psychiatric Clinics of North America, 8*(2), 347-363.

Bagnato, S. J., & Neisworth, J. T. (2000, Spring). Assessment is adjusted to each child's developmental needs. *Birth through 5 Newsletter, 1*(2), 1.

Bagnato, S. J., Neisworth, J. T., & Munson, S. M. (1997). *LINKing: Assessment and early intervention.* Baltimore: Paul H. Brookes.

Diamond, K., & Squires, J. (1993). The role of parental report in the screening and assessment of young children. *Journal of Early Intervention, 17*(2), 107-115.

National Association for the Education of Young Children (NAEYC) and National Association of Early Childhood Specialists in State Departments of Education (NAECSSDE). (2003). *Early childhood curriculum, assessment, and program evaluation: Building an effective, accountable system in programs for children birth through age eight.* Washington, DC: Author.

Neisworth, J. T., & Bagnato, S. J. (2004). The mis-measure of young children: The authentic assessment alternative. *Infants & Young Children, 17*(3), 198-212.

Perrone, V. (1991, Spring). On standardized testing. *Childhood Education, 67,* 132-142.

Ramey, C. T., & Ramey, S. L. (1998). Early intervention and early experience. *American Psychologist, 53*(2), 109-120.

Suen, H. K., Lu, C. H., & Neisworth, J. T. (1993). Measurement of team decision making through generalizability theory. *Journal of Psychoeducational Assessment, 11,* 120-132.

Thomas, A., & Grimes, J. (2002). *Best practices in school psychology* (4th ed.). Washington, DC: National Association of School Psychologists (NASP).

DEC Recommended Practices and Examples: Assessment

Professionals and families collaborate in planning and implementing assessment.

A1. Professionals provide families with easy access by phone or other means for arranging initial screening and other activities.

Example:

- *The family is provided a phone number or e-mail address that will always be answered promptly by a knowledgeable person.*

A2. Professionals ensure a single point of contact for families throughout the assessment process.

Example:

- *From the very first contact with a family, one team member is identified to serve as coordinator (i.e., the single point of contact) for all assessment activities from referral to the initiation of services.*

A3. Families receive a written statement of program philosophy regarding family participation in assessment planning and activities.

Examples:

- *A brochure or written statement about family involvement in assessment is provided to families.*

- *A staff member verbally explains the philosophy of assessment when the brochure or written statement is provided and clarifies any questions the family may have.*

A4. Professionals meet and collaborate with families to discuss family preferences and reach consensus about the process, methods, materials, and situations of assessment that will meet the child's needs best.

Examples:

- *Families and professionals jointly plan the specifics of the assessment including the location, time of day, and strategies for assessment.*

- *Professionals are careful to incorporate culturally and linguistically appropriate procedures into the plans.*

A5. Professionals solicit information from families regarding the child's interests, abilities, and special needs.

Examples:

- *The team plans which assessments to use only after obtaining information from the family about what the child typically does and what the child likes to do.*

- *The team asks for and utilizes family suggestions for favorite toys, activities, and accommodations to use in the assessment.*

A6. Professionals review, with parental consent, agency information about the child and family.

Example:

- *The service coordinator requests and the team reviews records of the child's birth history, medical history, and information from other agencies.*

A7. Professionals and families identify team members and the team assessment style to fit best the needs and goals of the child and family.

Examples:

- *It is decided that the occupational therapist, speech language pathologist, early childhood special educator, and family members will conduct the assessment using a transdisciplinary play-based model.*

- *The physical therapist and early childhood special educator make a home visit to assess the child in a familiar setting and within familiar activities.*

A8. Families participate actively in assessment procedures.

Example:

- *The child's mother observes as the team assesses her daughter, and answers questions about what the child typically does at home.*

A9. Families choose their roles in the assessment of their children (e.g., assistant, facilitator, observer, assessor).

Examples:

- *Families may choose to watch the assessment, to serve as an informant, to participate by interacting with the child, or to provide support to the child by staying nearby. Prior to the day of the assessment, a professional explains what each role entails so that families can choose which they wish to assume and will know what to expect on the assessment day.*

- *Family members observe the assessment activities and comment on their child's performance.*

- *Family members make a list of the words their child understands.*
- *A family member helps the child eat a snack while the occupational therapist observes the child's chewing and swallowing abilities.*

A10. With each family's agreement, professionals help families identify their resources, concerns, and priorities related to their child's development.

Examples:

- *In meetings prior to the development of the IFSP or IEP, families share their concerns and priorities for their child as well as the resources available to help them with their child's development.*
- *The early interventionist shares checklists of possible needs and resources for the family to use.*

A11. Professionals, families, and other regular caregivers work as equal team members for purposes of assessment (i.e., give equal priority to family/caregiver's observations and reports, discuss assessment results, reach consensus about the child's needs and programs).

Example:

- *At the team meeting, the parent, early interventionist, speech/language pathologist, and physical therapist all identify current functioning and areas of need for the child. All information is considered in the assessment process rather than viewing some information as more "correct" than other information.*

A12. Program administrators encourage the use of assessment procedures that ensure consultation and collaboration among families and professionals (e.g., the whole team discusses qualitative and quantitative information and negotiate consensus to make decisions).

Example:

- *The assessment team has an agreed upon model of teaming and consensus building that is followed.*

Assessment is individualized and appropriate for the child and family.

A13. Professionals use multiple measures to assess child status, progress, and program impact and outcomes (e.g., developmental observations, criterion/curriculum-based, interviews, informed clinical opinion, and curriculum-compatible norm-referenced scales).

Example:

- *Available measures include observations, criterion-curriculum-based instruments, interviews, curriculum-compatible norm-referenced scales, informed clinical opinion, and work samples.*

A14. Professionals choose materials and procedures that accommodate the child's sensory, physical, responsive, and temperamental differences.

Examples:

> *The child uses her augmentative communication device and adaptive equipment when her progress is assessed by the team.*

> *The child uses eye gaze to indicate choices on an assessment of receptive vocabulary.*

A15. Professionals rely on materials that capture the child's authentic behaviors in routine circumstances.

Examples:

- *Assessment includes observation of the child engaged in familiar activities in his typical environment rather than only behavior in contrived situations.*
- *The assessment is conducted in the classroom the child currently attends.*
- *Family members identify the child's favorite toys and these are used for assessment activities.*
- *A family member and the child look at picture books together while the speech therapist records the child's communication skills.*

A16. Professionals seek information directly from families and other regular caregivers using materials and procedures that the families themselves can manage to design IFSP/IEP goals and activities.

Examples:

- *Families provide information about potential learning opportunities for their child that occur in daily routines and that are feasible given the other demands of the family.*
- *Families choose to complete a questionnaire or checklist to help identify goals and learning activities.*
- *Assessment for program planning includes strategies for gaining information from families and other caregivers so that the IFSP/IEP goals pertain to the child's natural environment.*

A17. Professionals assess children in contexts that are familiar to the child.

Examples:

- *The professional observes the child in his usual early care and education environment.*
- *A family member reports that the child has some challenging behaviors in the early evening. The professional schedules a home visit at that time to try to understand the issues and potential solutions.*

A18. Professionals assess children after they have become familiar to the child.

Examples:

- *The assessment team members spend time with the child in play or in an informal activity to establish familiarity prior to assessment.*

- *Individuals who are familiar with and to the child are identified as members of the assessment team.*

A19. Professionals gather information from multiple sources (e.g., families, professional team members, agencies, service providers, other regular caregivers).

Examples:

- *The teacher and the babysitter make a list of the words the child uses, says, signs or gestures.*

- *The occupational therapist observes the child playing with toys in the classroom and then sets up a few testing items to clarify the child's performance.*

- *The child's physician, early care and education providers, babysitter, extended family members, and religious school teacher are also asked for input.*

A20. Professionals assess the child's strengths and needs across all developmental and behavioral dimensions.

Examples:

- *The team completes all sections of the curriculum-referenced instrument even though stated concerns are only in one domain.*

- *The team assesses a child across all developmental domains (i.e., social, motor, communication, adaptive, sensory, and cognitive) and all behavioral dimensions (e.g., temperament, problem solving, and self-regulation).*

Assessment provides useful information for intervention.

A21. Families and professionals assess the presence and extent of atypical child behavior that may be a barrier to intervention and progress.

Example:

- *The team assesses the occurrence of atypical behavior, challenging behavior, and self-stimulation in naturally occurring routines and activities throughout the day that are problematic.*

A22. Professionals use functional analysis of behavior to assess the form and function of challenging behaviors.

Examples:

- *Over a couple of days, the team members identify what happens just before and after they observe challenging behaviors (e.g., crying, hitting, throwing objects) by the child. They discuss whether the behavior is to obtain attention, avoid a specific activity, or to serve another function. Then the team plans strategies to reduce the behavior and evaluate their hypothesis.*

- *For a week, the child's mother and father write down what happens right before the child's tantrums and what happens afterward. The early interventionist reviews these notes with them, and they form a "best guess" about the purpose or function of the tantrumming behavior. Based on this information, the early interventionist helps the parents develop a plan for reducing the occurrence of the child's tantrums.*

A23. Program supervisors, in concert with the EI/ECSE team, use only those measures that have high treatment validity (i.e., that link assessment, individual program planning, and progress evaluation).

Examples:

- *The team uses curriculum-based instruments that link directly to the curriculum.*

- *Assessment tools used are those that provide information that directly assists with program planning.*

A24. Professionals assess not only immediate mastery of a skill, but also whether the child can demonstrate the skill consistently across other settings and with other people.

Examples:

- *The team assesses whether new words learned at home are also used in the caregiving setting.*

- *The team assesses the child's ability to walk in the classroom, on the playground, to and from the car, and so forth.*

A25. Professionals appraise the level of support that a child requires in order to perform a task.

Examples:

- *The team assesses whether or not a child can request juice independently or with varying amounts of help.*

- *The team assesses whether the infant lifts his head on his own in response to interesting sounds or sights.*

- *Professionals assess the level of prompting, environmental modification, or reinforcement required for a child to consistently demonstrate a skill.*

A26. Professionals choose and use scales with sufficient item density to detect even small increments of progress (especially important for children with more severe disabilities).

Example:

- *A curriculum-based instrument has too few items to demonstrate progress of a child over time, so the team breaks down items on the measure into smaller steps so that progress will be more apparent.*

A27. Professionals and families rely on curriculum-based assessment as the foundation or "mutual language" for team assessments.

Example:

- *In conducting an evaluation to determine eligibility for special education, the team uses a curriculum-based instrument in addition to a norm-referenced instrument.*

A28. Professionals conduct longitudinal, repeated assessments in order to examine previous assumptions about the child, and to modify the ongoing program.

Examples:

- *The team completes the curriculum-based measure twice per year for each child.*
- *Teachers collect weekly data on a child's fine motor objectives.*
- *Family members and early care and education providers keep track of what the child eats to monitor caloric intake for a child who has trouble gaining weight.*

A29. Professionals report assessment results in a manner that is immediately useful for planning program goals and objectives.

Examples:

- *The team uses a curriculum-based measure in which items become learning objectives.*
- *The team report describes the child's needs and suggests learning activities.*

Professionals share information in respectful and useful ways.

A30. Professionals report assessment results so that they are understandable and useful for families.

Examples:

- *Reports are translated into the dominant language of the family.*
- *Reports use minimal technical jargon and include definitions of terms if needed.*
- *Reports give specific information about the child's abilities and needs rather than just scores or developmental ages.*

chapter

3

A31. Professionals report strengths as well as priorities for promoting optimal development.

Example:

- *Team members always take the time to include information about a child's areas of strength in their reports as well as discussing areas of need.*

A32. Professionals report limitations of assessments (e.g., questions of rapport, cultural bias, and sensory/response requirements).

Examples:

- *Team members report the results of an assessment with caution due to the child's physical impairment, which may have prevented a valid assessment.*

- *The team decides that an assessment should be conducted in the child's dominant language as well as in English so that a comparison of the results can be made.*

A33. Professionals write reports that contain findings and interpretations regarding the interrelatedness of developmental areas (e.g., how the child's limitations have affected development; how the child has learned to compensate).

Examples:

- *A child who is visually impaired may currently be demonstrating a delay in vocabulary development due to his inability to see objects and people around him.*

- *A child whose speech is delayed may not be able to express all that she knows.*

A34. Professionals organize reports by developmental/functional domains or concerns rather than by assessment device.

Example:

- *The physical therapist, early interventionist, and speech/language pathologist write their report by organizing all of their information together by developmental domain.*

A35. Families have adequate time to review reports, ask questions, or express concerns before the team uses the information for decision making.

Example:

- *In advance of the team meeting, information is shared and family members are provided the opportunity to ask questions or express concerns with at least one member of the team.*

A36. Family members may invite other individuals to evaluation meetings or meetings to discuss children's performance or progress.

Example:

- *In preparation for the evaluation meeting, the service coordinator asks the family if they would like to invite anyone to attend. Those invited may include other family members, friends, spiritual advisors, or other professionals.*

chapter 3

Professionals meet legal and procedural requirements and meet Recommended Practice guidelines.

A37. Professionals inform families about state EI/ECSE rules and regulations regarding assessment.

Example:

- *Written information about state regulations is given to families prior to the eligibility assessment in written form or through other formats. The family has the opportunity to talk with a team member about the regulations if there are questions.*

A38. Professionals, when required by regulations to apply a diagnosis, employ measures and classification systems that are designed and developmentally appropriate for infants and young children.

Example:

- *Assessment teams have guidance from their state that makes disability categories appropriate for young children.*

A39. Psychologists rely on authentic measures of early problem-solving skills (instead of traditional intelligence tests) that link directly to program content and goals and that sample skills in natural, rather than contrived, circumstances (e.g., play-based).

Examples:

- *The assessment team always includes an authentic measure of child functioning in assessment to determine eligibility.*
- *The psychologist observes the child in her early education setting as part of the assessment process.*

. . . .

A40. Professionals, when appropriate, choose only those norm-referenced measures that are developed, field-validated, standardized, and normed with children similar to the child being assessed.

Example:

- *The assessment team is careful to choose instruments that are appropriate to each child rather than always using the same instruments for every child.*

. . . .

A41. Professionals monitor child progress based on past performance as the referent rather than on group norms.

Examples:

- *The assessment team considers assessment information from at least three points in time to monitor child progress.*

- *Rather than comparing a child's performance on an instrument to other children at the same age, the team analyzes the child's rate of development in relation to his previous rate of development.*

. . . .

A42. Professionals defer a definitive diagnosis until evaluation of the child's response to a tailored set of interventions.

Example:

- *The assessment team is cautious about identifying a category of disability for a child on the basis of one assessment only and has the option of using a "developmental delay" category so that services may be provided. More information will be learned about the child during intervention.*

. . . .

A43. Program administrators provide supervisory support for team members to enable them to maintain ethical standards and recommended practices.

Examples:

- *Inservice opportunities are provided for team members so they can maintain the skills necessary for appropriate assessment.*

- *Team members are encouraged to complete quality assessments. The need to complete assessments quickly is not allowed to compromise the quality of those assessments.*

A44. Professionals and families conduct an ongoing (formative) review of the child's progress at least every 90 days in order to modify instructional and therapeutic strategies.

Example:

- *The team has review meetings scheduled every three months to review child progress and plan needed changes if identified.*

A45. Professionals and families assess and redesign outcomes to meet the ever changing needs of the child and family.

Example:

- *A child's mother is returning to work, necessitating changes in the service plan. The team makes the needed changes to the intervention plan as requested by the family.*

A46. Professionals and families assess the child's progress on a yearly (summative) basis to modify the child's goal-plan.

Example:

- *The team summarizes the child's progress in preparation for the annual meeting to revise the IFSP or IEP.*

Assessment Glossary

Assessment. The process of collecting information, ideally from multiple sources and means, for making informed decisions for individuals, families, and programs.

Authentic assessment. An assessment that examines naturally occurring skills in natural, everyday settings using the child's own toys and activities rather than from something external (e.g., a set of test questions).

Authentic measures. Materials that allow appraisal of functional, useful behavior in natural, routine circumstances.

Curriculum-based (sometimes referred to as **curriculum-referenced**). A form of criterion-based assessment in which the standards to be achieved are the objectives that comprise the program of instruction or therapy.

Curriculum-compatible norm-referenced scales. Materials used to assess and compare a child's status with a larger peer group and that provide direct linkage with program curricular goals.

Early intervention/early childhood special education (EI/ECSE). Specialized practices, knowledge, and skills needed to meet the individualized needs of young children with special needs and their families.

Function. The effect the behavior has on the environment or the purpose of the behavior as seen from the child's perspective.

Functional analysis of behavior. A method that uses direct observation and recording of behavior to identify circumstances (antecedents) that may trigger and support (reinforce) problem behavior. Functional assessment provides information for conducting functional analysis, in which environmental variables can be manipulated to test findings of the functional assessment.

Individualized Family Services Plan/Individualized Education Program (IFSP/IEP). The written individualized plans for children with disabilities required under IDEA. Individualized Family Services Plans are required for children ages birth to age 3, while Individualized Education Programs (IEPs) are required for children ages three and older.

Informed clinical opinion. The use of quantitative and qualitative information to make judgments regarding eligibility or program decisions when child characteristics challenge more direct appraisal. This approach requires some familiarity with the child as well as sufficient professional knowledge for making informed judgments.

Item density. The number of assessment items within an age or developmental range; greater density permits finer detection of change.

Screening. A rapid process for identifying individuals who require closer examination for possible disabilities or special needs. Screening is only used to determine further assessment, and not for diagnosis or placement.

Assessment Resources

Position Statements

"Division for Early Childhood (DEC) Position Statement on Developmental Delay as an Eligibility Category"

"DEC Concept Paper on Developmental Delay as an Eligibility Category"
   The DEC position statements are found on the DEC Web site at http://www. dec-sped.org. Click on "Position Statements."

"National Association for the Education of Young Children (NAEYC) Position Statement on Early Childhood Curriculum, Assessment and Program Evaluation "
   The NAEYC position statements are found on the NAEYC Web site at http://www.naeyc.org/resources/position_statements/positions_intro.asp.

"National Association of School Psychologists (NASP) Position Statement on Early Childhood Assessment"
   The NASP position statements are found on the NASP Web site at http://www. nasponline.org/information/position_paper.html.

Print Materials

Alternative Approaches to Assessing Young Children
A. Losardo & A. Notari-Syverson (2001)
   Six alternative assessment methods for young children (naturalistic, focused, performance, portfolio, dynamic, and curriculum-based language) are detailed in this book. Chapters offer thorough descriptions of each approach, along with summaries of advantages and limitations, guidelines for implementation, suggestions for use in inclusive environments and samples of data collection forms. A companion Web site is available. (Baltimore: Paul H. Brookes)

Assessing and Fostering the Development of a First and a Second Language in Early Childhood: Training Manual
Child Development Division, California Department of Education (1998)
   This resource is designed to help train students, staff, and parents to assess and foster language development in young children from culturally and linguistically diverse backgrounds. Team members demonstrate and describe a six-step sequence through which they gather information, engage the participation of family members, and adjust the curriculum to support young language learners. A companion videotape, *Observing Preschoolers: Assessing First and Second Language Development*, provides helpful, culturally sensitive insights about how children learn and perform and how teachers can assist in these processes.

   CDE Press
   P.O. Box 271
   Sacramento, CA 95812-0217
   Phone: (800) 995-4099
   FAX: (916) 323-0823
   Web: http://www.cde.ca.gov/cdepress/ (Click on "Child Development.")

Assessing Infants and Preschoolers With Special Needs
M. McLean, M. Wolery, & D. B. Bailey (2004)

A new edition of a familiar resource, this book is broken down into four sections, covering issues from basic information about assessment to particulars regarding assessing young children with special needs. The text covers a variety of developmental domains, illustrating how assessment and child development are integrally linked. Finally, the resource emphasizes how individuals can use assessment results to plan instructional programs for infants and preschoolers with special needs. (Upper Saddle River, NJ: Pearson Education)

Assessment: Gathering Meaningful Information (Young Exceptional Children Monograph Series No. 4)
M. M. Ostrosky & E. Horn (Eds.) (2002)

Identifying and assessing children who are disabled, have developmental delays, or who are gifted/talented are among the most important steps in supporting each child's development. This collection of articles offers strategies for team assessments, insights on the impact of environment and cultural/linguistic differences on information gathering, and other helpful topics. (Longmont, CO: Sopris West)

Assessment for Early Intervention: Best Practices for Professionals
S. J. Bagnato & J. T. Neisworth (1991)

Written for psychologists, this book is a self-instructional guidebook relevant to all professionals who must acquire the unique perspectives and best practices to work with families and their infants and preschoolers with developmental disabilities. With content that is immediately applicable, *Assessment for Early Intervention* moves beyond diagnosis (which is often premature) to prescribe broad interventions for improving the quality of life for the child and the family. (New York: Guilford)

Diagnostic Classification: 0–3
Zero to Three/National Center for Clinical Infant Programs (1994)

This 134-page paperback is a supplement or alternative to DSM IV diagnostic classification that is focused especially on very young children. Issues of regulation and affect, mood, gender identity, adjustment, and trauma are presented as primary diagnoses. Axes II, III, IV, and V deal with Relationships, Medical, Psychosocial Stressors, and Functional Emotional Levels, respectively. The model employed is consistent with much of early childhood theory and approaches and is considered more in tune with children, birth to three, than the pathological model used in other classification systems.

> Zero to Three/National Center for Clinical Infant Programs
> 2000 M Street, NW, Suite 200
> Washington, DC 20036
> Phone: (202) 638-1144

Early Childhood Assessment
C. S. Lidz (2003)

This book has an emphasis on observing and appraising the "whole child," and includes guidelines on interviewing caregivers, observing parent-child interaction, conducting dynamic assessment, writing reports, and evaluating outcomes. There is also substantial material related to curriculum, standardized testing, play, and socioemotional and neuropsychological functioning. Four appendices present position statements on assessment by major professional organizations. (Hoboken, NJ: John Wiley & Sons)

LINKing Assessment and Early Intervention: An Authentic Curriculum-Based Approach
S. J. Bagnato, J. T. Neisworth, & S. M. Munson (1997)
> Pulling the best properties from widely known assessment and curriculum models, this book identifies critical markers for judging quality: authenticity, collaboration, convergence, equity, sensitivity, and congruence. Applying this unique six-standard index, the authors provide descriptive snapshots of the "best" curriculum-embedded and curriculum-compatible assessment and intervention systems criteria. Close-ups of actual forms, checklists, guidelines, and questionnaires allow readers to become familiar with various formats, while case vignettes illustrate the process. (Baltimore: Paul H. Brookes)

New Visions for the Developmental Assessment of Infants and Young Children
S. J. Meisels, & E. Fenichel (Eds.) (1996)
> This book offers clear and current rethinking of the key issues from five perspectives, one of which is from the family point of view. Cultural considerations, information gathering strategies, and policy considerations are also addressed.

> Zero to Three
> P.O. Box 960
> Herndon, VA 20172
> Phone: (800) 899-4301
> FAX: (703) 661-1501
> Web: http://www.zerotothree.org

Reach for the Stars, Planning for the Future
J. Grisham-Brown & D. G. Haynes (1999)
> This is a first-of-its-kind guidebook about building on the assessment process to create strengths-based plans for young children. The strategies and forms provided are designed to help families to imagine positive and productive futures for their children and support steps toward those futures through planning with program personnel.

> American Printing House for the Blind
> P.O. Box 6085
> Louisville, KY 40206-0085
> Phone: (800) 223-1839
> FAX: (502) 899-2274
> Web: http://www.aph.org/

Skilled Dialogue: Strategies for Responding to Cultural Diversity in Early Childhood
I. Barrera, R. M. Corso, & D. Macpherson (2003)
> Understanding how to respond to cultural diversity is one key to successful family-based practices. This resource gives early childhood professionals the knowledge they need to improve that understanding. Through this book, practitioners will better understand the challenges of collaboration with family members whose values, beliefs, and backgrounds may differ from their own. Further, they will discover a repertoire of skills and strategies for reframing differences between practitioners and families. The chapter entitled "Respectful, Reciprocal, and Responsive Assessment" is a particularly rich and timely source of new ideas. (Baltimore: Paul H. Brookes)

Videotapes

Breaking the News
Institute for Families of Blind Children (1990)
> Don't be put off by the fact that this resource was developed for pediatric ophthalmologists! It's a short (15 minutes), powerful videotape on the challenges of sharing difficult diagnostic information sensitively. The section on sharing information with compassion is particularly strong.

> Institute for Families of Blind Children
> Mail Stop 111
> P.O. Box 54700
> Los Angeles, CA 90054-0700
> Phone: (323) 669-4649
> FAX: (323) 665-7869
> Web: http://www.instituteforfamilies.org

But He Knows His Colors: Characteristics of Autism in Children Birth to Three
C. McClain & P. Osbourn (1993)
> Teaching families, educators, early interventionists, and other practitioners about the spectrum of characteristics seen in young children with autism was the purpose for developing this videotape. It provides the opportunity to observe four children, all under the age of three, in a variety of settings and assessment situations.

> Child Health and Development Media, Inc. (CHADEM)
> 5632 Van Nuys Boulevard., Suite 286
> Van Nuys, CA 91401
> Phone: (800) 405-8942
> FAX: (818) 989-7826
> Web: http://www.childdevmedia.com

First Years Together: Involving Parents in Infant Assessment
Project Enlightenment (1989)
> This 19-minute videotape accomplishes several purposes. It provides parent perspectives on what they like and do not like about assessment procedures. It demonstrates professionals collaborating with family members in formal and informal assessment situations. It also demonstrates using assessment as an opportunity to plan interventions and support parent strengths and accomplishments.

> Child Health and Development Media, Inc. (CHADEM)
> 5632 Van Nuys Boulevard., Suite 286
> Van Nuys, CA 91401
> Phone: (800) 405-8942
> FAX: (818) 989-7826
> Web: http://www.childdevmedia.com

Observing Preschoolers: Assessing First and Second Language Development
California Department of Education (1998)

> In 30 minutes, this videotape illustrates a thoughtful process for learning more about young children through observation, documentation, and discussion. This is a useful resource for supporting the development of observation skills and for learning to distinguish between children who are different and children who have delays or disabilities.
>
> > CDE Press
> > P.O. Box 271
> > Sacramento, CA 95812-0217
> > Phone: (800) 995-4099
> > FAX: (916) 323-0823
> > Web: http://www.cde.ca.gov/cdepress/ (Click on "Child Development.")

Portraits of the Children: Culturally Competent Assessment
National Association of School Psychologists (NASP) (2003)

> A videotape and CD-ROM are the key components of this multimedia professional development resource package. The video includes four culturally diverse case studies, featuring children from preschool to high school ages. Interviews with leading psychological assessment experts and experienced general educators, related services personnel, ESL specialists, administrators, and parents create meaningful discussion on the use of interpreters; bilingual assessment; distinguishing language difference from language delay; and the role of culture, race, and language on educational performance.
>
> > Council for Exceptional Children (CEC)
> > Department K03082W
> > P.O. Box 79026
> > Baltimore, MD 21279-0026
> > Phone: (888) 232-7733
> > TTY: (866) 915-5000
> > E-mail: services@cec.sped.org
> > Web: http://www.cec.sped.org/bk/catalog2/assessment.html#S5573

A Three-Way Conversation: Effective Use of Cultural Mediators, Interpreters, and Translators
Spectrum Project and Project A.C.T. (1999)

> Cultural mediators, interpreters, and translators are essential to the participation of culturally and linguistically diverse young children and families in the assessment process. This videotape explores the effective use of these resources, offering comments and insights from both parents and service providers. The brief vignette on communication provides a "wake-up call" with regard to culturally appropriate assessment. Video clips are paired with thought-provoking questions to promote discussion.
>
> > Western Media Products
> > P.O. Box 591
> > Denver, CO 80201
> > Phone: (800) 232-8902
> > FAX: (303) 455-5302
> > Web: http://www.media-products.com

Transdisciplinary Arena Assessment Process: A Resource for Teams
Child Development Resources, Inc. (1992)
   This 43-minute videotape demonstrates a six-step family-centered transdisciplinary
   approach to arena assessment IFSP development. The accompanying viewing guide
   provides an overview of the transdisciplinary approach and a summary of the
   process, as well as supporting activities and supplemental materials.

   Child Development Resources (CDR)
   P.O. Box 280
   Norge, VA 23127-0280
   Phone: (757) 566-3300
   FAX: (757) 566-8977

Web Sites

CLAS: Culturally and Linguistically Appropriate Services
   This Web site leads readers to a dynamic and evolving database of useful materials.
   Try the following subjects: "Child Assessment," "Family Assessment," and
   "IFSPs/IEPs."

   http://clas.uiuc.edu/

Early Identification
   The National Early Childhood TA Center has compiled a variety of helpful and
   informative resources at this site. Publications on key topics (e.g., eligibility,
   informed clinical opinion; information from funded projects; and examples of state
   assessment practices are examples of what's available.

   http://www.nectac.org/topics/earlyid/earlyid.asp

Get it Got it Go!
   These Web sites offer gateways to a comprehensive system for continuously measuring the skills and needs of individual children from birth to eight. The system
   includes: (1) growth and development indicators (IGDIs) for monitoring the
   progress of individual young children; (2) solutions-oriented assessments that allow
   families and early elementary educators to identify features of classroom and home
   settings they can change to improve children's developmental outcomes; and (3)
   dynamic data management tools to use online.

   Juniper Gardens Web site: http://www.lsi.ku.edu/jgprojects/igdi/
   Get it, Got it, Go! (Preschool) Web site: http://ggg.umn.edu

*Infant Behavioral Assessment and Intervention Program: An Education and Training
Program for Early Intervention Professionals*
   This site provides assessment and curriculum materials focused on supporting the
   neurobehavioral organization and development of infants who are born with very
   low/extremely low birthweight or disabilities and their families.

   http://www.ibaip.org

A Look at Social, Emotional, and Behavioral Screening Tools for Head Start and Early Head Start

This thoughtful resource from the Center for Children and Families at the Education Development Center, Inc. (EDC) provides guidance for choosing a screening tool in the areas of social, emotional, and behavioral development. Topics covered include the purposes of screening; features to look for in a screening tool; and a review of six commonly used tools in terms of availability, purpose, features, and psychometric properties.

http://ccf.edc.org/workpub.asp#look

New Visions for Parents

The helpful resources available through this Web site include a letter for parents about developmental assessment, a guidebook (*New Visions: A Parent's Guide to Understanding Developmental Assessment*), information on preparing for the assessment process, and a list of frequently used terms.

http://www.zerotothree.org/newvisions.html

Preparing Practitioners for Getting the Most Out of Child Evaluations

Author B. Crais offers a variety of tools and strategies for teaching/training about Recommended Practices in family-based evaluation and assessment.

http://www.fpg.unc.edu/~scpp/pdfs/Reforming/12-309_336.pdf

Statewide Readiness Assessment

A range of resources (e.g., position statements, articles, conference proceedings, Web sites links) on this evolving aspect of assessment are available at this site.

http://www.nectac.org/topics/readiness/Readiness.asp

Notes

Chapter 4

DEC Recommended Practices: Child-Focused Practices

Photo by David Naylor

Introduction

Mark Wolery

Child-focused practices include the decisions and strategies used to structure and provide learning opportunities for children. These practices guide how children are taught (i.e., the strategies and practices used to ensure learning), when and where the instructional practices and arrangements are implemented, and how children's performance is monitored to make decisions about modifying the interventions and identifying or revising goals.

Guiding Principles

This chapter is based on three guiding principles. First, *a primary function of early intervention (EI) and early childhood special education (ECSE) is to promote children's learning and development* (Bailey & Wolery, 1992; Shonkoff & Meisels, 2000; Widerstrom, Mowder, & Sandall, 1997). In short, children should learn important skills and have more advanced developmental abilities as a result of participating in EI/ECSE. Clearly, EI/ECSE has other functions, but a major purpose of specialized services is to promote children's learning and positively influence their developmental trajectories. This chapter focuses directly on the Recommended Practices for organizing and implementing interventions and strategies that promote these outcomes.

Focus group members: Lise Fox, Howard Goldstein, Louise Kaczmarek, Diane Sainato, Susan Sandall and Mark Wolery

chapter

4

Second, *children's experiences of interacting with the social and physical environment have a primary influence on their learning and development* (Horowitz & Haritos, 1998). Other forces such as children's health and their genetic inheritance also are important influences, but children's experiences are critical and have a range of influences. Some experiences assist children in learning desirable skills and patterns (styles) of interacting with the world, other experiences result in little apparent learning, and still others help them learn undesirable skills and patterns. Experiences that enhance learning or impede learning can and do occur anywhere and at any time. Experiences that facilitate learning and development are not restricted to children's contacts with intervention professionals or intervention programs; they occur throughout the day wherever children are (McWilliam, Wolery, & Odom, 2001). The tasks of early intervention professionals are: (1) to maximize the likelihood that all children's experiences, when- and wherever they occur, promote learning of desired skills and patterns; and (2) to minimize the likelihood that children will have interactions that impede learning of desirable skills and patterns.

The Practices in this chapter describe strategies and approaches that, when used systematically, accomplish these tasks. Thus, the planful, purposeful, and careful use of

Photo by David Naylor

the Recommended Practices is critical in influencing children's interactions with the world and thus their learning and development. In making this statement, however, an important qualification must be noted; specifically, not all of the interactions children have with the world around them must be planned by professionals. Clearly, most parents provide their children with an array of experiences in the home (e.g., games they play at bath time, family routines, eating with the family) and community (e.g., participating in events such as going shopping, attending religious services, going to story hour at the library) that promote learning of desirable skills. Professionals must be sure not to impose interventions that actually interfere with such events. This can be accomplished by working closely with families to identify goals, objectives, and teaching approaches and contexts.

Third, *the field now has a good deal of research for guiding practitioners' decisions related to organizing and influencing children's experiences* (Barnett, Bell, & Carey, 1999; Guralnick, 1997; Kozloff, 1994; Odom & McLean, 1996; Shonkoff & Meisels, 2000). This research often has been conducted in service programs addressing desired skills of real children. Further, much of this research was conducted with valid measures and rigorous procedures (Odom & Strain, 2002). As a result, the field has a solid foundation from which to derive Recommended Practices. The existence of this research foundation means practitioners' decisions and work should not be based solely on their experiences and beliefs; rather, clear guidance is available from the literature for making many critical decisions and for using particular practices.

Organization of the Practices

Using this ever-expanding research base, this chapter contains Recommended Practices for influencing children's ongoing interactions with the social and physical world to ensure that they have experiences that will enhance their learning of desirable skills and styles of interacting. In this chapter, the Recommended Practices are organized around three major "take-home messages":

1. Adults design environments to promote children's safety, active engagement, learning, participation, and membership.
2. Adults use ongoing data to individualize and adapt practices to meet each child's changing needs.
3. Adults use systematic procedures within and across environments, activities, and routines to promote children's learning and participation.

These messages carry some specific implications that deserve explicit note. Each message specifies that adults do specific things (i.e., design environments, individualize and adapt practices, and use systematic procedures) in very purposeful ways to produce specific outcomes. Child-focused intervention is broadly described as an intentional act on the part of adults who care for and interact with children. Implementing child-focused practices involves each of these functions. Designing environments is not enough, individualization and use of specific procedures must also occur; however, individualizing or using specific procedures is not adequate if the children's environments have not been designed to incorporate the recommended procedures. Individualization that ignores the use of specific procedures may not work. Thus, each of these three messages contains recommendations that if used in isolation are not adequate for providing high-quality intervention; the recommendations must be applied as a whole.

Child-focused intervention is broadly described as an intentional act on the part of adults who care for and interact with children.

Implementing child-focused interventions is a complex process; it is demanding and it requires careful attention to many different issues. Because of the complexity of these procedures and because many early childhood professionals have not had opportunities to learn these procedures and apply them in natural contexts, they may need training and support to be able to effectively design and implement these procedures.

These three messages are useful ways of organizing and thinking about this difficult task of designing interventions, solving problems, improving services, and ensuring that children's goals are achieved. In addition to the research that supports these practices, additional support comes from solid theoretical foundations, experience, and the judgments of knowledgeable experts.

chapter

4

Relationship to Other Chapters

Despite the comprehensive nature of the Recommended Practices in this chapter, they do not address some critical issues related to applying child-focused interventions. These practices do not describe in detail the Practices that should be used in assessing children and their environments to identify goals and plan the implementation of individualized intervention strategies (McLean, Wolery, & Bailey, 2004). This information is critical, because it helps ensure that the Practices included here are not misapplied. More specific information on identifying goals and objectives for individual children is included in Chapter 3. The assessment chapter includes specific practices related to assessment strategies that are designed for the purpose of identifying children's intervention goals (specifically Recommended Practices A13-29). In addition, the chapters on family-based practices (Chapter 5) and interdisciplinary practices (Chapter 6) include information about how to involve families and other team members in developing intervention goals for individual children.

This chapter does not include information on how to assist families in supporting their children's experiences (Dunst, Trivette, & Deal, 1994). When attempting to ensure that children's experiences promote learning of desired goals, there is a danger of placing expectations on parents to assume narrow roles similar to that of teachers or interventionists. While parents clearly and appropriately teach their children many things, the emphasis should be on ensuring that families live normalized lives while having positive interactions between themselves and their children and providing experiences that have enhancing effects. Recommended Practices for supporting and assisting families are presented in Chapter 5.

. . . the emphasis should be on ensuring that families live normalized lives while having positive interactions between themselves and their children. . . .

This chapter also does not include information on how to work with other adults (e.g., child care staff, therapists, community play group staff) to promote children's learning and development (Bruder, 1994). Nonetheless, working effectively with such individuals is central to promoting children's learning through their ongoing experiences. Nor does this chapter describe practices related to the delivery of specialized therapies, or how those specialized therapies are embedded into children's ongoing experiences (McWilliam, 1996). Recommended Practices for working with other adults and implementing specialized therapies are found in the other Recommended Practices strands. Finally, this chapter does not provide guidance related to placement decisions. The recommendations in this chapter assume such decisions have been made carefully; it does provide guidance, however, on how any placement should be organized and operated.

Some Key Terms

In the Recommended Practices, the term *adults* is used several times. This term is defined broadly to include all of the persons who are responsible for caring for, educating, or providing therapy to young children with disabilities. As such, it includes parents, teachers, therapists, and other caregivers. It includes all of these various adults because of the assumption that all interactions children have with their environment are potentially beneficial or harmful to their learning and development. When the term *interventionist* or *professional* is used, it refers specifically to the professionals (teachers, therapists, etc.) who are responsible for planning and carrying out children's individualized EI/ECSE programs.

The recommendations in this chapter also refer to intervention *strategies*. A strategy is an organized procedure for guiding adults' behavior in interacting with, and promoting the learning of, young children with disabilities. Such strategies have conceptual and research foundations; however, those that are listed should not be considered the sum total of what is possible. Other strategies can be devised, and individualized strategies not listed here could be used and evaluated with individual children to address specific goals. Strategies are different from practices in that they are more specific about what adults should do and how the strategies should be applied for addressing specific goals of individual children. References to more detailed information about these strategies are included in the reference list. In addition, citations to research that support these practices can be found on the Division for Early Childhood (DEC) Web site (www.dec-sped.org).

Summary

The Practices in this chapter will guide adults in planning and implementing effective child-focused interventions that enhance children's learning and development. The Practices can and should be used in conjunction with the others in this book to guide program development and improvement.

References

Bailey, D. B., & Wolery, M. (1992). *Teaching infants and preschoolers with disabilities* (2nd ed.). Columbus, OH: Macmillan.

Barnett, D. W., Bell, S. H., & Carey, K. T. (1999). *Designing preschool interventions: A practitioner's guide.* New York: Guilford.

Bruder, M. B. (1994). Working with members of other disciplines: Collaboration for success. In M. Wolery & J. S. Wilbers (Eds.), *Including children with special needs in early childhood programs* (pp. 45-70). Washington, DC: National Association for the Education of Young Children (NAEYC).

Dunst, C. J., Trivette, C. M., & Deal, A. G. (1994). *Supporting and strengthening families (Vol. 1): Methods, strategies and practices.* Cambridge: Brookline Books.

Guralnick, M. J. (1997). *The effectiveness of early intervention.* Baltimore: Paul H. Brookes.

Horowitz, F. D., & Haritos, C. (1998). The organism and the environment: Implications for understanding mental retardation. In J. A. Burack, R. M. Hodapp, & E. Zigler (Eds.), *Handbook of mental retardation and development* (pp. 20-40). New York: Cambridge University Press.

Kozloff, M. A. (1994). *Improving educational outcomes for children with disabilities: Principles of assessment, program planning, and evaluation.* Baltimore: Paul H. Brookes.

McLean, M., Wolery, M., & Bailey, D. (2004). *Assessment of infants and preschoolers with special needs* (3rd ed.). Columbus, OH: Pearson/Merrill/Prentice Hall.

McWilliam, R. A. (1996). *Rethinking pull-out services in early intervention: A professional resource.* Baltimore: Paul H. Brookes.

McWilliam, R. A., Wolery, M., & Odom, S. L. (2001). Instructional perspectives in inclusive preschool classrooms. In M. J. Guralnick (Ed.), *Early childhood inclusion: Focus on change* (pp. 503-527). Baltimore: Paul H. Brookes.

Odom, S. L., & McLean, M. E. (Eds.). (1996). *Early intervention/early childhood special education: Recommended practices.* Austin, TX: Pro-Ed.

Odom, S. L., & Strain, P. S. (2002). Evidence-based practice in early intervention/early childhood special education: Single-subject design research. *Journal of Early Intervention, 25,* 151-160.

Shonkoff, J. P., & Meisels, S. J. (2000). *Handbook of early childhood intervention* (2nd ed.). Cambridge, UK: Cambridge University Press.

Widerstrom, A. H., Mowder, B. A., & Sandall, S. A. (1997). *Infant development and risk* (2nd ed.). Baltimore: Paul H. Brookes.

DEC Recommended Practices and Examples: Child-Focused Practices

Adults design environments to promote children's safety, active engagemen learning, participation, and membership.

. . . .

C1. Physical space and materials are structured and adapted to promote engagement, play, interaction, and learning by attending to children's preferences and interests, using novelty, using responsive toys, providing adequate amounts of materials, and using defined spaces.

Examples:

- *The classroom has clearly defined learning centers. Visual cues in the flooring (e.g., bright area rugs, vinyl flooring, colored masking tape) or low pieces of furniture (e.g., shelves) define the learning centers.*

- *Toys and books are rotated (e.g., rotated in and out of storage, toys exchanged with another teacher) on a regular basis to provide novelty and interest to children. Toys and books are clean and in good repair.*

- *When learning centers are not a choice (e.g., during times when large group activities are occurring, when staffing is reduced, when behavior is a problem, when messy centers are closed early to clean them), they are visually closed. This can be done by placing lids on sand and water tables, turning shelves around, using "stop" and "go" signs, or draping sheets over centers that are not currently choices.*

- *Boxes of related props are used in the dramatic play area (e.g., hospital, vet's office, pizza parlor, grocery store, etc.) to keep the center interesting.*

- *Most toys and materials are accessible to children so that they can get them without adult help, although some toys should be visible and require the child to ask an adult for access.*

- *Sufficient amounts of toys are available so children's play is allowed to continue (e.g., enough blocks to allow children to build complex constructions), and to minimize conflicts between children over toys.*

- *Duplicates of highly preferred toys should be available, especially for toddlers, to minimize peer conflicts and maximize engagement and imitation.*

C2. The social dimension of the environment is structured and adapted to promote engagement, interaction, communication, and learning by providing peer models, peer proximity, responsive adults, and imitative adults; and by expanding children's play and behavior.

Examples:

- *Small groups are arranged so that children have peer models at their table who are situated so the children can see one another and interact.*

- *Peers are taught to be communicative partners for children using signing or augmentative or adaptive communication systems (AAC).*

- *Toys are selected that promote social interaction versus isolated play (e.g., wagons, balls, puppets, board games).*

- *Adults play with children, watch what children do, repeat what children are doing with their materials, and then model elaborations or variations of that play—sometimes by describing verbally what they are doing in the elaboration or variation.*

- *The home visitor shows an older sister how to help her younger brother manipulate blocks by giving cues on how to model building a house with blocks and asking him to build one like hers.*

- *Especially in infant-toddler programs, assignment of teachers or caregivers to children or groups of children remains consistent.*

C3. Routines and transitions are structured to promote interaction, communication, and learning by being responsive to child behavior and using naturalistic time delay, interrupted chain procedure, transition-based teaching, and visual cue systems.

Examples:

- *Clear visual cues including gestures, photographs, written labels, or an object cue are used to support children during transitions, to help children understand the routine, and to help children manage their time as needed.*

- *Time delay strategies are used to increase children's spontaneity and decrease their dependence on adult prompts. Time delays are brief intervals of time (e.g., a couple seconds) that are inserted between the need for a behavior and a prompt to help children perform the behavior. These prompts should and can be faded or removed over time.*

- *Transition times are kept minimal and are made as beneficial as possible by embedding interesting and instructional activities within them (e.g., teaching children to count the number of children who are lined up, teaching children to help each other during routines).*

- *When a transition begins, the teacher asks the children a quick question, waits for a response and/or models a response, and then lets the children proceed to the next area or activity (transition-based teaching).*

- *Caregivers label steps of routines (e.g., hand washing) by stating what children are doing or signing songs.*

- *To promote communicative exchanges, caregivers withhold help the child needs during routines while looking expectantly at the child and waiting for the child to request help or say the next step of the routine (interrupted chain procedure).*

- *Caregivers alert children to upcoming transitions (whether getting ready for small group time or getting ready to take a bath, for example) by telling them what will happen or by using a visual cue.*

- *Home visitors and parents use the naturally occurring routines of bedtime or meal-time to have children practice skills such as reaching, grasping, or requesting.*

- *Home visitors help parents make usual routines and transitions (e.g., getting in and out of a car seat) predictable by having regular sequences of events (including visual cues) in those routines.*

C4. Play routines are structured to promote interaction, communication, and learning by defining roles for dramatic play, prompting engagement, prompting group friendship activities, and using specialized props.

Examples:

- *Adults use children's preferences to increase engagement and to promote interactions with peers. For example, a teacher uses a child's preference for trains by turning the dramatic play area into a train station. The child now interacts with peers to "purchase" train tickets, to take turns blowing the train whistle and turning on the train, and to help build a pretend train station.*

- *Adults provide individual picture cues (e.g., photographs of the activities) to provide support and structure during free choice time for specific children.*

- *Adults join children in their play to keep children playing.*

- *Adults assist and encourage children to give toys to one another and to take offered toys from one another to teach social exchanges and sharing.*

- *Adults use small group activities that involve turn taking and social interactions between children during the activities.*

- *The home visitor and parent identify the child's favorite toys and storybooks to use to encourage joint attention (i.e., the parent and the child look at the same pictures).*

- *Home visitors help parents involve siblings and other children in the child's play.*

- *Home visitors help parents join in children's play by following children's lead in play activities.*

C5. Environments are designed and activities are conducted so that children learn or are exposed to multiple cultures and languages by, among other practices, allowing children and families to share their cultures and languages with others, to the extent they desire.

Examples:

- *Books are available that reflect multiple cultures and languages.*

- *Parents are welcomed in the classroom and professionals offer opportunities for parents and children to share practices from their cultures with others.*

- *Puzzles, dolls, dramatic play props, musical instruments and songs, kitchen utensils and menus, and decorations in the classroom reflect the variety of languages and cultures of the families in the program.*

- *At the beginning of the year, families are given the opportunity to decorate their children's cubbies to reflect the child's own personality and style.*

- *Parents are encouraged to participate in excursions into the community, and such excursions are to places reflecting the cultural mix of the community.*

C6. Learning environments meet accepted standards of quality including curriculum, child-staff ratios, group size, and physical design of classroom.

Examples:

- *Programs adopt curricula that are based on sound principles of child development and are consistent with the NAEYC's developmentally appropriate practice (DAP) guidelines.*

- *Programs hire enough staff and have an up-to-date substitute list so that when staff are absent, replacements are easily found and the program can maintain appropriate staff-child ratios. There is sufficient coverage so that when adults take breaks, or need to take children to the bathroom, the child-staff ratio does not become too great.*

- *The physical environment is safe for all children and is checked on a regular basis to ensure upkeep.*

- *In classroom programs attention is given to keeping children in consistent groups over time (several months to a couple years) to encourage membership and belonging.*

- *Programs ensure that the physical environment is accessible to all children, and classrooms allow for easy traffic flow between areas and activities.*

C7. Interventionists ensure the physical and emotional safety and security of children while children are in their care.

Examples:

- *Adequate supervision and careful monitoring are provided throughout the day. Staff "count" heads throughout the day and are frequently scanning the room to make sure all the children are present and safe.*

- *Transitions between the classroom and other areas (e.g., the playground) are monitored and supervised carefully to ensure children's safety and to prevent the development and maintenance of behavior problems.*

- *Adults respond empathetically to children who are hurt or in distress.*

- *Adults model through their own behavior how to treat others and how to appropriately express emotions.*

- *Adults regularly monitor and inspect their materials and environments for safety risks to minimize the likelihood of harm and injury.*

- *Adults smile frequently at children, show genuine pleasure to be in the company of children, and show authentic approval of each child's accomplishments.*

- *Home visitors assist families in monitoring their environments for safety risks that may expose children to harm and injury.*

- *Home visitors model and show genuine affection and care for children and for other members of the family.*

C8. A variety of appropriate settings and naturally occurring activities are used to facilitate children's learning and development.

Examples:

- *Teaching and learning opportunities are embedded throughout children's daily routines and activities regardless of where children spend time. For example, parents and caregivers can prompt children to use new words while driving in the car, eating dinner, taking a bath, or playing in the park.*

- *Intervention is provided in settings that families identify as routine and that families identify as possible teaching and learning opportunities. Care is taken to ensure that interventions are designed to "fit into" families' routines.*

- *Assistance provided outside of natural environments (e.g., clinics) includes practices that assist families in interacting with their children to meet goals at home and in the community.*

- *Assistance provided outside of natural environments (e.g., clinics) includes practices that are both feasible for and acceptable to families and that do not disrupt families' usual routines when interacting with their children.*

chapter

4

...rvices are provided in natural learning environments as appropriate. These
...nclude places in which typical children participate such as the home or
community settings.

Examples:

- *Supports are provided for children in their community child care setting. Some
  examples of supports might be regular visits from one of the child's therapists or
  early intervention providers, training of staff related specifically to including children with disabilities, specialized equipment loaned to the program by the early
  intervention system, securing input from the staff about the usual activities and
  routines of the day, and integration of intervention recommendations into those
  activities and routines.*

- *Programs are available for children in their neighborhoods. Children receive the
  support they need to attend the same school with their siblings and/or neighbors.*

- *The child's therapist provides suggestions for helping the child participate in a
  "mommy and me" group, storytime, or similar activity.*

- *Home visitors assist families in devising strategies to help the family participate in
  their usual routines with the child; for example, helping the family with strategies
  for attending religious services, helping families find qualified babysitters, assisting families in devising ways to accomplish usual activities such a grocery shopping with the child.*

C10. Interventionists facilitate children's engagement with their environment to
encourage child-initiated learning that is not dependent on the adult's
presence.

Examples:

- *Adults provide interesting toys, materials, and activities that encourage children to
  make choices independently and to want to continue playing.*

- *Adults provide fun and interesting activities for children that provide contingent
  feedback as a result of the child's actions (e.g., motion-activated mobiles, rattles,
  musical games).*

- *Adults modify and adapt the curriculum and the environment to increase the
  children's meaningful participation, which includes partial participation with support, with materials and people (e.g., structuring the physical, social, and tempo-
  ral environments; adapting materials; simplifying an activity; encouraging peers
  to support the child; using specialized equipment; using children's preferences).*

- *Many toys and materials are in organized learning centers with open shelves and
  at eye level so that children can find them and make independent selections.*

- *Adults encourage and reinforce children for initiations and engagement with
  materials by providing choices; making suggestions; giving children time to make
  choices; and providing positive, descriptive feedback.*

- *Adults are responsive to children's initiations by "reading" and interpreting their nonverbal cues, anticipating their desires but waiting for children to give a clear signal of that desire, and following the child's lead in play.*

- *Home visitors discuss and model the value of child initiations with materials and with others to help families value children's initiations.*

C11. Environments are provided that foster positive relationships, including peer-peer, parent/caregiver-child, and parent-caregiver relationships.

Examples:

- *Adults model positive interactions by commenting on children's behaviors, particularly sharing with, helping, and listening to others.*

- *Professionals establish positive relationships with parents and other professionals in proactive ways such as giving choices for communication systems, welcoming visitors in the classroom, and planning convenient social activities.*

- *Professionals communicate the accomplishments of children often to parents in formal (e.g., written notes and certificates) and informal (e.g., phone calls) ways.*

- *Home visitors begin their visits with parents by sharing thoughts, ideas, and updates.*

- *Home visitors interact with the adults in the family and listen to and respond to their questions honestly and with accurate information.*

- *Home visitors assist families in interacting with other professionals (e.g., for a transition IEP meeting) by giving families information about the process and about different team members' roles.*

- *Home visitors engage in courteous behavior with families by following through, being on time, keeping appointments, and meeting their responsibilities to families.*

Adults use ongoing data to individualize and adapt practices to meet each child's changing needs.

C12. Practices are individualized for each child based on: (a) the child's current behavior and abilities across relevant domains instead of the child's diagnostic classification; (b) the family's views of what the child needs to learn; (c) interventionists' and specialists' views of what the child needs to learn; and (d) the demands, expectations, and requirements of the child's current environments. The practices as well as goals are individualized.

Examples:

- *Teams have goals/objectives based on individualized observation and assessment and planning for each child rather than a set of goals for all children.*

- *Teams set goals that help children adapt to their home and community settings.*

- *Teams solicit and actively encourage parents' input on goals multiple times before formal meetings to determine goals are conducted.*

- *Teams give considerable weight to the assessment results obtained from interviews with familiar adults and observations in normal and familiar circumstances.*

- *Teams describe the specific situations and conditions under which children exhibit given behaviors and do not assume behaviors are well-generalized.*

- *Teams identify practices and interaction patterns that appear to work well with the child in planning interventions that will be used.*

- *Teams conduct preference inventories and assessments to identify children's preferences and potential reinforcers.*

- *Teams secure information about children's regular schedules and the settings in which they spend significant time and use this information in planning intervention programs.*

C13. Practices target meaningful outcomes for the child that build upon the child's current skills and behavior and promote membership with others.

Examples:

- *Professionals and family members collaboratively identify goals and objectives during the IFSP/IEP process. Parents are asked to talk about their goals, dreams, and preferences for their children.*

- *Children's future environments are considered when planning instructional programs so children's goals and objectives are designed to support their success in future as well as current environments.*

- *The team identifies skills that will help the child perform with increasing independence at home, in the community, or in school.*

- *Professionals and families consider the settings in which children regularly spend time and determine the expectations needed in those environments to promote children's participation in all activities.*

C14. Data-based decisions are used to make modifications in the practices. Child performance is monitored and data are collected to determine the impact of the practices on the child's progress, and monitoring must be feasible and useful within the child's environments (i.e., ongoing monitoring must be user friendly) and is used to make modifications of intervention if needed.

Examples:

- *Adults collect data frequently enough to determine if children are making progress so that they can make modifications in the instructional program if it is not effective.*

- *Teams work to develop data sheets and other data collection strategies that work for teachers as well as strategies that work for families and other caregivers.*

- *Teams consider multiple methods for documenting children's progress, such as frequency counts, per opportunity probes, work samples, checklists, videotapes, and photographs.*

- *Members of the team who have regular (e.g., at least weekly) contact with the child review the data often and make necessary adjustments if progress is not occurring.*

- *Teams monitor how well the intervention practices are being implemented (i.e., fidelity) to ensure correct and consistent usage and the likelihood of effectiveness.*

C15. Recommended practices are used to teach/promote whatever skills are necessary for children to function more completely, competently, adaptively, and independently in the child's natural environment. These skills should include teaching those that maximize participation and membership in home, school, and community environments—including those that are typical or similar to other persons' in that environment. Attention should be given to the breadth and sophistication of the child's skills. Examples of important skills across many children are

- Being actively engaged with materials, objects, activities, and other people (peers and adults)

- Being an initiator (i.e., child initiates play, social interactions, communicative exchanges, etc. without assistance from adults)

- Being responsive to the initiations and behavior of others, including peers and adults

- Reading the cues of the environment and responding appropriately based on those cues without being directed by adults

- Having social interactions and relationships with family, peers, and others

- Communicating with others, including peers and adults

Examples:

- *Teams observe children in the settings in which they regularly spend time to identify skills children need for participating actively in the activities and routines of those settings.*

- *Adults monitor their own behavior and interactions with children to ensure they are not promoting lack of child initiation, passivity, helplessness, dependence, nonengagement, or challenging behaviors.*

- *The team examines the settings in which the child regularly spends time to identify ways to adapt the environment or materials in order to allow the child to initiate more interactions with materials, peers, and adults.*

- *Home visitors assist families, as the families desire, in including children in all their usual activities and routines.*

C16. Children's behavior is recognized, interpreted in context, and responded to contingently, and opportunities are provided for expansion or elaboration of child behavior by imitating the behavior, waiting for the child's responses, modeling, and prompting.

Examples:

- *During snack time, the child looks at the applesauce on the snack tray. The teacher recognizes this as interest and points to the applesauce, saying, "We have applesauce." The teacher waits and the child says, "apple." The teacher says, "applesauce please," and the child responds, "applesauce please." The teacher gives the child the applesauce while also giving her positive feedback about her response.*

- *Adults use progressive match strategies, in which they imitate the children's behavior and then add steps. The teacher imitates the child scooping and pouring water in the sensory table over and over, and then the teacher scoops and pours the water into a jar and waits for the child to imitate. The teacher can then suggest a more complex play sequence that involves adding a peer to the activity and promoting turn taking.*

- *A parent imitates her child's sounds and actions until the child notices, and then stops and waits for the child to request her to continue.*

- *A baby kicks his legs in excitement when playing a game with his parent. The home visitor helps the parent understand the child's wish to repeat the game.*

Adults use systematic procedures within and across environments, activities, and routines to promote children's learning and participation.

C17. Interventionists are agents of change to promote and accelerate learning, and that learning should be viewed in different phases that require different types of practices. Phases are

- acquisition—learning how to do the skill
- fluency—learning to do the skill smoothly and at natural rates
- maintenance—learning to do the skill after instruction has stopped
- generalization—learning to apply the skill whenever and wherever it is needed

Examples:

- *IFSP/IEP objectives reflect different phases of learning—learning how to do behaviors, doing them well, and applying them when they are needed.*

- *Data collection on an objective continues even after the child acquires the skill to monitor the ongoing use (i.e., maintenance) of the skill.*

- *Planning for generalized use of target behaviors begins when objectives are written, not after acquisition has been accomplished.*

- *Teams explicitly monitor whether newly acquired competencies are maintained and applied when and where children need the skills.*

- *Teams view their roles as that of helping families and assisting children in learning important and useful skills for appropriate home and community circumstances.*

C18. Practices are used systematically, frequently, and consistently within and across environments (e.g., home, center, community) and across people (i.e., those who care for and interact regularly with the child).

Examples:

- *Professionals collaborate with family members to determine instructional practices to increase the probability that strategies can and will be used at home and the center.*

- *The intinerant teacher cross-trains and shares instructional programs with child care providers to ensure that practices are consistent across settings.*

- *If the family desires, professionals work with the family to identify the adults who are regularly in the child's life (e.g., the grandfather or babysitter) and include them in the IFSP/IEP development to increase the likelihood that practices will be used across people.*

- *Professionals solicit information from families about things they are doing that are "working" with their children so that professionals can incorporate those practices into their interactions with children (e.g., list of commonly used words at home, verbal and physical cues used to initiate toileting).*

C19. Planning occurs prior to implementation, and that planning considers the situation (home, classroom, etc.) to which the interventions will be applied.

Examples:

- *Instructional programs reflect antecedents and consequences that would occur naturally in classrooms and homes. If requesting is the target skill, teachers provide examples and demonstrations of how mand-model instructional strategies could be used in home settings. For example, parents can set up situations in which children will have to request more food at the dinner table, more water in the bathtub, and ask for assistance getting something out of the refrigerator. At school, the teacher might place the child's favorite toy out of reach so the child will have to request the toy.*

- *Consideration of family routines, lifestyles, supports, and resources are considered when choosing communication systems for children, as some require extensive time, organization, and training to be effective. Families are involved in identifying the strategies or systems to ensure that they will "work" within the family's routines.*

- *Recommendations to families and to other caregivers about intervention practices are made only after it is determined that the practices are feasible in light of the demands on the families and other caregivers at that time.*

- *Planning has enough specificity to include who will implement a practice with whom, when it will be done, what will be done, and how regular monitoring will be performed to see if the practice is effective.*

. . . .

C20. Practices are used that are validated, normalized, useful across environments, respectful, and not stigmatizing of the child and family and that are sensitive to cultural and linguistic issues.

Examples:

- *When cooking activities are planned at school, professionals talk with parents of children with restricted diets to determine acceptable foods and recipes so that all of the children can participate and no child is stigmatized.*

- *Professionals plan activities around the holiday celebrations that each child celebrates, or does not plan holiday activities at all versus solely celebrating those of the dominant culture.*

- *Professionals validate the children's home languages by learning some words of the languages and teaching them to the other children. For example, when counting the days on the calendar, the teacher counts them in both English and Vietnamese.*

- *Professionals learn about the family's usual child rearing practices such as introduction of self-feeding or timing of toilet training and incorporates this knowledge into their planning.*

- *Practice recommendations to families are made so that they preserve the role of adults as parents as compared to turning them into teachers or therapists.*

- *Teachers use strategies that are known to be effective and collect data to determine if the strategy works with the individual child.*

. . . .

C21. Consequences for children's behavior are structured to increase the complexity and duration of children's play, engagement, appropriate behavior, and learning by using differential reinforcement, response shaping, high-probability procedures (i.e., behavioral momentum), and correspondence training.

Examples:

- *Staff and parents "catch children being good" by commenting on their appropriate behavior as frequently as possible. Adults tailor the positive feedback by making it descriptive and individualized. For example, some children enjoy being acknowledged in front of others, while some children might prefer a quiet pat on the shoulder.*

- *Natural reinforcers (i.e., reinforcers that are part of the activity or routine such as a toy the child is requesting) are used. These types of reinforcers increase children's motivation and assist in teaching children to use new skills in different situations.*

- *Staff provide children with additional materials as their play continues in order to expand that play and promote learning.*
- *Staff use praise and other reinforcers in varied, genuine, enthusiastic, and contingent ways.*
- *Staff help children plan their play and activities, reinforce that planning, and reinforce children for following through on the plan.*
- *Staff observe and become aware of children's usual behavior (e.g., play, social and communicative interactions) and systematically and consistently reinforce more advanced variations of those behaviors.*
- *Staff observe children to identify materials or activities children find reinforcing and use those materials and activities to increase children's engagement and learning.*

C22. Systematic naturalistic teaching procedures such as models, expansions, incidental teaching, mand-model procedure, and naturalistic time delay are used to promote acquisition and use of communication and social skills.

Examples:

- *At snack, adults display the snack items and wait for the children to request them (e.g., by pointing, speaking, signing, or using their alternate communication systems). If the child makes an appropriate request, descriptive feedback and access to the requested material is provided to the child. If not, a planned correction is used to help the child learn to request.*
- *When playing with interlocking blocks, adults model the color names and ask children to imitate the verbal models.*
- *The teacher arranges for a cooperative peer with a "busy ball" game to sit down in front of a child who is learning to take turns with peers. When the target child initiates play by grabbing at the ball, the teacher asks the child to use words to ask the peer for the toy. The child is given time to respond. When the child asks, "Can I play?" the teacher prompts the peer to share the toy with the target child.*
- *A parent and young preverbal child are taking turns with sounds. The home visitor describes or models how to expand the child's sounds into words.*
- *Home visitors assist parents in using naturalistic teaching procedures by describing them briefly, modeling them with the child, watching the parent use them with the child, and giving the parent encouragement and feedback.*

C23. Peer-mediated strategies are used to promote social and communicative behavior.

Examples:

- *Adults involve peers in promoting children's social interactions. The teacher teaches peers critical social skills (e.g., asking another child to play, taking turns, talking to a child, staying in proximity). When peers and the target child play together, the teacher carefully monitors and judiciously reinforces their interactive play.*

- *Teachers use peer tutoring to promote children's communication skills. Teachers demonstrate to peers how to use descriptive talk to comment on their peer's behavior during play to provide a model of specific communication and language objectives.*

- *Teachers employ peer modeling to increase children's imitative play. During free choice, teachers have peers perform a desired skill for the target child and encourage the target child's attention to the important behavior (e.g., "Wow, look what Tommy is doing with the blocks. You can do that too!").*

- *Professionals implement group contingencies for the performance of target children's social behavior. For example, all of the children in the class receive "high fives" when the target children share toys with peers during free choice time.*

- *Professionals teach developmentally sophisticated peers how to initiate play and social interactions with other children, how to have positive exchanges with other children, and how to persist in playing with other children.*

- *Professionals teach developmentally sophisticated peers to verbally describe what they are doing when they are playing near children with disabilities.*

- *Adults engage and play with the children with low rates of peer interaction and invite peers to join them to promote and support exchanges between the children (e.g., giving/taking toys, asking each other for more materials, asking another child to look at a construction or product).*

- *Professionals teach developmentally sophisticated peers to interpret nonverbal children's communicative attempts (e.g., looking as an indication of preference, reaching as expression of a desire for a toy).*

C24. Prompting and prompt fading procedures (e.g., modeling, graduated guidance, increasing assistance, time delay) are used to ensure acquisition and use of communicative, self-care, cognitive, and social skills.

Examples:

- *Adults determine the level and type of prompt children need to exhibit appropriate performance, and then use that prompt with one of the methods (listed above) for delivering and removing prompts systematically.*

- *Adults use an effective prompting strategy to promote correct responding and then reinforce children contingently for appropriate performance.*

- *Adults reinforce both prompted and unprompted behaviors that are being taught to ensure that children are successful.*

- *Adults monitor their own behavior to ensure that they are not providing unneeded prompts for behaviors children can already do independently, but perhaps not proficiently; for example, allowing the child to put on her shoes after nap herself although the teacher could do so more quickly.*

- *Adults check that children are actively attending to them, the task, or the activity before asking them to respond and before using prompting strategies.*

- *Adults use the prompt/prompt fading procedures throughout the day for the targeted skills rather than only in isolated sessions or small group activities.*

. . . .

C25. Specialized procedures (e.g., naturalistic strategies and prompt/prompt fading strategies) are embedded and distributed within and across activities.

Examples:

- *Adults provide opportunities to learn and practice targeted skills during routine, planned, and child-initiated activities. For example, children learning to make requests are provided opportunities throughout the day (e.g., what they want for breakfast, the shirt they want to wear, who they want to sit by on the bus, what color scissors they want to cut with, what song they want to sing at circle).*

- *Professionals develop activity matrices to schedule instructional opportunities for identified objectives throughout the daily schedule. On the activity matrix, the schedule of class activities is listed down one side (e.g., arrival, circle time, small group, outside, free choice, snack, story, departure) and the children's names are listed across the top. In the intersecting cells, the child's objective is listed for the identified teaching opportunities (e.g., responding to a peer's greeting is listed in the cells for arrival and circle), and the instructional procedure to be used is noted.*

- *Adults identify classroom areas or activities in which particular goal behaviors are likely to be needed and are appropriate, and they ensure those goal behaviors are promoted when the child is in those areas.*

- *Professionals and families collaboratively develop family-guided routine schedules to identify times throughout the child's day when instruction on target skills can occur (e.g., bath time, riding in the car, getting ready for nap).*

- *Each activity and routine of the day includes more than one objective that is taught. For example, toileting time is used for teaching dressing/undressing, social turn taking with the adult monitoring the toileting, and vocabulary development. Mealtimes and snacks are used for self-feeding goals as well as child-child conversations, more elaborate language usage, and cognitive skills such as naming the foods, their colors, and size. Play time is used for teaching sustained and more elaborate engagement with toys, how to play with new toys, social interactions, cognitive skills, and language skills.*

chapter
4

C26. Recommended instructional strategies are used with sufficient fidelity, consistency, frequency, and intensity to ensure high levels of behavior occurring frequently.

Examples:

- *Professionals assess their own use of instructional procedures to ensure they are performing them correctly, or they ask other professionals to observe and provide them with feedback.*

- *Professionals develop fidelity checklists of the steps involved in using procedures and monitor their own behavior related to correct use of those procedures.*

- *Professionals teach other caregivers (e.g., teaching assistants) how to use instructional practices, model the use of those practices with them, observe their use of the practices, and give them feedback to ensure correct use.*

- *Professionals and families work together to develop written instructional plans that specify the strategies to be used to ensure that everyone involved is using the strategies correctly. Those plans are sufficiently detailed to allow a trained person to follow them accurately.*

- *Team members collect, summarize, and analyze data with sufficient frequency to determine if instructional strategies are effective with individual children.*

- *Team members collect, summarize, and analyze data with sufficient frequency to determine if instructional strategies should be modified to promote learning and development.*

- *Team members plan and schedule instructional opportunities so that instruction occurs often enough to result in sufficient practice and learning.*

- *Teams restructure their schedule and activities to ensure that all the children are receiving adequate opportunities to learn the behaviors in their objectives.*

C27. For problem behaviors, interventionists assess the behavior in context to identify its function, and then devise interventions that are comprehensive in that they make the behavior irrelevant (child's environment is modified so that problem behavior is unnecessary or precluded), inefficient (a more efficient replacement behavior is taught), and ineffective (i.e., reinforcement and other consequent events are used).

Examples:

- *Professionals collect data on the antecedents (A), behavior (B), and consequences (C) (the "ABCs of behavior") to determine what functions problem behaviors might be serving for children. For example, following an ABC analysis, the teacher determines that activities that involve a lot of watching (A) result in tantrumming (B), which results in the child being removed from the activity (C). The teacher makes the child's escape behavior (e.g., tantrumming) at circle time irrelevant by planning interactive and fun circle times that are no longer than ten minutes.*

- *After determining that the function of a child's spitting behavior is to obtain her sister's attention, the parent makes the spitting inefficient by teaching the child to instead gently touch her sister's arm to gain her attention (which is easier than spitting).*

- *After determining that a child's swearing is used to obtain the teacher's attention, the teacher makes the behavior ineffective by ignoring the bad words and providing high rates of positive attention to the child when he uses appropriate words.*

- *Professionals ensure that children have access to environments with interesting and preferred activities and materials that are both age and developmentally appropriate and that encourage children to participate or partially participate with those activities or materials. Professionals also ensure that children receive a great deal of attention, acknowledgment, and support for being engaged and participating.*

- *Professionals assess their own behaviors to ensure that they are not promoting or maintaining challenging behaviors (e.g., attending to children for minor disruptions, instigating transitions without adequate warning and cues, having unclear expectations, having too few materials resulting in child-child conflicts).*

- *Adults anticipate when children are likely to have significant problems, and support them by teaching and encouraging positive replacement behaviors. For example, if children are likely to be aggressive when peers take their toys, the teacher carefully monitors those children and observes for such occurrences, then helps the aggressive children to ask appropriately for the toys back rather than hitting the offending peers. It is critical that the offending peers then return the toys and that potentially aggressive children learn that words will be effective in retrieving toys.*

Child-Focused Practices Glossary

Acquisition. The initial phase of learning. It refers to learning the basic requirements and movements of a skill or behavior; learning how to do something.

Active engagement. Children manipulating materials and/or interacting with others in ways that promote learning.

Assessment. The process of collecting information, ideally from multiple sources and means, for making informed decisions for individuals, families, and programs.

Behavior. The actions people (children and adults) do; this term refers to both desirable or adaptive actions (e.g., speaking, playing with toys, interacting with peers) and undesirable or challenging actions (e.g., tantrums, aggression, self-injury).

Behavioral momentum. The theoretical principle underlying the effectiveness of the high-probability request procedure, often used as a synonym for the high-probability request procedure.

Consistency. The regularity with which a given instructional procedure or intervention practice is used.

Contingently. A relationship between two events; if the first occurs, then the second occurs soon thereafter. It usually is associated with adults' responses to children; for example, adults deliver reinforcers contingently, meaning that when the child performs a given behavior, adults quickly respond to that behavior.

Correspondence training. A procedure that reinforces a match (correspondence) between what children say and do. There are several variations of the procedure, including the "plan, do, and review" approach, which involves asking the child what he or she is going to do ("plan"), providing an opportunity for the child to engage in the behaviors listed in the plan ("do"), and after the session asking the child what he or she did ("review"). Reinforcement can be delivered at each step of the procedure.

Data-based decisions. Decisions that are made based on the results of collecting, summarizing, and analyzing information about children's performance on their goals.

Differential reinforcement. Providing positive consequences (reinforcers) contingent upon a given behavior for the child and not for other behaviors, or delivering a reinforcer for a behavior in one situation but not in other situations.

Distributed. Delivering trials (i.e., opportunities for children to respond) on a given behavior over time with opportunities to perform other behaviors between the trials for the target behavior.

Embedded. Identifying times and activities when a child's goals *and* the instructional procedures for those goals can be inserted into children's ongoing activities, routines, and transitions in a way that relates to the context. It involves distributing opportunities to learn goals and apply instructional procedures for those goals across different activities, routines, and transitions of the day.

Engagement. In the broad sense, this term refers to children actively manipulating materials, participating in an activity, or interacting with others in appropriate ways that lead to goal achievement.

Expansions. Listening to what a child says, and after the child speaks, repeating what the child has said and adding new words to the child's statement.

Fidelity. How accurately a person (usually an adult) uses an instructional procedure or other intervention practice.

Fluency. A phase of learning. It refers to learning how to perform acquired behaviors rapidly, smoothly, and at rates needed to be useful in the child's usual environment.

Frequency. How often an event occurs in reference to a unit of time. For example, how many times per minute a behavior occurs, or how many times per day a given instructional procedure is used.

Function. The effect the behavior has on the environment or the purpose of the behavior as seen from the child's perspective.

Functional analysis of behavior. A method that uses direct observation and recording of behavior to identify circumstances (antecedents) that may trigger and support (reinforce) problem behavior. Functional assessment provides information for conducting functional analysis, in which environmental variables can be manipulated to test findings of the functional assessment.

Generalization. A phase of learning. It refers to learning to use a skill outside of the context in which it was initially acquired. This is often thought of as performing a behavior in another setting, with other people, and/or with materials different from those used in initial instruction.

Graduated guidance. A response prompting procedure used with chained behaviors (a series of behaviors sequenced together to form a more complex skill). It involves prompting the child with the amount and intensity of prompts needed to ensure the behaviors occur and immediately removing those prompts (but reapplying them as needed) to ensure the series of behaviors are done correctly. As the child becomes more proficient the adult "shadows" (follows) the child, ready to immediately apply and remove prompts as necessary.

Group contingencies. Consequences (usually positive reinforcers) that are delivered to a group. The reinforcers can be provided based on the performance of all members of the group, the performance of a subgroup of the members, or the performance of an individual in the group.

Group friendship activities (also known as **affection training activities).** Involves two major components: First, it involves short discussions with children about the value of having friends and what friends are. Second, it involves adapting usual group games and songs to increase the social and physical contact between children when the games are played or the songs are sung. These songs/games are performed with enthusiasm and excitement and with frequent references to the value of having friends.

High-probability procedure. This procedure involves providing reinforcement for relatively easy or readily done behaviors (i.e., high-probability behaviors) before asking the child to engage in a behavior that is less likely to occur. Usually, the adult asks the child to do three or four high-probability behaviors in rapid fashion and provides enthusiastic reinforcement for each before quickly asking the child to perform the less likely behavior.

Incidental teaching. The environment is structured to increase the probability that a child will initiate to the adult. When the child initiates, the adult requests more elaborate behavior (usually a more elaborate request). If more elaborate behavior is forthcoming from the child, the adult praises the child and responds to the content of the child's initiation. If more elaborate behavior is not forthcoming, the adult prompts the child, allows the child to respond, and then responds to the content of the child's initiation.

Increasing assistance. Another name for the system of least prompts, which involves developing a hierarchy of prompts that are ordered from the least to the most assistance needed to perform a behavior. For each trial, the adult initially gives the child an opportunity to perform the behavior without prompts; if the child does not respond, the adult delivers the least controlling prompt and another opportunity for the child to respond. Again, if the child does not respond or starts to respond incorrectly, the adult delivers the next more controlling prompt. This continues on each trial until the child responds correctly or the most controlling level of prompt is provided.

Intensity. As it relates to instructional procedures or practices, this term refers to how often a given procedure or practice is used (in one setting or in multiple settings). As it relates to the totality of intervention, this term often refers to the number of hours of intervention per week and the number of weeks of intervention.

Interrupted chain procedure. A procedure that is implemented during a behavior chain (i.e., a series of behaviors sequenced together to form a more complex skill). The adult interrupts the child's performance of the chain to provide an opportunity for the child to do a target behavior—often a communicative behavior. The adult looks expectantly at the child after interrupting the chain.

Maintenance. A phase of learning. It refers to continuing to perform behaviors that have been acquired after instruction on those behaviors has stopped.

Mand-model procedure. This procedure involves observing the child's focus of attention, asking a non-yes/no question (i.e., a mand) of the child about the focus of his or her attention, and waiting for an answer from the child. If no answer is forthcoming, then a model of the answer is provided. The procedure is embedded into children's play or interactions.

Models. This term is used in two distinct ways. First, it refers to the people (adults, other children) who perform behaviors one wants a given child to imitate. Second, it refers to the behavior of another (an adult or peer) that is done with the intention that the child will imitate the behavior. When used in this second way, models often are prompts provided to show children how to do a target behavior.

Naturalistic time delay. A procedure implemented during children's ongoing interactions with the environment and at a point in which adult assistance or help has been regularly given in the past. It involves the adult waiting (delaying the help) for the child to initiate a target behavior at the point when help has regularly been given. During the delay, the adult looks expectantly at the child. If the child does not initiate during this delay, the adult provides a prompt (i.e., the regularly occurring help) and allow the child to continue the sequence.

Natural learning environments. Settings in which children without disabilities spend time. Common places include the home, child care programs, family daycare homes, and in community settings (e.g., stores, barber's shops, doctor's offices, parks, etc.) and programs (e.g., children's hour at the library, gymnastics classes, etc.) available to all children in the society. Activities and routines may need to be adapted to ensure that children with disabilities are able to be integral members of the activity or routine.

Participation. Being a part of the activities and routines of any setting in which children spend time. Children's involvement in the activities and routines may need to be adapted to ensure they are able to be an integral member of the activity or routine.

Peer-mediated strategies. A collection of procedures, all of which involve using peers to promote the behavior of a child with disabilities. This may involve having peers model specific behaviors for the child with disabilities to imitate, it may involve teaching the children to initiate social interactions to the child with disabilities, it may involve teaching the children to respond to social initiations by the child with disabilities, it may involve teaching children to tutor the child with disabilities.

Play sequences. Play that involves more than one step (e.g., for a child playing in housekeeping: [1] pick up a doll, [2] feed the doll with a bottle, and [3] burp the doll).

Prompt fading. The process by which teacher assistance (prompts) is removed when teaching children specific skills. Several systematic procedures exist for delivering and removing prompts, including simultaneous prompting, constant time delay, progressive time delay, system of least prompts (increasing assistance), and graduated guidance.

Prompting/prompt strategies. Any assistance or help given by another person (usually an adult) to assist children in knowing how to do a given behavior or to perform a target behavior in the presence of a target stimulus. Prompts take many forms, including verbal cues or hints, gestures, models of the target behavior, pictures, partial physical prompts, and full physical prompts. Prompts are divided into two broad classes based on their effects on children's behavior: controlling prompts and noncontrolling prompts. Controlling prompts ensure the child will respond correctly when those prompts are delivered, and noncontrolling prompts increase the probability of correct responses but do not ensure correct responding.

Reinforcement. A consequence for a behavior that increases the probability that the behavior will occur more frequently, with more intensity, or for longer durations. Positive reinforcement involves adding something to the environment (e.g., praise, access to a toy), and negative reinforcement involves removing something from the environment (e.g., allowing a child to leave an area after putting a toy on the shelf).

Replacement behavior. A behavior that is more adaptive than a regularly occurring behavior yet fulfills the same function (produces the same effect) as the regularly occurring behavior. An adaptive behavior can be taught to replace a problematic or challenging behavior (e.g., teaching a child to say, "my toy" when a peer takes his or her toy rather than biting the peer), and a more complex adaptive behavior can be taught to replace a less complex adaptive behavior (e.g., teaching a child to say, "bye-bye" rather than just waving when the child leaves for the day).

Response shaping. This procedure involves reinforcing successive approximations of a target behavior. Initially, the child's current behavior is reinforced until it occurs consistently, and then a slightly more complex variation of the behavior is reinforced and the original form of the behavior is not reinforced. Over time, progressively more complex forms of the behavior are reinforced and the less complex forms are not reinforced.

Time delay. This term refers to three different strategies. First, it refers to an adult waiting for a child to initiate a behavior, often during interactions or play. Second, constant time delay refers to a procedure in which the adult initially provides sufficient help (a prompt) for a child to perform correctly and then on subsequent trials delays the assistance for a fixed (constant) number of seconds. Third, progressive time delay refers to a procedure in which the adult initially provides sufficient help (a prompt) for a child to perform correctly and then on subsequent trials gradually (progressively) increases the time before giving help. With both constant and progressive time delay procedures, correct responses (prompted or unprompted) are reinforced.

Transition-based teaching. A procedure in which a single opportunity to perform a target behavior is delivered to the child at the onset of a transition from one activity or area to another; it can be delivered when the child initiates a transition or when a transition is initiated by an adult. Often, a prompt is needed to get the child to perform the behavior, but the natural consequence is continuing with the transition.

Visual cue systems. The use of stimuli children can see (e.g., objects or pictures) to communicate to children what behaviors are expected or to signal changes in activities and identify the upcoming activity.

Child-Focused Practices Resources

Position Statements

"Division for Early Childhood (DEC) Position Statement on Inclusion"

"DEC Position Statement on Interventions for Challenging Behavior"

"DEC Concept Paper on Identification of and Intervention With Challenging Behavior"
   The DEC position statements are found on the DEC Web site at http://www.dec-sped.org. Click on "Position Statements."

Print Materials

An Activity-Based Approach to Early Intervention (3rd ed.)
K. Pretti-Frontczak & D. Bricker (2004)
   This book offers a systematic method for assessing young children with special needs and helping them reach their goals. Readers will find thorough, research-based information on activity-based intervention (ABI) and the strategies needed to use it effectively. (Baltimore: Paul H. Brookes)

An Administrator's Guide to Preschool Inclusion
R. A. Wolery & S. L. Odom (2000)
   This guide was developed to help administrators who are responsible for setting up, monitoring, supporting, and maintaining inclusive programs for preschool children with and without disabilities. It delineates barriers and roadblocks, while at the same time offering strategies, supports, and illustrations. One very useful feature is the section on collaboration and consultation. (Chapel Hill, NC: University of North Carolina, FPG Child Development Center, Early Childhood Research Institute on Inclusion. Download from FPG Publications http://www.fpg.unc.edu/~ publicationsoffice/pdfs/AdmGuide.pdf or e-mail FPG Publications at pubs@mail.fpg.unc.edu.)

Blending Practices for Teaching Young Children in Inclusive Settings
J. Grisham-Brown, M. L. Hemmeter, & K. Pretti-Frontczak (in press)
   This book provides teachers with comprehensive strategies for teaching young children with and without disabilities in inclusive early childhood settings. The book emphasizes how teachers can use statewide preschool standards as the basis for curriculum design. It provides specific examples for individualized, as well as class-wide, curriculum planning. Detailed information is provided for how classroom personnel can assess and plan for the individual needs of all children. As well, there are specific chapters on family involvement, addressing challenging behavior, and data collection. (Baltimore: Paul H. Brookes)

Building Blocks for Teaching Preschoolers With Special Needs
S. Sandall & I. Schwartz (2002)
> Whether you're new to teaching in an inclusive classroom or a seasoned veteran, this guidebook provides clear ideas on including young children with disabilities in any curriculum. Teachers, caregivers, other early childhood team members, and consulting teachers will enjoy this book's easy-to-read style and examples of using the methods described in real settings. (Baltimore: Paul H. Brookes)

Cultural Diversity and Social Skills Instruction: Understanding Ethnic and Gender Differences
G. Cartledge & J. F. Milburn (1996)
> Here's a book that offers ideas for teaching social skills from a culturally sensitive perspective. It affirms that the behaviors of culturally and linguistically diverse young children need to be viewed from a cultural perspective and addresses how instruction should affirm and empower children. The authors address differences in social skills according to ethnicity, gender, and other variables. (Champaign, IL: Research Press)

DEC Recommended Practices Program Assessment: Improving Practices for Young Children With Special Needs and Their Families
M. L. Hemmeter, G. E. Joseph, B. J. Smith, & S. Sandall (2001)
> Help in assessing and improving the quality of services provided to young children with disabilities and to their families is what this publication offers. It can be used to determine the strengths, needs, and supports of a program. Whether readers work at a Head Start, child care center, public school, or other early childhood/early intervention program, the examples and reproducible forms help to enhance the quality of the program. (Longmont, CO: Sopris West)

Designing Preschool Interventions: A Practitioner's Guide
D. W. Barnett, S. H. Bell, & K. T. Carey. (1999)
> Practical and ecological are the two words most often used to describe this text. One reviewer said it "captures the essence of what it takes to provide high-quality intervention services to preschoolers experiencing developmental delays and disabilities as well as those who are at risk." Both relevant research and practical examples are cited in chapters that cover topics from the classroom as an ecosystem to designing effective interactions. (New York: Guilford)

Early Childhood Inclusion: Focus on Change
M. J. Guralnick (Ed.) (2001)
> Several chapters in this book deserve mention. M. B. Bruder's chapter ("Inclusion of Infants and Toddlers: Outcomes and Ecology") offers suggestions for adults who, within and across environments, support opportunities, activities, and routines to promote learning and participation for the youngest children. McWilliam, Wolery, and Odom ("Instructional Perspectives in Inclusive Preschool Classrooms") explore key considerations for preschoolers, such as individualized instruction, skills to be taught, and factors influencing implementation. And Guralnick ("Social Competence With Peers and Early Childhood Inclusion: Need for Alternative

Approaches") offers new insights for developing social skills in infants, toddlers, and young children. (Baltimore: Paul H. Brookes)

The Exceptional Child: Inclusion in Early Childhood Education (5th ed.)
K. E. Allen & G. E. Cowdery (2005)

Teachers, parents, and all personnel who strive to design and implement quality programs for children who are developing normally and for those with developmental or behavioral challenges will benefit from this resource. The authors emphasize offering each child individualized learning opportunities that are developmentally appropriate and workable within inclusive classrooms. Particular attention is paid to including parents in the design of their children's learning programs and to the inclusion of exceptional children in the classroom setting. A current, extensive list of Web sites complements the content of the book. (Albany, NY: Delmar)

Including Children With Special Needs in Early Childhood Programs
M. Wolery & J. S. Wilbers (1994)

Here's a book that will appeal to teachers and caregivers alike. It provides a thoughtful synthesis of the research and clear implications and applications for daily practice. The chapters on designing inclusive environments and implementing instruction for young children with special needs are particularly useful.

National Association for the Education of Young Children (NAEYC)
P.O. Box 932569
Atlanta, GA 31193
Phone: (866) 623-9248
FAX: (770) 442-9742
Web: http://www.naeyc.org/
E-mail: naeyc@pbd.com

Natural Environments and Inclusion (Young Exceptional Children Monograph Series No. 2)
S. Sandall & M. Ostrosky (Eds.) (2000)

With IDEA '97 prompting inclusive settings for children with disabilities, it is important to consider the natural settings in which these children are being taught and cared for, child care centers and preschools in particular. This monograph focuses on aspects of inclusion that include strategies for implementing inclusive environments within natural settings, ways to ensure that preschools nurture positive attitudes and provide valuable experiences, and examples of state and federal regulations that clarify changes in early intervention. (Longmont, CO: Sopris West)

One Child, Two Languages: A Guide for Preschool Educators of Children Learning English as a Second Language
P.O. Tabors (1997)

Help for early childhood educators in understanding the process of second language acquisition in young children is what this book provides, along with organizational and curricular strategies for developing supportive environments for young, diverse language learners. Based on extensive research, the author offers a variety of resources, including vignettes, teaching cases, classroom observations, suggestions for teaching/training, and strategies for involving parents. (Baltimore: Paul H. Brookes)

Practical Ideas for Addressing Challenging Behaviors (*Young Exceptional Children Monograph Series No. 1*)
S. Sandall & M. Ostrosky (Eds.) (1999)

This monograph offers ideas on how to more effectively prevent, identify, and address challenging behaviors by taking a positive behavioral approach. Strategies for addressing challenging behaviors within inclusive settings include utilizing developmentally appropriate management techniques, using preventive measures and intervention strategies, and enlisting families in designing and carrying out interventions. (Longmont, CO: Sopris West)

Skillstreaming in Early Childhood: Teaching Prosocial Skills to the Preschool and Kindergarten Child
E. McGinnis & A. P. Goldstein (1990)

The Skillstreaming approach is designed to help young children develop competence in dealing with interpersonal conflicts, learning to use self-control, and contributing to a positive learning environment. Modeling, role playing, performance feedback, and transfer are featured approaches. The curriculum contains 40 skill lessons and includes six skill groups: beginning social skills, school-related skills, friendship-making skills, dealing with feelings, alternatives to aggression, and dealing with stress. (Champaign, IL: Research Press)

SPIES: Strategies for Preschool Intervention in Everyday Settings
S. Rule & T. Smith (1998)

SPIES was developed to introduce adults to intervention strategies that can be used with infant, toddler, and preschool children who have disabilities, special health needs, or are at risk for the development of a disability. Using everyday settings as the context for intervention, these training materials (participant manuals, instructors manuals, and videotapes) introduce strategies adults can use in the context of daily routines wherever they happen—in homes, preschools, child care settings, and in the community. The *SPIES* curriculum is divided into six modules: creating teaching opportunities, providing help, incidental teaching, tracking progress, prior to preschool, and planning across the day. An abbreviated version (CD-ROM disc and participant manual for all six modules) and Spanish language captioning are also available.

> Center for Persons With Disabilities
> Utah State University
> 6818 Old Main Hill
> Logan, UT 84322-6818
> Phone: (435) 797-1993 (voice) or (435) 797-1981 (TDD)
> FAX: (435) 797-3944
> Web: http://www.cpd.usu.edu/SPIES/
> E-mail: connie@cpd2.usu.edu

Teaching Other People's Children: Literacy and Learning in a Bilingual Classroom
C. Ballenger (1998)

What happens when a teacher does not share a cultural background with her young students? Ballenger's narrative shares the experiences of one North American teacher who spent three years teaching Haitian children in an inner-city preschool. This engaging account, which does a splendid job of reinforcing the importance of thoughtful research, uses first person narrative to explore the complexities of family-based practices. (New York: Teachers College Press)

Teaching Strategies: What to Do to Support Young Children's Development (*Young Exceptional Childrens* **Monograph, Series No. 3**)
M. Ostrosky & S. Sandall (Eds.) (2001)
A series of articles describing effective and acceptable teaching strategies for young children including methods for classrooms and other intervention settings. A variety of curriculum domains are addressed. (Longmont, CO: Sopris West)

Understanding and Affecting the Behavior of Young Children
T. J. Zirpoli (1995)
Designed to provide teachers and caregivers with a basic understanding of the factors and variables that affect young children's behavior, this text examines a wide variety of guidance approaches, while emphasizing the efficacy of behavioral interventions. There are four major goals acknowledged by guidance practitioners as pivotal for helping children today: (1) understanding behavior in the context of young children's current social conditions; (2) understanding behavior in the context of normal development; (3) understanding behavior in the context of culture and ability/disability; and (4) understanding the assessment methods that are effective with young children. (Englewood Cliffs, NJ: Prentice-Hall)

Widening the Circle: Including Children With Disabilities in Preschool Programs
S. L. Odom (Ed.) (2002)
This book is a really useful blend of practical applications and lessons learned from the five-year Early Childhood Research Institute on Inclusion. The chapters cover such topics as individualizing instruction, social relationships, community participation, cultural and linguistic diversity, classroom ecology and child participation, and collaborative relationships among adults. The one-page "Quality Indicator Questionnaire" for examining inclusion could be a great resource for those considering or tracking changes at the program level. (New York: Teachers College Press)

Videotapes

Activity-Based Intervention
D. Bricker, P. Veltman, & A. Munkres (1995)
An array of visual examples for using daily activities to maximize growth and development are what this video offers. Segments illustrate how activity-based intervention can be used to turn everyday events and natural interactions into opportunities to promote learning in young children of all abilities. (Baltimore: Paul H. Brookes)

DEC Recommended Practices: Selected Strategies for Teaching Young Children With Special Needs
Division for Early Childhood (DEC) (2002)
This 18-minute video is designed to assist early childhood teachers and other early childhood/early intervention partners in helping all children achieve important

learning objectives and grow as individuals. The video is based on comprehensive literature reviews and focus groups of parents, teachers, researchers, and administrators about what best promotes learning for young children with special needs. It demonstrates different learning environments and teaching procedures from *DEC Recommended Practices in Early Intervention/Early Childhood Special Education* and *DEC Recommended Practices Program Assessment*, including peer-mediated strategies, consequences, prompting strategies, naturalistic teaching procedures, and much more. (Longmont, CO: Sopris West)

Family-Guided Activity-Based Intervention for Infants and Toddlers
J. Cripe (1995)

> Using this practical videotape, early childhood professionals will be able to teach parents and other caregivers how to use daily routines and activities to help young children with special needs gain vital skills. (Baltimore: Paul H. Brookes)

Language Is the Key
K. Cole (1999)

> Preservice and inservice audiences can discover strategies for increasing language and building language/literacy skills with children (birth to 4) through these materials. The set, which is available in English, Spanish, and Korean, includes two 20-minute videos (*Talking and Play* and *Talking and Books*). An accompanying manual includes handouts, agendas, and other resources to support effective use of the videos, along with suggestions for enhancing cultural sensitivity, using interpreters/translators, and coaching others in skill development.

> Washington Learning Systems
> 2212 Queen Anne Avenue, No. #726
> Seattle, WA 98109
> Phone: (206) 310-7401
> FAX: (206) 283-9243
> Web: http://www.walearning.com
> E-mail: mmaddox@walearning.com

Observing Young Children: Learning to Look, Learning to Listen
L. J. Colker (1995)

> This 30-minute videotape and accompanying guide help new and experienced early childhood educators to observe and learn about children as a way to individualize programs and adjust environments. Observation techniques are described and guided practice opportunities are provided. This resource is also appropriate for self-instruction.

> Teaching Strategies, Inc.
> P.O. Box 42243
> Washington, DC 20015
> Phone: (800) 637-3652
> FAX: (202) 364 7273
> Web: http://www.teachingstrategies.com

Possibilities: A Mother's Story

Orelena Hawks Puckett Institute (2002)

This five-minute video illustrates the experiences of a child and his family when they participate in a project designed to increase access to and participation of children with disabilities in community recreation and leisure activities. A compelling story for inclusion and a great opportunity to discuss routines-based intervention strategies are provided in a compact package.

Winterberry Press
P.O. Box 2277
Morganton, NC 28680
Phone: (800) 824-1174 or (828) 432-0065
FAX: (828) 432-0068
Web: http://wbpress.com
E-mail: info@wbpress.com

Talking With Preschoolers: Strategies for Promoting First and Second Language Development

California Department of Education, Child Development Division (1998)

This videotape is designed to help preschool team members and family members to develop skills and strategies for meeting the needs of culturally and linguistically diverse children. The tape is organized in short segments on different aspects of language, listening, and literacy development, suitable for introducing key concepts.

CDE Press
P.O. Box 271
Sacramento, CA 95812-0217
Phone: (800) 995-4099
FAX: (916) 323-0823
Web: http://www.cde.ca.gov/cdepress/ (Click on "Child Development.")

Web Sites

Circle of Inclusion

Designed for early childhood service providers and families of young children, this Web site offers demonstrations of and information about the effective practices of inclusive programs. What will you find at this site? Articles and activities to download. Links to other inclusion sites to visit. Personnel and families with firsthand experiences to share.

http://www.circleofinclusion.org

Early Childhood Research Institute on Inclusion (ECRII)

Inclusion research briefs, bibliographies, and publications (e.g., *Portraits of Inclusion Through the Eyes of Children, Families and Educators*) are all available to download at this multifaceted site.

http://www.fpg.unc.edu/~ecrii

Inclusion: Yours, Mine, Ours

Support, confidence, and resources to successfully include children with special needs in community programs are what this site offers. You can get answers to inclusion questions, find examples of successful strategies, subscribe to a free newsletter, or browse a detailed bibliography of inclusion "how-to" books.

http://rushservices.com/Inclusion/homepage.htm

Keys to Inclusion

The National Early Childhood Technical Assistance Center (NECTAC) Web site was developed to build administrative supports for inclusion and natural environments. Features include examples of legislation and policies, effective practices, fiscal resources, collaborative activities, and research.

http://www.NECTAC.org/inclusion

Kids Together, Inc.

Access a variety of resources for families, teachers, administrators, and programs at this site. You'll find information about legislation, assistive technology, accessing community resources, and more. Also, check out the great cartoons illustrating common challenges of inclusion.

http://www.kidstogether.org

Research Training Center on Early Childhood Development

This site was established to create a bridge between research evidence and early childhood intervention practices. It provides downloadable articles on the latest research, presents the facts on a variety of techniques and strategies, and provides solutions and ideas written in a user-friendly, newspaper article format that is designed for practitioners and parents. There is an emphasis on the relationship between characteristics of the practice and the results that can be expected. Included are carefully explained, easy steps and creative ideas that parents and practitioners can use right away to implement a particular early childhood practice recommended by the Research Training Center.

http://www.researchtopractice.info/

TaCTICS (Therapists as Collaborative Team Members for Infant/Toddler Community Services)

With support from a U.S. Department of Education grant, this site shares tools using the child/family's daily routines, activities, and events as a context for assessment and intervention.

http://tactics.fsu.edu

Chapter 5

DEC Recommended Practices: Family-Based Practices

Photo by David Naylor

Introduction

Carol M. Trivette and Carl J. Dunst

There has been considerable discussion among early intervention and early childhood special education professionals regarding the best practices for working with families of young children with developmental disabilities and children at risk for developmental delays. The following statement captures the key elements of family-based practices: Family-based practices provide or mediate the provision of resources and supports necessary for families to have the time, energy, knowledge, and skills to provide their children learning opportunities and experiences that promote child competence and development. Resources and supports provided as part of early intervention/early childhood special education (EI/ECSE) are done in a family-centered manner so family-based practices will have child, parent and family strengthening and competency-enhancing consequences.

Guiding Principles

Two aspects of this definition of family-based practices are important to underscore. The first relates to the nature of the resources and supports that are considered important for improving family functioning. A broad-based view of resources and supports is suggested, including various types of informal and formal supports or resources needed by family members to promote their child's development. The second aspect

Focus group members: Harriet Boone, Carl J. Dunst, Marilyn Espe-Sherwindt, Richard Roberts, and Carol M. Trivette of these practices is the focus on how and in what manner supports and resources are provided in order to support and enhance the competency of parents and strengthen the family.

Resources and Supports

According to Bronfenbrenner (1979), families need both informal and formal resources and supports so that they have both knowledge and skills, and the time and energy to promote the development of their children. Social support refers to the information, advice, guidance, and material assistance provided by social network members including persons, groups, and institutions that come into contact with families. Social network members include informal sources, such as family members, friends, and neighbors, and formal sources of support, such as early childhood professionals and agencies.

The model shown in Figure 1 depicts the direct and indirect influences of social support on personal and family well-being, parent-child interactions, and child behavior and development that are now supported by research findings (Dunst, 1999; Trivette, Dunst, & Hamby, 1996). According to this model, social support and resources directly influence the health and well-being of parents; both support and health/well-being influence parenting styles; and support, health/well-being, and parenting styles directly and indirectly influence child behavior and development (Dunst, 1999, 2000; Trivette, Deal, & Dunst, 1986).

Figure 1. Model depicting the direct and indirect influences of social support and intrafamily factors on parents and family well-being, parenting styles, and child behavior and development.

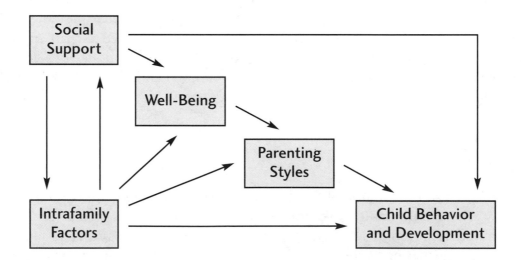

Research evidence now indicates that social support has positive effects on parental well-being, that a parental sense of well-being is directly related to responsive styles of interaction, and that both parental responsiveness and facilitation styles of interaction are related to child development. For example, Dunst (1999) reported findings demonstrating the direct and indirect influences of social support (as well as family socioeconomic status) on parental well-being and parent interactional style, and the positive influence of highly supportive and minimally directive parenting styles on child development. Providing or mediating the supports that parents need ensures that they have the resources necessary to have the time and both the physical and psychological energy to engage in child rearing responsibilities and parenting activities (Bronfenbrenner, 1979).

Research evidence now indicates that social support has positive effects on parental well-being. . . .

Family-Centered Helpgiving

The second guiding principle of family-based Recommended Practices concerns the manner in which the resources and supports are provided to parents and families. There is now considerable understanding about the fact that *how* interventions are done matters as much as *what* is done if helpgiving is to have positive effects on families and young children (Brickman et al., 1983; Dunst & Trivette, 1988; Dunst, Trivette, Gordon, & Starnes, 1993; Karuza & Rabinowitz, 1986; Rappaport, 1981). The effects of *how* something is done beyond the effects of *what* is done are referred to as value-added benefits (Dunst & Trivette, 1996).

Photo by David Naylor

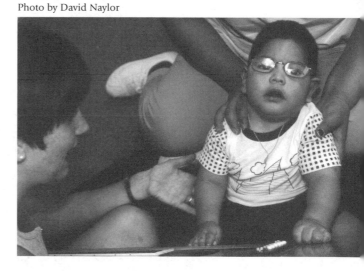

Research indicates that when family-centered practices are used in working with families there are more positive consequences in terms of families valuing the support and help they receive from early intervention practitioners (Dunst, Brookfield, & Epstein, 1998). For example, a number of studies have used structural equation modeling (Bentler, 1995) to demonstrate the mediating effects of family-centered helpgiving on a number of parent, family, and child outcome measures (Dunst, 2000; Dunst et al., 1993; King, Rosenbaum, & King, 1997; Thompson et al., 1997).

The provision of resources and supports to parents and families that enables them to promote the development of their children is one aspect of family-based practices. The value-added effect of using practices that strengthen the competency of families while providing them support and resources is the other focus of family-based practices. Professionals must strengthen families' abilities to support the development of their children in a manner that is likely to increase families' sense of parenting competence, not families' sense of dependency on professionals or professional systems.

Organization of the Practices

Seventeen family-based Recommended Practices were identified as a result of the work conducted in this strand. The individual practices were organized into four categories, or "take-home messages," around the major themes found in the Practices. The four themes are: (1) shared responsibility and collaboration; (2) strengthened family functioning; (3) individualized and flexible practices; and (4) strengths- and asset-based practices.

Shared Responsibility and Collaboration

The Practices in this category focus on the types of interactions that occur between families and professionals that promote working together to jointly develop and achieve goals and outcomes as opposed to the individual actions of one party. The attainment of these outcomes occurs when the family and early childhood practitioners share relevant information on a regular basis as part of identifying and achieving outcomes. To ensure full collaboration, professionals have a significant responsibility to share all relevant information in a way that matches the family's style of understanding and processing said information.

Strengthened Family Functioning

These practices promote a way of working with families that provides supports and resources that develop and strengthen parenting competence and confidence, and other aspects of positive parent and family functioning. The Practices reflect the importance of informal supports and natural community life by suggesting that early intervention and early childhood special education practices should strengthen these important aspects of families' lives. Practices should operate in ways that enhance families' abilities to have the time to engage in activities they like to do as a family, including time for extended family and friends.

Individualized and Flexible Practices

The essence of these practices is the understanding that families as well as the individual family members may have diverse backgrounds, beliefs, and opinions about what is important and how intervention activities should be implemented. Specific interventions must be derived from an understanding of what each family or family member wants for the child. Therefore, intervention practices must be individualized and be specific to a family's unique situation. The Practices in this area indicate that practitioners must be careful not to make assumptions that families have beliefs and values similar to other families or to the professionals. Further, the Practices must be provided in ways that minimize family stress and optimize healthy functioning. Practitioners must examine with each individual family the family's wishes, desires, beliefs, and concerns, allowing these to determine what and how interventions are provided to both the child and family.

Strengths- and Assets-Based Practices

This set of practices emphasizes the fact that interventions must be based on the strengths and assets of children, parents, and the family in order to have optimal benefits and outcomes. Assets are the abilities, talents, strengths, interests, preferences, gifts, aspirations, competencies, and so forth that people build on or use to achieve their desired life dreams or goals (Dunst & Trivette, 1996).

Effective family-based practices move beyond simply identifying the strengths and assets of children and families to using these strengths and assets as the building blocks for acquiring new information and skills. For example, a parent facilitating a child's participation in an activity based on a child's enjoyment of music is an example of building on a child's asset. Interventions that use the strengths and assets of the family and child are more likely to have positive competency-enhancing outcomes, for both the parent and child.

chapter
5

Summary

This chapter provides professionals with four sets of Recommended Practices concerning the types of interactions with families that are most likely to have positive outcomes for children and families. The Practices are based on collaborating evidence from early childhood intervention and other fields that suggest the ways in which practitioners and families should interact in order to optimize positive benefits from their work together.

. . . family-based practices help inform professionals about what is important when supporting families. . . .

These practices also provide a framework that early childhood practitioners can use to reflect on their own personal practices. Organizing the Practices by four major themes provides professionals with direction in order to focus their understanding and practices on the important aspects of working with families. Taken together, family-based practices help inform professionals about what is important when supporting families, and provide a way of thinking about interactions with families that allows for personal reflection and growth.

References

Bentler, P. (1995). *EQS structural equation modeling manual.* Encino, CA: Multivariate Software, Inc.

Brickman, P., Kidder, L. H., Coates, D., Rabinowitz, V., Cohn, E., & Karuza, J. (1983). The dilemmas of helping: Making aid fair and effective. In J. D. Fisher, A. Nadler, & B. M. DePaulo (Eds.), *New directions in helping (Vol. 1): Recipient reactions to aid* (pp. 18-51). New York: Academic Press.

Bronfenbrenner, U. (1979). *The ecology of human development: Experiments by nature and design.* Cambridge: Harvard University Press.

Dunst, C. J. (1999). Placing parent education in conceptual and empirical context. *Topics in Early Childhood Special Education, 19,* 141-147.

Dunst, C. J. (2000). Revisiting "rethinking early intervention." *Topics in Early Childhood Special Education, 20,* 96-104.

Dunst, C. J., Brookfield, J., & Epstein, J. (1998, December). *Family-centered early intervention and child, parent, and family benefits: Final report.* Asheville, NC: Orelena Hawks Puckett Institute.

Dunst, C. J., & Trivette, C. M. (1988). Helping, helplessness, and harm. In J. C. Witt, S. N. Elliott, & F. M. Gresham (Eds.), *Handbook of behavior therapy in education* (pp. 343-376). New York: Plenum.

Dunst, C. J., & Trivette, C. M. (1996). Empowerment, effective helpgiving practices, and family-centered care. *Pediatric Nursing, 22,* 334-337, 343.

Dunst, C. J., Trivette, C. M., Gordon, N. J., & Starnes, A. L. (1993). Family-centered case management practices: Characteristics and consequences. In G. H. Singer & L. L. Powers (Eds.), *Families, disability, and empowerment: Active coping skills and strategies for family interventions* (pp. 89-118). Baltimore: Paul H. Brookes.

Karuza, J., & Rabinowitz, V. (1986). Implications of control and responsibility on helping the aged. In M. Baltes & P. Baltes (Eds.), *The psychology of control and aging* (pp. 373-396). Hillsdale, NJ: Erlbaum Associates.

King, G. A., Rosenbaum, P. L., & King, S. M. (1997). Evaluating family-centered service using a measure of parents' perceptions. *Child: Care, Health, and Development, 23*(1), 47-62.

Rappaport, J. (1981). In praise of paradox: A social policy of empowerment over prevention. *American Journal of Community Psychology, 9,* 1-25.

Thompson, L., Lobb, C., Elling, R., Herman, S., Jurkiewicz, T., & Hulleza, C. (1997). Pathways to family empowerment: Effects of family-centered delivery of early intervention services. *Exceptional Children, 64*(1), 99-113.

Trivette, C. M., Deal, A., & Dunst, C. J. (1986). Family needs, sources of support, and professional roles: Critical elements of family systems assessment and intervention. *Diagnostique, 11,* 246-267.

Trivette, C. M., Dunst, C. J., & Hamby, D. W. (1996). Social support and coping in families of children at risk for developmental disabilities. In M. Brambring, H. Raub, & A. Beelman (Eds.), *Early childhood intervention: Theory, evaluation, and practice* (pp. 234-264). Berlin, Germany: de Gruyter.

chapter

5

DEC Recommended Practices and Examples: Family-Based Practices

Families and professionals share responsibility and work collaboratively.

. . . .

F1. Family members and professionals jointly develop appropriate family-identified outcomes.

Examples:

- *IFSPs or IEPs are individualized to address the needs expressed by different family members (e.g., to help the child's mother develop a time management plan or the child's father to develop coping skills).*

- *Information is shared by both professionals and families prior to the IFSP/IEP meeting so that everyone has time to reflect and develop clarifying questions for the meeting.*

- *Goals are developed at the IFSP/IEP meeting rather than having goals prewritten and reviewed at the meeting.*

- *Professionals and family members communicate about priorities, needs, and concerns prior to the formal IFSP/IEP meeting.*

. . . .

F2. Family members and professionals work together and share information routinely and collaboratively to achieve family-identified outcomes.

Examples:

- *Professionals use communication journals to share information with parents about how their child is progressing and, in turn, for parents to share information about how their child is doing at home.*

- *Family members share information with professionals about modifications that can be made for their child to be successful in different environments.*

- *Professionals have access to phones with which they can call and speak privately to parents on a regular basis.*

- *Professionals videotape sessions of children in center-based programs for parents to view if they cannot accompany their child.*

- *Family members and professionals identify new activity settings in which the child will participate during home visits. Professionals communicate with parents to inquire about how the activity settings are working for the child and family.*

chapter

5

F3. Professionals fully and appropriately provide relevant information so parents can make informed choices and decisions.

Examples:

- *Professionals share information about parents' rights in the format (e.g., written, video, conversation) and language with which parents are most comfortable.*

- *Professionals provide information such as assessment options; program alternatives; and agency, district, or state policies, etc. so that parents can make informed choices based on complete knowledge.*

- *Professionals provide many opportunities for parents to ask questions and discuss their child's activities and progress.*

- *Professionals help parents get in touch with other parents who may serve as sources of support and information.*

F4. Professionals use helping styles that promote shared family/professional responsibility in achieving family-identified outcomes.

Examples:

- *Programs implement procedures that provide a variety of emotional, informational, and material resources for families as well as children in order to meet their specific needs.*

- *Professionals and families work together to embed naturalistic instruction within family-guided activity settings.*

- *Professionals gather information about accessible parent education and training activities, and help families take advantage of such activities if they desire.*

- *Home visits are provided by a single service provider using a transdisciplinary approach.*

F5. Family/professionals' relationship building is accomplished in ways that are responsive to cultural, language, and other family characteristics.

Examples:

- *Professionals use appropriate family interviewing techniques in order to learn the priorities of the family.*

- *Professionals identify and use interpreters as necessary to ensure that families have full information about available resources.*

- *Professionals attempt to learn at least some words and phrases in the family's preferred language.*

- *Professionals invite all family members to program activities, meetings, and special events.*

- *Professionals encourage family members to include the people they would like to participate in meetings and other activities.*

- *Professionals honor each family's decision-making style.*

Practices strengthen family functioning.

F6. Practices, supports, and resources provide families with participatory experiences and opportunities promoting choice and decision making.

Examples:

- *Home visits focus on sharing information and providing help so that the family feels confident they can assist their child in-between visits.*

- *Professionals help families learn about resources and supports that address their particular parenting needs and how to access these resources.*

- *Professionals help families identify ways to share their parenting accomplishments and successes with other parents.*

F7. Practices, supports, and resources support family participation in obtaining desired resources and supports to strengthen parenting competence and confidence.

Examples:

- *Programs provide families with a variety of choices for participating such as membership on advisory groups, volunteering, building or repairing toys or equipment, talking with other families, etc.*

- *Professionals ask families to identify resources and supports available in their community that have been helpful to them so that these resources can be shared with other families.*

- *Professionals work with families to design unique methods to provide resources and supports to all families such as written or electronic newsletters, bulletin board displays, verbal exchanges, and informational meetings.*

F8. Intrafamily, informal, community, and formal supports and resources (e.g., respite care) are used to achieve desired outcomes.

Examples:

- *Connections to informal supports and resources such as family, friends, and neighbors are encouraged by professionals.*

- *Family members and friends are identified to assist with transportation to medical appointments.*

- *A religious group is identified in the family's community that offers respite services for families.*

- *Professionals help families set up babysitting cooperatives.*

- *A professional offers to meet with the church nursery staff so that a child can better participate in Sunday School.*

chapter

5

. . . .

F9. Supports and resources provide families with information, competency-enhancing experiences, and participatory opportunities to strengthen family functioning and promote parenting knowledge and skills.

Examples:

- *The program offers families information about how to interpret research reports from journals, Internet, or other sources.*

- *Professionals learn about and advertise parent education activities that take place in the community.*

- *Professionals work with other child or parent organizations to cosponsor activities that meet the parenting needs of a wide range of families.*

- *Professionals help parents find the ways to answer their specific parenting questions.*

- *The family room at the program has a computer with Internet access that families can use.*

. . . .

F10. Supports and resources are mobilized in ways that are supportive and do not disrupt family and community life.

Examples:

- *A program allows the family to choose whether they want support for their child through home visits, classroom participation, and/or community opportunities.*

- *Child care and food are provided so that families are able to attend meetings or training activities.*

- *Programs offer evening or weekend options for activities and/or services.*

- *Program schedules are designed to support parents' participation (or continued participation) in everyday activities such as church groups, recreational events, etc.*

Practices are individualized and flexible.

. . . .

F11. Resources and supports are provided in ways that are flexible, individualized, and tailored to the child's and family's preferences and styles, and promote well-being.

Examples:

- *Programs offer genuine options or look to other programs or services to expand the available options. Programs move beyond a "one size fits all" approach.*

- *Speech resources are available to a child and family in various ways (e.g., part of everyday home activities, within the child's regular classroom activities).*

- *During the early stages of a child's new feeding program, the home visitor changes her visiting schedule to be available when the child is typically eating lunch.*

- *A program makes their newsletter available in several formats (e.g., print, electronic, video) and in the major languages of their families.*

F12. Resources and supports match each family member's identified priorities and preferences (e.g., mother's and father's priorities and preferences may be different).

Examples:

- *The professional talks with each family member in order to gather information concerning his or her needs and priorities.*
- *The program offers or provides access to a variety of support activities such as Dad's or Grandparent's Night Out, sibling workshops, etc.*
- *Information is provided in various formats matching individual preferences (e.g., the father requests information in print format, the grandmother wants information from a videotape).*

F13. Practices, supports, and resources are responsive to the cultural, ethnic, racial, language, and socioeconomic characteristics and preferences of families and their communities.

Examples:

- *Program staff learn about the beliefs and values of families in their communities in order to consider how early intervention and early childhood practices may be viewed by families.*
- *The program director organizes a task force of family and staff members to develop policies related to holidays.*
- *Classroom settings include picture displays, food, books, and play materials that reflect the lives of the children in the class.*
- *Professionals attend community activities, meetings, and events to learn more about the cultures in their community.*

F14. Practices, supports, and resources incorporate family beliefs and values into decisions, intervention plans, and resources and support mobilization.

Examples:

- *The program staff incorporate and accommodate children's cultural dietary restrictions.*
- *Families have the opportunity to discuss and prioritize IFSP/IEP goals to help team members understand what is important to the family.*
- *Professionals support parents' interests in alternative treatments by helping parents gather and evaluate the available evidence concerning the effectiveness of such treatments.*

Practices are strengths- and assets-based.

. . . .

F15. Family and child strengths and assets are used as a basis for engaging families in participatory experiences supporting parenting competence and confidence.

Examples:

- *The child's interests are used when developing learning activities in the home, community, and classroom.*

- *Parents are asked on a regular basis to complete a strengths inventory of their child in order to plan better interventions.*

- *A child's grandfather, who was once a librarian, is asked if he would like to read to the children during story time.*

. . . .

F16. Practices, supports, and resources build on existing parenting competence and confidence.

Examples:

- *The feeding specialist arranges a meeting that includes the father, who is the family's cook, so that he can discuss how he adjusts food preparation to accommodate his child's specialized feeding interventions.*

- *Information about a situation (e.g., toilet training) is provided to a family that is specific to their situation and builds on what the family is currently doing within that area.*

. . . .

F17. Practices, supports, and resources promote the family's and professional's acquisition of new knowledge and skills to strengthen competence and confidence.

Examples:

- *The program director recruits a committee of family members and staff to assess the educational interests of families and to develop methods for meeting these needs.*

- *The program offers access to parent education activities that are provided individually or in small or large groups.*

- *Family members have a bulletin board or other forum where they can share parent training/education activities.*

- *Family members and staff assess the staff's need for education about family issues, and families help provide training for the staff.*

Family-Based Practices Glossary

Family-centered. A philosophy or way of thinking that leads to a set of practices in which families or parents are considered central and the most important decision maker in a child's life. More specifically it recognizes that the family is the constant in a child's life and that service systems and personnel must support, respect, encourage, and enhance the strengths and competence of the family.

Formal support. Formal support networks are made up of professionals (e.g., early interventionists, doctors, teachers, social workers) or organizations (e.g., public health clinics, mental health agencies, child welfare agencies) whose responsibility it is to provide needed social support for children and their families.

Helpgiving. The manner or style in which help or assistance is provided to individuals or families with the intent that the help will have positive consequences for individuals or families.

Informal support. Informal support networks are made up of family, friends, neighbors, church members, association members, coworkers, or others who are not paid to do so but provide social support to children and their families.

Social support. Information, advice, guidance, and material assistance provided by members of the social network. Social networks are unique from one person to another or one family to another. Members may include other family members, friends, professional helpers, members of one's church or temple, etc.

chapter
5

Family-Based Practices Resources

Position Statement

"Division for Early Childhood (DEC) Position Statement on Responsiveness to Family Cultures, Values, and Language:
> The DEC position statements are found on the DEC Web site at http://www.dec-sped.org. Click on "Position Statements."

Checklists and Measures

Brass Tacks: Program Policies and Practices
P. J. McWilliam & P. Winton (1992)
> This instrument can help individuals and team members in two key areas: (1) determining the extent to which interactions, practices, and policies are family-centered; and (2) identifying specific areas for improvement. Four key areas of interaction (first encounters, identifying goals, intervention planning, and day-to-day service provision) are targeted, and suggestions for prioritizing and tracking changes are included.

> Publications Office
> FPG Child Development Center
> CB #8185
> University of North Carolina
> Chapel Hill, NC 27599-8185
> Phone: (919) 966-4221
> FAX: (919) 843-5784
> E-mail: pubs@mail.fpg.unc.edu

Family-Centered Services: Guiding Principles and Practices for Delivery of Family-Centered Services
L. C. Pletcher & S. McBride (2000)
> To assist practitioners and programs with the application of key principles of family-centered practice, these Iowa colleagues created an annotated checklist, which offers thoughtful, practical examples of how to support each principle.

> Linnie Hanrahan
> Iowa State Department of Education
> Grimes State Office
> Des Moines, IA 50319
> Phone: (515) 281-3021
> FAX: (515) 242-6019
> E-mail: Linnie.Hanrahan@ed.state.ia.us

Print Materials

By Design: Family-Centered, Interdisciplinary Preservice Training in Early Intervention
A. Whitehead, B. Ulanski, B. Swedeen, R. Sprague, G. Yellen-Shiring, A. Fruchtman, C. Pomije, & P. Rosin (1998)

This guide for faculty and trainers was developed by the Family-Centered Interdisciplinary Training Project in Early Intervention. It describes all the strategies used to stimulate, support and evaluate learning by students from different disciplines (e.g., seminars, team activities, family mentor experience, community placement, supervision). All materials for replicating these strategies are included, along with evaluation data from the project to guide implementation.

> The Waisman Center
> Early Intervention Program
> 1500 Highland Avenue, Room S101G
> Madison, WI 53705
> Phone: (608) 263-5022, ext. 132
> Web: http://www.waisman.wisc.edu/birthto3/products.html
> E-mail: sanders@waisman.wisc.edu

Enabling and Empowering Families: Principles and Guidelines for Practice
C. Dunst, C. Trivette, & A. Deal (1988)

This book was written to assist practitioners who work with families in understanding and applying the principles of family systems assessment and intervention. It blends theory and practice with pointers for applying the principles and case studies illustrating how to apply them. Tested principles and operating guidelines and assessment are provided. The book's values-driven system enables professionals to help each family to identify their needs, locate the formal and informal resources and supports to meet those needs, and develop decision-making and problem-solving abilities to effectively access needed resources. (Cambridge: Brookline Books)

Families, Professionals, and Exceptionality: Collaborating for Empowerment (4th ed.)
A. P. Turnbull & H. R. Turnbull, III (2001)

The fourth edition (the 5th edition is scheduled for release in August 2005) of this classic and enduring text and its companion instructor's manual offer many activities related to family-centered practices. Each of 14 topical chapters (e.g., historical and current roles of parents, family functions, referral and evaluation) includes ideas for student projects and class discussions, assignments, and discussion questions. A course syllabus, including requirements, topical outlines, weekly assignments, and class project options, is also provided. (Des Moines, IA: Merrill/Prentice Hall)

Fathers & Early Childhood Programs
J. Fagan & G. Palm (2004)

Detailed information on practical strategies and useful approaches for involving fathers in early childhood programs is offered in this book. Readers will discover background information (history, theory, research) and resources for promoting meaningful paternal participation (e.g., tools and instruments, models, case studies, examples of father involvement activities). (Albany, NY: Delmar)

A Path to Follow: Learning to Listen to Parents
P. A. Edwards (1999)

When professionals learn to listen to the stories parents tell about their children and their lives, they can learn about the strengths, needs, and resources of the family and child. The authors explain that with this information, one can also learn how to effectively involve parents in their children's education and to develop family-professional collaboration. Teachers, directors, and administrators, as well as faculty and students, can benefit greatly from this book not only because it talks about the importance of listening to families, but because it also outlines ways to obtain the kind of information professionals seek. (Portsmouth, NH: Heinemann)

A Place to Begin: Working With Parents on Issues of Diversity
J. Gonzalez-Mena & D. Pulido-Tobiassen (1999)

Have you ever wanted to bring up a potentially sensitive issue with a parent or have a conversation—but weren't sure how to begin? Have you ever wanted to learn more about a parent's ideas about childrearing? This resource may guide you in discovering effective methods and materials. Handouts are included in English, Spanish, Vietnamese, and Chinese.

California Tomorrow
1904 Franklin Street, Suite 300
Oakland, CA 94612
Phone: (510) 496-0220, ext. 23
FAX: (510) 496-0225
Web: http://www.californiatomorrow.org
E-mail: info@californiatomorrow.org

Skilled Dialogue: Strategies for Responding to Cultural Diversity in Early Childhood
I. Barrera, R. M. Corso, & D. Macpherson (2003)

Understanding how to respond to cultural diversity is one key to successful family-based practices. This resource gives early childhood professionals the knowledge they need to improve that understanding. Through this book, practitioners will better understand the challenges of collaboration with family members whose values, beliefs, and backgrounds differ from their own. Further, they will discover a repertoire of skills and strategies for reframing differences between practitioners and families. The chapter entitled "Respectful, Reciprocal and Responsive Assessment" is a particularly timely source of new ideas. (Baltimore: Paul H. Brookes)

The Spirit Catches You and You Fall Down: A Hmong Child, Her American Doctors, and the Collision of Two Cultures
A. Fadiman. (1997)

The clash between a small county hospital in California and a refugee family from Laos over the care of Lia Lee, a Hmong child diagnosed with severe epilepsy, is chronicled in this book. Lia's parents and her doctors both want what is best for her, but the lack of understanding between them leads to tragedy. Powerful writing and a thoughtful reader's guide featuring questions for discussion make this a useful resource for learning about the complexities of family-based practices. (New York: Farrar, Straus and Giroux)

Supporting and Strengthening Families: Methods, Strategies, and Practices
C. Dunst, C. Trivette, & A. Deal (1994)

> The theory, methods, strategies, and practices involved in adopting an empowerment and family-centered resource approach to supporting families and strengthening individual and family functioning are championed in this book. Topics include the meaning and key characteristics of empowerment; family support programs; individual family support plans; family needs, strengths, and resources; and effective helpgiving practices. (Cambridge: Brookline Books)

Videotapes

Credo for Support
N. Kunc & E. Van der Klift (1995)

> This powerful four-minute (closed captioned) video set to music offers a series of suggestions for people who care about and support someone with a disability. It prompts viewers to question the common perceptions of disability, support, collaboration, and professionalism. This video can be a provocative catalyst for a dialogue on these issues.

> Axis Consultation & Training, Ltd.
> 340 Machleary Street
> Nanaimo, BC Canada V9R 2G9
> Phone: (250) 754-9939
> Web: http://www.normemma.com/axisbio.htm
> E-mail: normemma@normemma.com

Delivering Family-Centered, Home-Based Services
L. Edelman (1991)

> Five vignettes, developed for viewing one at a time followed by discussions and activities (included in the facilitator's guide), are included in this set of materials. Each vignette illustrates what can happen when service providers fail to use family-centered practices. They offer an opportunity to show an interaction and then invite a discussion of how the interaction might have occurred in a more family-based manner.

> Kennedy Krieger Institute
> Training and Products Division
> 7000 Tudsbury Road
> Baltimore, MD 21244
> Phone: (410) 298-9286
> FAX: (410) 298-9288
> Web: http://www.kennedykrieger.org/accessible/kki_misc.jsp?pid=1601

Language and Culture: Respecting Family Choices
C. Perez-Mendez & S. M. Moore (2003)

> How do bilingual/bicultural families make choices about what languages their children speak at home and at school? How can educators and providers support and

inform this decision-making process? Should these choices be different for a child with an identified disability? What are the long-term cultural consequences of preserving the language(s) of one's heritage, or of losing them? This video addresses these issues through interviews with a wide variety of people, from recent immigrants to the great-grandchildren of Native Americans.

> Landlocked Films, LLC
> 1505 Mariposa Avenue
> Boulder, CO 80302
> Phone: (303) 447-2821
> FAX: (303)-440-3961
> Web: http://www.landlockedfilms.com/Educational.htm
> E-mail: orders@landlockedfilms.com

One of the Family
Colorado Department of Education, Early Connections for Infants, Toddlers and Families. (1998).

> Four culturally diverse families, each with a young child with disabilities, warmly describe the values that motivate them: including their children in all family activities, treating them as children first, expecting the most from them, looking for a normal family life, and choosing to work with professionals who support their values. Viewers can use this video to gain fresh perspective on family-based practices.

> Western Media Products
> P.O. Box 591
> Denver, CO 80201
> Phone: (800) 232-8902
> FAX: (303) 455-5302
> Web: http://www.media-products.com

Web Sites

DEC Recommended Practices in Early Intervention/Early Childhood Special Education: Parent Checklist

> What should parents (and professionals) look for as features of family-based programs and practices? Here's a concise list to use in identifying exemplary practices and targeting others for change and improvement.

> http://www.dec-sped.org/pdf/recommendedpractices/parentchecklist.pdf

Family Village (A Global Community of Disability-Related Resources)

> The Family Village community includes informational resources on specific diagnoses, communication connections, adaptive products and technology, adaptive recreational activities, education, worship, health issues, disability-related media and literature, and much more! The resources featured are always changing, but the emphasis on supporting family-based practices remains constant.

> http://www.familyvillage.wisc.edu

Family Voices

This Web site of families and friends speaking on behalf of children with special needs can be a great place to find resources and information. While much of the emphasis is on health issues, this site offers much more, including policy briefs, instructional resources, fact sheets, and information links.

http://www.familyvoices.org

Family-Guided Approaches to Collaborative Early-Intervention Training and Services (FACETS)

The FACETS Web site is designed to support meaningful family participation and decision making in the intervention planning process. It offers strategies for ensuring effective interdisciplinary and interagency collaboration throughout the intervention process, along with "how-to" information and training for family members, early interventionists, related service providers, and administrators.

http://www.parsons.lsi.ku.edu/facets

FamilyNet

Covering relationships, parenting, and home life for gay, lesbian, bisexual, and transgender people and their families is the purpose of this Web site. It offers a range of information and resources that can be used to support family-based practices.

http://www.hrc.org/familynet

Federation for Children With Special Needs

The Federation was organized in 1975 as a coalition of parent groups representing children with a variety of disabilities. Their Web site offers a variety of services and resources for parents, parent groups, and others who are concerned with supporting family-based practices.

http://www.fcsn.org

Guiding Practitioners Toward Valuing and Implementing Family-Centered Practices
S. L. McBride & M. J. Brotherson

Previously offered in *Reforming Personnel Preparation in Early Intervention*, this chapter, which highlights key concepts, methods, and materials, is now available online. The title says it all.

http://www.fpg.unc.edu/~scpp/pdfs/Reforming/10-253_276.pdf

Institute for Family-Centered Care

The Institute serves as a central resource for family members, administrators, policymakers, and members of the health care field, including medical education. This site shares information, facilitates problem solving, and promotes dialogue among individuals and organizations working toward family-centered care.

http://www.familycenteredcare.org

Kids Together, Inc.

Get a family- and consumer-eye view on family-based practices at this creative Web site. Cartoons, essays, links, and many other offerings can help practitioners to see thing from a different angle. Be sure to look at "When a Professional Says" (www.kidstogether.org/profsay.htm), which is located in the "Perspectives" section.

http://www.kidstogether.org

Chapter 6

DEC Recommended Practices: Interdisciplinary Models

· · · · · · · · · ·

Introduction

· · · · · · · · · · · · · · ·

Robin A. McWilliam

Professionals from multiple disciplines provide services for children birth to 5 and their families. This strand focuses on *consultative practices* from the four major specialized disciplines in EI/ECSE: early childhood special education, occupational therapy, physical therapy, and speech-language pathology. (Although numerous other specializations will not be emphasized, some practices will be applicable to them.) Models for delivering both *home-based* and *classroom-based* (e.g., child care programs, preschools) service delivery are addressed. These models exist on continua from segregated and multidisciplinary services to integrated and transdisciplinary services. Practices for adult consumers of specialized services (e.g., family members, early childhood professionals) are incorporated into this strand. These Recommended Practices are the foundation upon which professionals go about their daily routines and activities (Rapport, McWilliam, & Smith, 2003).

It is important to clarify what is meant by the term *interdisciplinary models*. The term refers to professionals from multiple professional disciplines who represent special expertise working together to help children with disabilities and their families accomplish important outcomes. The term *transdisciplinary* (one of the Recommended Practices) refers to the specific ways that team members interact. Trandisciplinary services require all professionals to collaborate and provide integrated routines-based interventions in children's natural environments.

Focus group members: Mary Beth Bruder, Pip Campbell, Eva Horn, Leslie Jackson, Louise Kaczmarek, Gerry Mahoney, Robin A. McWilliam, and Mark Wolery.

IDEA requires some level of interdisciplinary teamwork. In both infant-toddler and preschool services, individuals from different disciplines are involved not only in assessment but in service delivery. In infant-toddler services, states must provide services to meet the child's individualized needs, many of which are carried out by specialists: home visits, special instruction, speech-language pathology and audiology, occupational therapy, physical therapy, psychological services, service coordination, medical services, screening and assessment, health services, social work, vision services, assistive technology, and transportation. In preschool services, individuals from these disciplines might be involved with an individual child, but the most common interdisciplinary challenges are among therapists (e.g., occupational, physical, speech-language) and educators (i.e., regular, special). Even before the passage of the original early intervention law (P.L. 99-457), researchers, practitioners, and university faculty members were paying attention to the importance of inclusion (e.g., Stoneman, Cantrell, & Hoover-Dempsey, 1983). This alerted the field that collaboration between specialists (e.g., early childhood special educators, psychologists, therapists) and generalists (e.g., classroom teachers, teachers' assistants, family members) was complex and necessary.

The Recommended Practices within this strand address two principal service delivery settings: home- and classroom-based. Home-based services consist of professionals' going to the child's home to provide help to the family. Sometimes, the actual locale is different; community settings or a relative's house might be used instead of the family's home. The type of help the family receives depends on the profession (discipline), the needs being addressed, and—probably most saliently—the philosophy of the home visitor. Classroom-based services consist of professionals going to the child's group care or classroom program. Settings include family daycare homes, child care centers, Head Start programs, and preschools. These practices were written to apply to a broad variety of classroom models, from self-contained to inclusive settings.

Guiding Principles

Four theoretical principles summarize the Practices.

Collective Responsibility: Teamwork

The first principle is that early intervention involves collective responsibility, meaning that teamwork is required (Allen, Holm, & Schieflebusch, 1978; Bruder, 1996; Campbell, 1987). The notion is that different perspectives result in better decision making, and no one can do everything. The team consists of the individuals needed to conduct assessment as well as the individuals involved in providing services. An inclusive definition would also embrace resource providers who are not professional service providers (e.g., extended family members, community merchants, other parents). The child's guardians are always central team members.

Transdisciplinary

It is not enough simply to have individuals from different disciplines. The second principle is that a transdisciplinary model of service delivery is recommended (McCormick & Goldman, 1979). It is important to avoid fracturing (or segregating) services along disciplinary lines. This acknowledges that early intervention involves development, habilitation, and supporting families. Traditional medical model or school-based model practices, in which different team members perform largely independently, are antithetical to Recommended Practices in EI/ECSE. A critical value embedded in transdisciplinary practices is the exchange of competencies between team members. Thus, not only is intervention more holistic and complete, but team members' abilities are also enhanced. The expertise that individual members bring to a team is vital; without it, the team lacks specificity, resources, and the wisdom of knowledge accumulated through a field of concentrated study (i.e., a discipline).

It is not enough simply to have individuals from different disciplines.

Functionality

Whereas the first two principles pertain to service delivery (i.e., how services are provided), the third pertains to the content of early intervention. The philosophy is that intervention should be functional (Warren & Horn, 1996; Warren & Rogers-Warren, 1985). The challenge concerning this principle is the definition of functionality. Primarily, functional interventions are those that are necessary for the child's engagement, independence, and social relationships in the context in which he or she lives and those that are immediately useful to the child. Functionality is stressed to ensure that children receive intervention aimed at valued outcomes or outcomes that matter in their daily lives. Professionals need to know a range of effective approaches and be able to match them to children's needs.

Practicality and Parsimony for Regular Caregivers

The fourth principle stems directly from the previous one. Interdisciplinary services must be practical for regular caregivers and the simplest possible to implement while still being effective (Bricker, Pretti-Frontczak, & McComas, 1998; McWilliam, 1992). This concept of practicality is based on the belief that young children learn through ongoing interactions with their natural environment rather than in isolated lessons or sessions. Therefore, it is not the consultant who has the direct impact on the child; it is the child's natural caregivers (e.g., parents, teachers, child care providers, etc.). Specialists must support these caregivers so the child receives an adequate amount of quality help in areas determined by the team. Specialists must focus on those activities or strategies that are meaningful and practical to caregivers. Because most issues in early intervention can be addressed in more than one way, specialists from different disciplines must arrive at suggestions that are compatible with caregivers' resources, desires, and routines.

In summary, the Practices in this strand emphasize teamwork, loose boundaries between disciplines, functional intervention, and support for caregivers.

Organization of the Practices

This chapter is organized into practices that support working together, crossdisciplinary boundaries, a focus on function, and that highlight regular caregivers and routines. Supporting this organization is a philosophical bedrock that appears in contemporary discussions of interdisciplinary issues in early intervention. The Recommended Practices in this section are supported by the literature reviews, scientific experts, and stakeholder focus groups described in Chapter 2. In comparison to other strands, the interdisciplinary strand has a smaller empirical literature base. The need for documenting the efficacy of interdisciplinary work is strong.

To further strengthen the bridge from theory to practice, it is important to clarify some terms:

● *Environmental resources and constraints.* Interventions are described as being based on environmental resources and constraints, among other factors. This means that they take into account caregivers' interests and abilities as well as the limitations of the natural physical environments.

● *Model of service delivery.* In home- and community-based settings, the model of service delivery describes the professional's practices vis-à-vis the child and the parents. It ranges from direct work with the child; through triadic intervention (i.e., the professional, the child, and the parent all working together); to consultation with the parent. In classroom-based settings, the model of service delivery describes the professional's practices vis-à-vis the child, the teaching staff, and the other children. A six-model continuum has defined service (McWilliam, 1992), from most segregated to most integrated: one-on-one pull-out, small group pull-out, one-on-one in the classroom, group activity, individualized within routines, and pure consultation.

● *Natural learning environments* are the places and activities in which children without disabilities of the same age and their families would participate (e.g., homes, community settings, child care centers, family daycare homes, preschools).

● The *team* consists of the individuals responsible for either assessing or providing services to the child and family, including the parents themselves. (The word *parents* is used for simplicity to refer to the child's guardians). Additional terms are defined later in this chapter.

This chapter helps teams make decisions about how to work together for individual children and families. Another use of the chapter is to develop a program philosophy around the use of professionals from the many disciplines who bring specialized expertise to enhancing child development and family functioning.

References

Allen, K. E., Holm, V. J., & Schieflebusch, R. L. (1978). *Early intervention—a team approach.* Baltimore: University Park Press.

Bricker, D., Pretti-Frontczak, K., & McComas, M. (1998). *An activity-based approach to early intervention* (Rev. ed.). Baltimore: Paul H. Brookes.

Bruder, M. B. (1996). Interdisciplinary collaboration in service delivery. In R. A. McWilliam (Ed.), *Rethinking pull-out services in early intervention: A professional resource* (pp. 27-48). Baltimore: Paul H. Brookes.

Campbell, P. H. (1987). The integrated programming team: An approach for coordinating professionals of various disciplines in programs for students with severe and multiple handicaps. *Journal of the Association for Persons With Severe Handicaps, 12,* 107-116.

McCormick, L., & Goldman, R. (1979). The transdisciplinary model: Implications for service delivery and personnel preparation for the severely and profoundly handicapped. *AAESPH Review, 4,* 152-161.

McWilliam, R. A. (1992). *Family-centered intervention planning: A routines-based approach.* Tucson, AZ: Communication Skill Builders.

Rapport, M., McWilliam, R., & Smith, B. (2003). Practices across disciplines in early intervention: The research base. *Infants and Young Children, 17*(1), 32-44.

Stoneman, Z., Cantrell, M. L., & Hoover-Dempsey, K. (1983). The association between play materials and social behavior in a mainstreamed preschool: A naturalistic investigation. *Journal of Applied Developmental Psychology, 4* 163-174.

Warren, S. F., & Horn, E. M. (1996). Generalization issues in providing integrated services. In R. A. McWilliam (Ed.), *Rethinking pull-out services in early intervention: A professional resource* (pp. 121-146). Baltimore: Paul H. Brookes.

Warren, S. F., & Rogers-Warren, A. K. (Eds.). (1985). *Teaching functional language.* Baltimore: University Park Press.

DEC Recommended Practices and Examples: Interdisciplinary Models

Teams including family members make decisions and work together.

I1. Families and professionals, including regular caregivers, work as team members in planning, delivering, and evaluating EI/ECSE services.

Examples:

- *Team members meet to talk about children's current abilities, progress, and other concerns.*

- *Team members meet regularly but might also communicate regularly by e-mail or telephone.*

- *Team members share ideas and concerns and develop possible teaching or helping strategies.*

- *Team members incorporate and integrate each other's ideas into a single working plan.*

- *A team meets during nap time at the child care center.*

- *Team meetings have agendas and end with action plans.*

- *A parent convenes a team meeting to discuss the child's recent change in behavior.*

I2. All team members participate in the IEP/IFSP process.

Examples:

- *Meetings are held at convenient times and in convenient places. Team members take the time to get to know each other.*

- *The IFSP/IEP process is more than a meeting. It's about talking about, planning for, and intervening on behalf of the child.*

- *A team member may participate via written information or telephone/conference call as well as through his or her physical presence.*

- *All team members have access to the same information in order to make informed decisions about the child.*

- *Team meetings are structured so that family members give their ideas first, if they desire.*

I3. Team members are knowledgeable about funding and reimbursement policies and advocate for policies that support recommended practices.

Examples:

- *Team members learn about reimbursement policies and help families as needed, understand the impact on families of using nonpublic funds (e.g., lifetime limits on insurance), and participate in activities to inform the public about ways to increase funding and other resources for early intervention/early childhood special education.*

- *Team members compile and update a resource book on funding options and policies.*

- *Members of the team attend meetings or other forums on funding issues and share information at staff meetings, team meetings, and with parents.*

I4. Team members support an optimum climate for all caregiving adults to ensure trust, collaboration, and open communication.

Examples:

- *Team members meet at times and places that are convenient for all team members. They get to know one another at times other than during crises or during required meeting times.*

- *If the child attends more than one program, team members arrange to visit the other program and develop strategies to keep each program informed.*

- *Team members attend workshops together.*

- *Team members use e-mail to communicate among themselves.*

- *The team acknowledges gaps in communication among team members, including parents and other caregivers, and develops plans to remedy any problems.*

I5. Team members make time for and use collaborative skills when consulting and communicating with other team members, including families and regular teachers and caregivers.

Examples:

- *Indirect service time is valued, scheduled, and considered part of professionals' workdays.*

- *Time is scheduled for the team to work and exchange ideas together.*

- *Team members work with regular caregivers, including family members and child care providers, to assess needs, develop and teach strategies, and evaluate effectiveness.*

- *The team uses preferred adult learning strategies such as demonstration, written information, and time to practice.*

- *Team members take advantage of continuing education opportunities to learn consulting skills.*

chapter

6

. . . .

I6. Team members support paraprofessionals so they are treated respectfully and their skills are used most effectively.

Examples:

- *Skills such as delegating tasks, teaching other adults, and providing feedback to adults may be new to team members. Thus, team members may need to recognize their own area of need, and learn new skills.*
- *Team members attend paraprofessional and supervisor training sessions.*
- *Team members help paraprofessionals develop growth plans.*
- *Team members give choices when possible.*
- *Team members model effective intervention strategies and coach paraprofessionals in their use.*

Professionals cross disciplinary boundaries.

. . . .

I7. Team members engage in role release (i.e., help others learn each other's skills) and role acceptance (i.e., are prepared to learn others' skills).

Examples:

- *An occupational therapist uses videotape to model appropriate strategies within the child's daily routine for training and feedback.*
- *All team members conduct mini-workshops and provide written materials for each other to learn commonly used practices or techniques.*
- *The physical therapist helps the child care provider adjust an adaptive chair so that the child can participate at the snack table.*
- *The speech therapist demonstrates a prompting procedure to parents that they can use at home during routine activities such as mealtime, bathtime, and storytime.*

. . . .

I8. Team members use a transdisciplinary model to plan and deliver interventions.

Examples:

- *Team members schedule time for teaching the parent or classroom teacher, to answer questions, and to provide feedback.*
- *The team uses feedback from regular caregivers to design "do-able" and useful interventions.*
- *The home visitor watches the parent and child read storybooks together, acknowledges successful turn taking, and suggests another step to elicit a more sophisticated response from the child: a technique recommended by the speech-language pathologist.*

Intervention is focused on function, not services.

I9. Team members focus on the individual child's functioning (e.g., engagement, independence, social relationships) in the contexts in which he or she lives, not the service.

Examples:

- *Assessment includes identification of the child's needs within daily routines and activities.*

- *Team members together write goals (outcomes) and objectives that are relevant, contextual, and integrated throughout the child's life.*

- *Goals (outcomes), objectives, and interventions address the child's need for participation in a variety of activities at home, school, child care, or in other community activities.*

I10. Team members change models of service delivery (e.g., location) as needed, continuously monitoring what the child can do, what the child is doing, and what the family needs, to decide how to serve them.

Examples:

- *The team reviews service delivery options (e.g., direct versus indirect through consultation), with family input, as part of regular monitoring of the child's progress on IFSP/IEP goals.*

- *The team schedules extra home visits for a child and family who are learning how to use an augmentative communication device.*

- *The team changes the child's sessions to itinerant services provided in a local child care program for a child and family who need full-time child care.*

I11. Team members select child and family priorities for intervention based on child and family functioning (not services) and determine what is interfering with growth or progress in each priority area.

Examples:

- *Child and family priorities, goals, outcomes, and objectives are based on needs related to participation in daily life; they are not predetermined by professional services such as physical therapy or speech therapy. Team members discuss the child's needs within the context of the routines and activities of daily life and then identify goals and services.*

- *The team interviews the family about their routines and how they can address their child's goals in those routines. Families and professionals work together to develop a plan for home that works with the family's schedule and routines.*

- *The team uses a classroom activity matrix and discusses the child's usual participation within daily activities and transitions.*

chapter

6

I12. Team members decide on supports (a) that meet the priorities; (b) that are based on environmental resources and constraints; and (c) that are known to be helpful.

Examples:

- *A team member listens to the family's concerns and provides informational and material supports that are needed to help the family support the child's learning and development.*

- *The parents want the child to stay in his current Head Start program, so the team decides to use an itinerant service delivery option to provide service and supports for the child in the Head Start classroom.*

I13. Team members decide on each intervention variable—how to intervene, who should intervene, when the intervention should occur, and where the intervention should occur—based on (a) relevance to the priority (i.e., the functioning the family desires); (b) environmental resources and constraints; and (c) likelihood that it will help.

Examples:

- *Team members use a classroom activity matrix.*

- *Specialized therapies and instruction are integrated within classroom activities and routines.*

- *Home visitors use family-guided routines that the family identifies as feasible for working on the child's skills.*

- *The occupational therapist posts photographs in the classroom writing center to demonstrate appropriate hand placement and grasp.*

I14. In IFSPs/IEPs, team members define therapy and specialized instruction to include indirect or consultative services.

Examples:

- *Team members help explain to families and other team members that services and supports can be both direct (direct teaching or therapy) and indirect (consultation) and that both can be effective.*

- *Team members help each other understand that children learn all the time and that the regular caregivers must be able to follow through so that the child continues to learn appropriately in between visits or sessions with specialists.*

- *The child receives therapy with the physical therapist once per week at the class's outdoor time. The therapist shows the teacher one new strategy each week.*

- *A speech therapist leads circle time in the classroom twice per week. She brings songs and stories highlighting particular language skills. The teacher and aide use some of the same songs and stories during the rest of the week.*

- *An occupational therapist visits a child and her teacher at the child care center once per month. The child care teacher and the occupational therapist have a weekly telephone call to discuss the child's progress.*

- *The developmental interventionist shows the family a new strategy that will make the family's routine during mealtime smoother.*

I15. Team members use the most normalized and least intrusive intervention strategies available that result in desired function.

Examples:

- *A physical therapist uses the swings and other playground equipment to help a child with his dynamic balance.*

- *The teacher helps a child learn to take turns by setting up and teaching the children to play table-top games during free choice time in the classroom.*

- *The speech therapist incorporates therapy while playing with the child during choice time in the classroom.*

I16. Team members use activities within the range of current functioning (i.e., individually appropriate activities).

Examples:

- *A child is fascinated by cars and trucks so his teacher uses cars and trucks when teaching the child colors.*

A family lives near a body of water, so the team helps the family find swimming and water safety lessons for the child.

The team works with the family to figure out when to start toilet training and how to keep track of the child's progress.

Regular caregivers and regular routines provide the most appropriate opportunities for children's learning and receiving most other interventions.

I17. Team members plan to provide services and conduct interventions in natural learning environments.

Examples:

- *The team and family plan a set of intervention strategies to increase requesting behaviors to be used during bathtime and snack, and at the park.*

- *The child attends a child care center and receives her specialized services from an itinerant teacher who consults with the child care teacher.*

- *The child is enrolled in an inclusive preschool in which the class is team taught by a special educator and a regular early childhood teacher.*

- *A home visitor arranges to meet the family at their neighborhood park where they practice motor skills using the playground equipment.*
- *The team identifies community activities and opportunities (e.g., T-ball, soccer, library story times, community music programs) where a child can observe and practice skills such as kicking a ball, listening to stories, or participating in movement or music activities with other children.*

I18. Team members focus on the between-sessions time (i.e., build in activities that can be carried out across time and contexts).

Examples:

- *Team members figure out ways to help regular caregivers learn how to help the child learn and practice new skills in between sessions or visits. Team members use their visiting time to demonstrate for and/or talk with the regular caregivers.*
- *The physical therapist videotapes part of the child's session and uses the tape to demonstrate to the child's parents how to hold the child's hips as he learns to crawl.*
- *Parents send in the names of their children's favorite books. The teacher and speech therapist make storybook bags that contain one of these storybooks, a few simple props, and suggested activities. These bags go back and forth to children's homes.*
- *The teacher begins a parent conference by asking parents to talk about what the child is learning at home.*
- *At every visit, home visitors ask how family routines are going.*

I19. Team members recognize that outcomes are a shared responsibility across people (i.e., those who care for and interact with the child) working with the child and family.

Examples:

- *The team meets regularly to review data they have collected on the effectiveness of specific strategies identified for individual children and make changes as necessary.*
- *The child's portfolio includes work samples, photographs, and notes from school, home, and the babysitter.*
- *At the annual review meeting, all team members contribute to updating the child's performance on all goals.*
- *Team members praise and acknowledge parents' contributions to the child's progress.*

Interdisciplinary Models Glossary

Consultative services. A model in which professionals provide training, technical assistance, and/or feedback to those individuals working directly with children (e.g., a consulting physical therapist might work with an early interventionist on issues related to positioning an infant with cerebral palsy).

Delivery formats. The means by which the curriculum is delivered (e.g., face-to-face, interactive television, Web-based).

Disciplines. A branch of knowledge, service, or teaching. In early intervention and early childhood special education, individuals from multiple professional disciplines provide services. Among these are early childhood education, early childhood special education, speech-language pathology, physical therapy, and occupational therapy.

Indirect services. Services provided to assist the child's learning and development but not provided directly to the child. Consultation or technical assistance provided to the classroom teacher or family member are examples of indirect services.

Interdisciplinary model. An approach in which members of a team employ their own perspectives and materials but who reach decisions collaboratively.

Least intrusive. The arrangement of instructional procedures that provides the minimum amount of assistance required for the child to perform the skill or behavior.

Natural learning environments. Settings in which children without disabilities spend time. Common places include the home, child care programs, family daycare homes, and in community settings (e.g., stores, barber's shops, doctor's offices, parks, etc.) and programs (e.g., children's hour at the library, gymnastics classes, etc.) available to all children in the society. Activities and routines may need to be adapted to ensure that children with disabilities are able to be integral members of the activity or routine.

Participation. Being a part of the activities and routines of any setting in which children spend time. Children's involvement in the activities and routines may need to be adapted to ensure that they are able to be integral members of the activity or routine.

Role acceptance. The willingness and ability to learn skills from other members of the team.

Role release. The willingness and ability to share control over a professional/occupational activity in order to facilitate in others the learning of one's knowledge and skills.

Service delivery models. Options for bringing professional assistance, information, or involvement to selected settings or locations (e.g., home- or center-based).

Transdisciplinary model. An approach in which team members share responsibilities and information to the extent that one team member can assume the role of another. Interventions focus on the whole child and family and are provided by a primary service provider. In home-based services, the primary service provider is a home visitor. For classroom-based services, it is the teacher. Children's goals and objectives are integrated in meaningful ways into a single plan. Specialists share their knowledge and skills, especially with the primary service provider and family members. Professionals provide guidance; they trust the regular caregivers to implement the interventions effectively.

Interdisciplinary Models Resources

Checklists and Measures

Skills Inventory for Teams (SIFT)

C. Garland, A. Frank, D. Buck, & P. Seklemian (1992)

"SIFT" is an inventory of skills needed to function as part of an early intervention team. The instrument is divided into Team and Team Member sections. The Team section examines overall team functioning; the Team Member section examines individual teamwork skills. Each section is organized with a screening scale and an assessment checklist. The screening scales help teams and individual team members identify key areas of need and strengths regarding teamwork. The checklists then help clarify and prioritize for improvement in the targeted areas. Directions and forms are provided, along with forms for creating development plans.

> Child Development Resources
> P.O. Box 280
> Norge, VA 23127-0280
> Phone: (757) 566-3300
> FAX: (757) 566-8710
> Web: http://www.cdr.org

Team Practices Profile

A. Frank & C. W. Garland (1997)

The core of this document is a self-rating checklist for early intervention teams. Completion of the checklist and identification of next steps can assist teams in moving toward more family-centered, transdisciplinary service delivery and promote better team problem solving.

> Child Development Resources
> P.O. Box 280
> Norge, VA 23127-0280
> Phone: (757) 566-3300
> FAX: (757) 566-8710
> Web: http://www.cdr.org

Print Materials

By Design: Family-Centered, Interdisciplinary Preservice Training in Early Intervention

A. Whitehead, B. Ulanski, B. Swedeen, R. Sprague, G. Yellen-Shiring, A. Fruchtman, C. Pomije, & P. Rosin (1998)

This guide for faculty and trainers was developed by the Family-Centered Interdisciplinary Training Project in Early Intervention. It describes strategies used to stimulate, support and evaluate learning by students from different disciplines (e.g., seminars, team activities, family mentor experience, community placement, supervision). All materials for replicating these strategies are included, along with evaluation data from the Project to guide implementation.

> The Waisman Center
> Early Intervention Program
> 1500 Highland Avenue, Room S101G
> Madison, WI 53705
> Phone: (608) 263-5022, ext. 132
> Web: http://www.waisman.wisc.edu/birthto3/products.html
> E-mail: sanders@waisman.wisc.edu

The Collaboration Guide for Early Career Educators
M. S. E. Fishbaugh (2000)

Today's personnel are required to work collaboratively with a variety of partners—other teachers, early intervention specialists, parents, paraeducators, community agencies—yet few are adequately prepared to do so. Each issue-focused chapter in this book covers key skills needed by team members, such as communicating effectively, resolving conflicts, coteaching and supervision. Goals, objectives, activities, reproducible forms, and vignettes also are included, making this a great resource for preservice, inservice, or personal use. Examples are varied and effectively target both general and special education issues, as well as the intersections between the two. (Baltimore: Paul H. Brookes)

Collaboration Handbook: Creating, Sustaining, and Enjoying the Journey
M. Winer & K. Ray (1994)

This resource is organized to support interpersonal, organizational, and community collaboration by offering case examples, activities, tools, and resources. It also offers thoughtful strategies for overcoming obstacles to collaboration, including trust, conflict, decision making, and change.

> Amherst H. Wilder Foundation Publishing Center
> 919 Lafond Avenue
> St. Paul, MN 55104
> Phone: (800) 274-6024
> E-mail: books@wilder.org

Consultation, Collaboration and Teamwork for Students With Special Needs (5th ed.)
P. Dettmer, L. P. Thurston, & N. Dyck (2005)

Information, checklists, self-assessments, and forms for promoting family-centered collaborations in work with children of all ages form the heart of this book. Liberally sprinkled throughout this text are scenarios and vignettes, which can be used as mini-cases, and applications, which are alternative assignments for extending learning into real life settings. (Needham Heights, MA: Allyn & Bacon)

DEC Personnel Preparation in Early Childhood Special Education: Implementing the DEC Recommended Practices
V. D. Stayton, P. S. Miller, & L. A. Dinnebeil (Eds.) (2003)

This book offers guidance to early childhood and early childhood special education programs that want to reflect the DEC Recommended Practices in their student

chapter 6

preparation. The chapter on "Interdisciplinary and Interagency Collaboration in Personnel Preparation" offers suggestions on what to teach and how to teach it, as well as model programs, extensive references, self-assessment checklists, and planning tools. (Longmont, CO: Sopris West)

Facilitator's Guide to Participatory Decision Making
S. Kaner with L. Lind, C. Toldi, S. Fisk, & D. Berger (1996)
Here's an eight-chapter source book that's packed with ideas for teams to use in making decisions together. Clear, useful materials for encouraging full participation, promoting mutual understanding, fostering inclusive solutions, and teaching new thinking skills are included.

New Society Publishers
P.O. Box 189
Gabriola Island, BC V0R 1X0 Canada
Phone: (800) 567-6772
Web: http://newsociety.com/index.html
E-mail: nsp@island.net

A Roadmap for Facilitating Collaborative Teams
P. Hayden, L. Frederick, & B. J. Smith (2003)
This manual provides reasons and resources for creating collaborative teams to promote meaningful change in local early childhood systems. It was developed based on research on effective practice related to systems change and teaming/collaboration. Strategies, activities, reproducible forms, guidance, and encouragement are all offered as resources for the collaborative planning journey. (Longmont, CO: Sopris West)

Young Exceptional Children (YEC) Monograph Series No. 6: Interdisciplinary Teams
E. Horn & H. A. Jones (Eds.) (in press)
Professionals from multiple disciplines must work together to provide the appropriate supports to young children with disabilities and their families. The articles in this monograph provide ideas for teams on how to work together for individual children and their families. Complimenting DEC's Recommended Practices, the strategies offered address practices that support working together across disciplinary boundaries, focusing on function, and highlighting regular caregivers and routines. (Longmont, CO: Sopris West)

Videotapes

The Goose Story

Training Resource Center/NJDA (1992)

> Interested in a resource that can inspire individuals to pursue interdisciplinary models? This four-minute video tells the story of how geese have developed a model of teamwork and cooperation that can be an inspiration to even the most cynical.

> > Eastern Kentucky University
> > National Juvenile Detention Association (NJDA)
> > 301 Perkins Building/EKU
> > 521 Lancaster Avenue
> > Richmond, KY 40475-3102
> > Phone: (859) 622-6259
> > Web: http://www.njda.com/

Interdisciplinary Teamwork: A Team in Name Only and Becoming an Effective Team

Virginia Institute for Developmental Disabilities (1990)

> The two parts of this video emphasize the effects of team process on the recipients of team service: young children with disabilities and their families. Both segments provide the opportunity to see a team in action, first not functioning effectively (Part 1: "A Team in Name Only") and then learning to work together (Part 2: "Becoming an Effective Team"). The video and training guide are designed to facilitate discussion and analysis of both positive and negative team processes (e.g., disagreement among team members, not honoring family priorities, using jargon, etc.). The guide provides background information, training objectives, a content outline, and suggested learning activities for preservice or inservice training.

> > Child Health and Development Media, Inc. (CHADEM)
> > 5632 Van Nuys Boulevard, Suite 286
> > Van Nuys, CA 91401
> > Phone: (800) 405-8942
> > FAX: (818) 989-7826
> > Web: http://www.childdevmedia.com

Just Being Kids

L. Edelman (Producer) (2001)

> Supports and services for infants and toddlers with special needs are best provided in the context of families' everyday routines, activities, and places. Each of the six stories in this video demonstrates collaboration between interdisciplinary early intervention team members and families to achieve meaningful goals for their child. Parents and providers reflect on their experiences in ways that offer examples for diverse audiences, including teachers, therapists, and service coordinators. A Facilitator's Guide offers background information on the stories, suggestions for discussion, and activities to enhance viewers' learning.

> > Western Media Products
> > P.O. Box 591

Denver, CO 80201
Phone: (800) 232-8902
FAX: (303) 455-5302
Web: http://www.media-products.com

Navigating New Pathways: Obstacles to Collaboration

J. Olson (1994)

Five short scenarios, each reflecting different team challenges in an inclusive community setting, form the core of this video. No pat answers are provided, but the video does provide lots of opportunities for discussion of team challenges in areas including communication, roles, collaboration, planning, differing philosophies, and training.

Idaho Center on Disabilities and Human Development
University of Idaho
129 West Third
Moscow, ID 83843
Phone: (208) 885-3588 or (800) 432-8324
Web: http://www.educ.uidaho.edu/cdhd/

Project Relationship: Creating & Sustaining a Nurturing Community

M. K. Poulsen & C. K. Cole (1996)

This 41-minute (five segment) videotape depicts a family and professionals working together to meet the needs of a young child with significant behavioral issues. Along with accompanying written material, the video provides a model for practitioners who want to develop their skills for planning effectively with each other and with families.

WestEd Center for Prevention and Early Intervention
429 J Street
Sacramento, CA 95814-2300
Phone: (916) 492-4000
Web: http://www.wested.org/cs/cpei/print/docs/220

Transdisciplinary Arena Assessment Process: A Resource for Teams

Child Development Resources (1992)

A six-step, family-centered, transdisciplinary approach to arena assessment and IFSP development is demonstrated on this videotape. The accompanying viewing guide provides an overview of the transdisciplinary approach, as well as supporting activities and supplemental materials.

Child Development Resources
P.O. Box 280
Norge, VA 23127-0280
Phone: (757) 566-3300
FAX: (757) 566-8710
Web: http://www.cdr.org

Web Sites

Building Effective Early Intervention Teamwork

Downloadable chapters from this out of print book share methods, models, and materials for addressing interdisciplinary practice in teaching, training, and staff development.

http://www.fpg.unc.edu/~scpp/pdfs/Reforming/14-363_392.pdf

Creating New Visions in Institutions of Higher Education: Interdisciplinary Approaches to Personnel Preparation in Early Intervention

Models for interdisciplinary collaboration in preservice education are offered in this chapter by J. Kilgo and M. B. Bruder.

http://www.fpg.unc.edu/~scpp/pdfs/Reforming/04-81_102.pdf

Family-Guided Approaches to Collaborative Early Intervention Training and Services (FACETS)

The FACETS Web site is designed to support meaningful family participation and decision making in the intervention planning process. It offers strategies for ensuring effective interdisciplinary and interagency collaboration throughout the intervention process, along with "how-to" information and training for family members, early interventionists, related service providers, and administrators.

http://www.parsons.lsi.ku.edu/facets

National Individualizing Preschool Inclusion Project

Information and materials on this Web site support collaboration and effective consultation among team members providing early intervention services and supports to families. Click on "Integrated Therapy" for useful resources.

http://www.IndividualizingInclusion.us

Chapter 7

DEC Recommended Practices: Technology Applications

. . . .

Introduction
. . . .

Kathleen Stremel

Technology has the potential to enhance and improve the lives of children and their families. Technology applications can be important vehicles to improve teaching and learning for children, families, and professionals. The Recommended Practices presented in this strand include recommendations across three types of technology applications: (1) assistive; (2) instructional/educational; and (3) informational. The 1997 reauthorization of IDEA emphasizes that assistive technology and services should be considered for all children with disabilities. Assistive technology has been expanded to include what has been traditionally thought of as instructional technology. A child's developmental, educational, and access needs must now be considered by a team to determine the maximum benefits of technology use (Zirkel, 1998). Additionally, the need to operate and maintain medical devices and equipment properly is an issue for families and professionals as they care for medically dependent infants.

This strand includes general policies, procedures, and Recommended Practices based on research. The strand emphasizes that decision making should be family-centered and guided by principles of individualization. The strand does not focus on specific devices, services, funding, or outcomes.

Focus group members: Darbi Breath, Lise Fox, Ann Hains, Mark Innocenti, Joan Karp, John Killoran, and Kathleen Stremel

Guiding Principles

It is important that assistive technology be *considered* for every child as the IFSP/IEP is being developed. Technology applications should be considered to enhance child development and access to natural learning opportunities and the participation in the general education curriculum across the following areas: (1) motor; (2) cognitive/perceptual; (3) communication/language; (4) medical; (5) social interactions; (6) adaptive; (7) daily life skills; (8) play; and (9) academic (Lesar, 1998). Additionally, cultural and family preferences must be incorporated into decision making about assessment, funding, implementation, and evaluation processes related to assistive technology services. Considerations for the use of low technology applications should be equal to high technology applications. Both technologies have the potential to

It is important that assistive technology be considered for every child. . . .

assist infants, toddlers, and young children to be successful in natural environments, typical settings, and in the general education curriculum. It is important to emphasize that technology is only a tool, not a solution.

Advances in the development of technology devices, services, and supports have the potential for enhancing the quality of life of young children and their families, but also present challenges to the professionals who provide services to young children (NSBA, 1997; USDE, 1998).

Organization of the Practices

The practices are organized across technological applications for children, their families, professionals, and service programs under the following headings:

- Professionals utilize assistive technology in intervention programs for children
- Families and professionals collaborate in planning and implementing the use of assistive technology
- Families and professionals use technology to access information and support
- Training and technical support programs are available to support technology applications

The Recommended Practices in this strand focus on multiple outcomes, which include, but are not limited to: (1) enhancing development across all domains; (2) increasing independence and access; (3) enhancing individualized child and family interaction/instruction; (4) supporting professionals and families to ensure successful use of technology; and (5) increasing family and professional access to information and networking.

The majority of the Practices focus on the use of technology to directly impact the lives of young children and their families, recognizing that the intended outcomes for infants and toddlers will be somewhat different than those for preschool-age and older children. There is also strong encouragement to use technology at the preservice and inservice levels of personnel preparation to increase the competencies of service providers, families, and administrators across the types of technological applications. In the 21st Century professionals are using distance technologies to remain current in their areas of expertise, to upgrade their certification, and to collaborate with families and other professionals. As technological application advances continue, there remains a need to validate tools that increase independence and interaction, enhance individual instruction, and lead to meaningful early intervention and early educational outcomes.

Relationship to Other Chapters

The Recommended Practices in this chapter rely extensively on the implementation of those practices described in several of the other chapters including assessment, child-focused practices, and interdisciplinary models. Technology is not intended to be the outcome. It is the *use* of the technology that is important, in that technology is a tool that can help reach and achieve desired outcomes. Therefore, the Practices in this chapter are useful as a platform for communication, diagnosis, intervention, and teaching. Technology can open doors and create paths for the Practices from other chapters.

Some Key Terms

Assistive technology is defined as any item, piece of equipment, or product, whether acquired commercially, off the shelf, modified, or customized, that is used to increase, maintain, or improve the functional capabilities of individuals with disabilities (P.L. 100-407, the Technology-Related Assistance for Individuals With Disabilities Act of 1988). The IDEA amendments of 1997 focus on expanding access. Thus, assistive technology has been expanded to include instructional technology.

High technology (*high tech*) and *low technology* (*low* or *light tech*) are general terms that are used by researchers and educators. High technology usually refers to complex electrical and electronic devices, such as computers, voice synthesizers, Braille readers, augmentative communication systems, and environmental control units. Low technology refers to more simple devices, supports, systems, and adaptations such as custom-designed hand tools; positioning devices; and other simple, inexpensive, easy-to-use devices (Galvin & Scherer, 1996).

The terms *distance education*, *distance learning*, and *distributed learning* refer to a system in which educator and learner are separated by physical distance; the concept is that distance education systems may bring together, in virtual space, learners, educators, and curriculum materials that are distributed throughout a wide arena, perhaps the whole globe.

Summary

The Practices in this chapter guide adults in planning for, and using, technology as a tool to enhance performance and desired outcomes for children. The Practices will be most useful when linked to other practices from this book in the development of programs and interventions for young children.

References

Galvin, J. C., & Scherer, M. J. (1996). *Evaluating, selecting, and using appropriate assistive technology.* Gaithersburg, MD: Aspen Publishers.

Individuals with Disabilities Education Act, Amendments of 1997, Public Law 105-17. U.S.C. 1401. Available on the Internet: http://www.ed.gov/offices/OSERS/IDEA/the_law.html.

Lesar, S. (1998). Use of assistive technology with young children with disabilities: Current status and training needs. *Journal of Early Intervention 21,* 146-159.

National School Boards Association (NSBA) (1997). *Technology for students with disabilities: A decision maker's resource guide.* Alexandria, VA: Author.

Technology-Related Assistance for Individuals With Disabilities Act of 1988, Pub. L No. 100-407, §105, Stat. 1044 (1988)

U.S. Department of Education (USDE), Office of Special Education Programs (OSEP). (1998). Integrating technology into the standard curriculum. *Research Connections, 3,* 1-8.

Zirkel, P. (1998). Assistive technology: What are the legal limits? *The Special Educator, 2*(5), 4.

DEC Recommended Practices and Examples: Technology Applications

Professionals utilize assistive technology in intervention programs for children.

. . . .

T1. Service agencies and personnel training programs use technology as a vehicle for more effectively serving children, families, and professionals.

Examples:

- *Videotape is used by professionals and parents as the basis for discussing the child and creating a plan of intervention.*

- *Telehealth or telemedicine (e.g., one physician having a satellite consultation with another physician) is used to provide a connection of providers to parents living in rural areas.*

. . . .

T2. State agencies arrange for leaders/teams to provide program staff with assistive and instructional technology as well as training and support for technology.

Examples:

- *Staff have access to the Internet to use for locating information and resources, communicating, and for planning children's programs.*

- *Agencies collaborate to operate assistive technology centers or library loan programs so that families and professionals can easily learn about adaptations and devices and borrow devices to try with children in the settings where children spend time (e.g., home and community).*

. . . .

T3. Service programs and professionals provide assistive technology for improving early intervention/early childhood special education services for all children with disabilities in order to increase:

- Communication and language
- Environmental access
- Social-adaptive skills
- Mobility and orientation skills
- Daily life skills
- Social interaction skills
- Health
- Position/handling

chapter

7

Examples:

- *Professionals use toys with voice output and simple plate switches to help the child understand and communicate her wants and needs.*

- *Professionals use a switch with animated toys to help the child learn cause and effect concepts.*

- *The teacher uses a picture system with magazine photos pasted to cards for a child who needs help transitioning between activities.*

- *The family and team use switches to turn on lights, the TV, or other small appliances, and accommodations to allow for access to playground equipment, for a child with limited mobility.*

- *The child uses an adaptive walker for ambulation or a power wheelchair so that he can move over longer distances.*

- *The teacher and family use adaptive feeding devices, such as modified handles on eating utensils and a switch to activate a blender, for a child with limited hand strength.*

- *The child uses a sidelyer, bolster, or stander as a means of alternative positioning to sitting in a wheelchair or stroller.*

T4. Service programs and professionals consider assistive technology applications to increase children's ability to function and participate in diverse and less restrictive environments.

Examples:

- *The teacher installs special software for the child to access the computer by touching the screen.*

- *The classroom staff uses low tech adaptations, such as picture and simple word cues, which are used as tools for prewriting, early literacy, and making choices.*

- *The child practices using power mobility toys for getting around outside on the playground.*

- *The child learns to use a switch with voice output so she can greet her peers.*

T5. Professionals consider chronological age-appropriateness and developmentally appropriate practices for infants, toddlers, and preschool children when selecting types of assistive technology in assessment and intervention.

Examples:

- *An occupational therapist helps the child, who has limited mobility, to activate a source of music by teaching him to roll on a pressure-activated mat.*

- *The five-year old child, who has limited hand strength, touchs a switch with her clenched hand to activate a tape player and listen to stories.*

T6. Professionals match assistive technology tools/devices to intervention and instructional objectives and evaluate to determine the effectiveness of the specific assistive technology tool/device.

Example:

- *A specific early intervention objective is written to increase the child's expressive communication through activation of a switch connected to a tape recorder with voice output. The adults in the classroom to collect ten-minute samples on a daily basis and review the data each week to measure the rate of switch access and communication.*

T7. Service programs and professionals consider the least intrusive, least intensive, yet effective low tech devices in making decisions about assistive technology for individual children.

Examples:

- *An inexpensive motorized play cart is used to teach mobility prior to considering the purchase of a motorized wheelchair.*

- *A trial is performed with a communication device that has four prerecorded messages prior to deciding on a more complex device with computer-generated voice output and additional messages.*

T8. Service programs and professionals consider the use of technology to assist in the assessment process.

Examples:

- *An FM system is used when conducting an assessment with the child with a hearing impairment.*

- *The child has limited motor control of his upper extremities. An optical pointer is attached to the child's head as a means of pointing to or selecting the desired picture or response in a multiple choice assessment.*

T9. Service programs and professionals have knowledge of sources for funding and consider procedures to coordinate resources for funding and re-use.

Examples:

- *Workshops are organized to inform professionals about public and private funding sources in the community and the procedures for accessing and using these sources.*

- *A local service organization is contacted to assist in funding an augmentative communication device for the child.*

Families and professionals collaborate in planning and implementing the use of assistive technology.

. . . .

T10. Professionals' use and selection of assistive technology is based on a family's preferences within assessment, implementation, and evaluation activities.

Examples:

- *A speech therapist provides the family with information on different communication devices to assist them in their selection of a device based on their child's needs and strengths.*

- *The family tries several different switch-activated toys suggested by the occupational therapist prior to selecting the one that they think their child will like best.*

. . . .

T11. Professionals provide assistance to individual families in the use, maintenance, and generalization of assistive technology to facilitate child development.

Examples:

- *Family members learn how to record names of family members or common words and phrases on a device used in the home to help the child communicate with them.*

- *Family members are asked to assist in recharging the battery on a power wheelchair when it is parked at home overnight.*

. . . .

T12. Professionals and families provide children access to assistive devices across settings. Teachers and parents place the devices/tools in the location where instruction and interaction take place.

Examples:

- *The child has a motorized toy vehicle to use at home, and another vehicle is available for use at school.*

- *The family places pictures used for communication in several locations in the home where the child spends most of her time (e.g., in the kitchen, bathroom, bedroom, family room).*

- *The teacher shows the parents how she has wrapped the markers and paintbrushes with pieces of foam so their child will have an easier time grasping them.*

T13. Service programs and professionals are responsive to the culture, language, and economics of the family when making decisions concerning assessment, funding, implementation, and evaluation of technology applications.

Examples:

- *Spanish is the primary language spoken in the child's home. Thus, Spanish is used during assessments pertaining to communication or use of a communication device.*

- *The culture of the family does not permit the use of actual photographs of people, so the speech therapist and the family select objects familiar to the child.*

- *The program staff is aware of the family's sources of funding and other funding options and is thoughtful about how to select and acquire funding for a communication device.*

Families and professionals use technology to access information and support.

T14. Service programs and professionals provide families choices and opportunities to use technology applications to access information and network with other families for support/advocacy.

Examples:

- *The program staff offer families the opportunity to join a LISTSERV created specifically for families to share information on resources, such as educational and respite programs for children with a particular diagnosis or disability.*

- *The program staff maintain a list of possible funding sources, including private foundations and organizations, on its Web site for families who are considering acquisition of assistive technology for their child.*

T15. Professionals and families use technology applications (e.g., teleconferencing and distance learning) to increase their knowledge base and skills.

Examples:

- *Parents are provided training on using Internet search engines to find diagnosis-related information.*

- *Parents participate in workshops with access through video conferencing.*

T16. Service programs and family organizations use information technology as a source of resources for families.

Examples:

- *Agency A has a "Family" section on their Web site.*

- *Agency B provides numerous links to other Web sites and resources directly on their site.*

. . . .

T17. Professionals have competencies to access technology for obtaining current research, reviewing effective practices, and networking with peers.

Examples:

- *Professionals use Internet search engines to locate sources of information and relevant literature.*

- *E-mail is used as a communication strategy for team members to add to reports and assessment information.*

Training and technical support programs are available to support technology applications.

. . . .

T18. State agencies and personnel training programs require licensure or credentials and continuing education units for technology specialists.

Examples:

- *The state education or Part C agency creates teams of professionals in school districts or regions throughout the state, and these people are recognized to be the "experts" in assessment for assistive technology.*

- *The state university offers additional coursework leading to an endorsement in technology as part of their teacher licensure personnel preparation program.*

. . . .

T19. State agencies, service programs, and personnel training programs infuse technology at the preservice and inservice levels to increase competencies of service providers, families, and administrators in assistive, instructional, and informational technologies.

Examples:

- *The state's Comprehensive System of Personnel Development (CSPD) plan includes "Technology Training" for teachers in infant-toddler or preschool programs.*

- *Technology is incorporated into workshops provided by the agency as a way to improve knowledge for families and program staff in the use of technology.*

- *A university initial teacher preparation program includes a course on the application of technology to classroom learning.*

. . . .

T20. Service programs provide maintenance services for repair and replacement of devices.

Examples:

- *The early intervention program has an agreement with a vendor to provide a loaner until a device is repaired.*

- *The school district has a contract with a local vendor for ongoing maintenance and repair of devices owned or purchased by the school district.*

. . . .

T21. Preservice/inservice programs provide training across transdisciplinary teams for parent involvement, training, and decision making in the area of technology.

Examples:

- *Team members are trained together to provide ongoing evaluation of children using assistive technology.*

- *A workshop is offered to all related service providers and family members on the use of technology in assessment.*

. . . .

T22. Service programs provide training and technical support to teachers and parents of specific children for ongoing support, transition, and operational maintenance in the area of assistive technology.

Examples:

- *Head Start teachers are provided inservice time to receive information on using a communication device with a particular child in the classroom.*

- *Teachers from an early childhood program provide inservice to kindergarten staff to better prepare for the child's transition with a specific piece of technology.*

chapter

7

Technology Applications Glossary

Assistive devices (or **assistive technology).** Any item, piece of equipment, or product system, whether acquired commercially, off-the-shelf, modified, or customized, that is used to increase, maintain, or improve functional capabilities of individuals with disabilities.

Distance education (also known as **distance learning** or **distributed learning**). A system in which educator and learner are separated by physical distance.

FM system. One of three types of large area assistive listening systems. The FM system is simply a variation on the commercial FM radio. (The other large area assistive listening systems are the induction loop and the infrared [IR] system.)

Generalization. A phase of learning. It refers to learning to use a skill outside of the context in which it was initially acquired. This is often thought of as performing a behavior in another setting, with other people, and/or with materials different from those used in initial instruction.

High technology or high tech. General terms that are used by researchers and educators. Refers to complex electronic devices such as computers, voice synthesizers, Braille readers, augmentative or adaptive communication (AAC) systems, and environmental control units.

Information technology (IT). Includes matters concerned with computer science and technology, and the design, development, installation, and implementation of information systems and applications.

Instructional technology. Any item, piece of equipment, or product that is used to increase, maintain, or improve the functional capabilities of a child with a disability.

Least intensive. A device that requires the least amount of work from the child for the same gain as a device that requires extensive work.

Least intrusive. The arrangement of instructional procedures that provides the minimum amount of assistance required for the child to perform the skill or behavior.

LISTSERV. An automatic mailing list server. When an e-mail is addressed to a LISTSERV, it is automatically broadcast to everyone on the list.

Low technology or **low tech.** General terms that are used by researchers and educators. Refers to more simple devices, supports, systems, and adaptations such as custom-designed hand tools; positioning devices; and other simple, inexpensive, easy-to-use devices.

Search engine (Internet). A type of software that creates indexes of databases or Internet sites based on the titles of files, key words, or the full text of files.

Technology Application Resources

Print Materials

Baby Power: A Guide for Families for Using Assistive Technology With Infants & Toddlers
P. Pierce (Ed.) (1994)

This free guide offers suggestions and guidelines for using assistive technology to help with different aspects of daily life. Each chapter includes basic information, strategies to try, sample goals, and helpful resources.

> North Carolina Department of Health and Human Services
> Early Intervention Branch, Women's & Children's Health Section
> 2302 Mail Service Center
> Raleigh, NC 27699-2302
> Phone: (919) 715-7500

Engineering the Preschool Environment for Interactive, Symbolic Communication: An Emphasis on the Developmental Period 18 Months to Five Years
C. Goossens', S. S. Crain, & P. S. Elder (1994)

Imagine a preschool environment where assistive technology is being used constantly by both the students and the instructors. This 202-page book gives the practical information needed to set up such an environment. It is written simply and clearly and is full of illustrations, "how-to" explanations, and examples.

> Mayer-Johnson, Inc.
> P.O. Box 1579
> Solana Beach, CA 92075
> Phone: (800) 588-4548 or (858) 550-0084
> FAX: (858) 550-0449
> Web: http://www.mayer-johnson.com/main/index.html
> E-mail: mayerj@mayer-johnson.com

TECH-IT-EASY: Technology for Infants and Toddlers Made Easy
D. Reinhartsen, S. Attermeier, B. Edmondson, & P. Pierce (1995)

Looking for step-by-step instructions on adapting toys and environments for very young children with special needs? This resource offers lots of specific ideas, resources, and references for the use of assistive technology and light tech applications.

> Center for Development and Learning
> CB #7255
> University of North Carolina at Chapel Hill
> Chapel Hill, NC 27599-7255
> Phone: (919) 966-5171
> Web: http://www.ec-link.org

chapter
7

Total Augmentative Communication in the Early Childhood Classroom
L. J. Burkhart (n.d.)

A wealth of strategies and simple adaptations for using multiple forms of communication are included in this book. Chapters describe application strategies for individual communication modes of sign language, speech, powered mobility, voice-output devices, and picture symbols, as well as ideas on how to integrate these modalities. One chapter discusses appropriate communication goals and creative methods for evaluating progress. Detailed directions are provided for construction of simple devices and adaptations, for emergent literacy and math skills, beginning writing adaptations, and communication. An appendix on facilitated communication suggests strengths, cautions, and ideas for integrating this tool into the total program.

> Linda J. Burkhart
> 6201 Candle Court
> Eldersburg, MD 21784
> FAX: (410) 795-8834
> Web: http://www.lburkhart.com
> E-mail: linda@Lburkhart.com

Videotapes

Freedom of Speech
West Virginia Documentary Consortium and Spectra Media (1997)

This is a 30-minute, closed-captioned video about the capacity of technology to assist individuals with disabilities in achieving their potential. Using stories from two families, this video delivers powerful messages about concerns, priorities, resources, and aspirations from parent and consumer perspectives.

> West Virginia Documentary Consortium and Spectra Media
> 2410 Woodland Avenue
> South Charleston, WV 25303
> Phone: (304) 744-7725
> FAX: (304) 744-7740

Welcome to My Preschool! Communicating With Technology
National Center to Improve Practice (NCIP) (1994)

Play this 14-minute, closed-captioned videotape to visit an inclusive preschool classroom where children with disabilities use assistive technology to communicate and fully participate. The video helps viewers reconsider options for water play, storybook reading, and other daily activities.

> National Center to Improve Practice (NCIP)
> Education Development Center, Inc.
> 55 Chapel Street
> Newton, MA 02458
> Phone: (800) 793-5076
> Web: http://www2.edc.org/NCIP/ (Click on "Video Profiles.")
> E-mail: ncip@edc.org

Web Sites

Alliance for Technology Access

This group and their Web site offer information, resources, strategies, and networking for connecting children with disabilities and technology tools.

http://www.ataccess.org

Assistive Technology and Diversity Issues

The National Early Childhood Technical Assistance Center (NECTAC) has compiled this mini-bibliography. It offers resources and strategies for considering each family's cultural, ethnic, and/or socioeconomic background when considering the use of assistive technology with young children.

http://www.nectac.org/~pdfs/topics/at.pdf

Assistive Technology for Infants and Toddlers

This four-page brief answers some common questions parents and practitioners may have about assistive technology. It defines assistive technology and discusses key related topics such as evaluation and costs.

http://www.fape.org/pubs

AT Quick Guides: Independence Through Assistive Technology

Each "AT Quick Guide" provides a brief overview of when and how assistive technology can be beneficial for a child who has developmental delays. Topics include communication, adaptive skills and cognition, fine motor, gross motor, self-help, and sensory development.

http://jfkpartners.org/PUBLICATIONS.asp

Children With Special Needs: Internet Guide for Parents and Professionals

The topics covered by this resource range from adaptive toys and sibling relationships to specific disability Web sites.

http://www.state.de.us/dhss/dms/epqc/birth3/files/internetguide.pdf

Early Childhood Guided Tour

The National Center to Improve Practice (NCIP) developed this site to illustrate ways that technology can help provide full access to rich language and literacy experiences for children with disabilities. Take a virtual tour of two inclusive classrooms to discover an array of resources and strategies.

http://www2.edc.org/NCIP/tour/toc.htm

Useful Web Sites for Parents of Children With Special Health Care Needs

A starting point for exploration of the World Wide Web is what this Web site offers. Search engines, subject guides, news groups, free home page opportunities, and affinity groups are some of the categories of available resources.

http://www.familyvillage.wisc.edu/websites.html

chapter 7

Selected Bibliography of Articles and Books on Assistive Technology

This rich bibliography features a variety of resources (e.g., articles, checklists, quality indicators, etc.) on a variety of topics (e.g., family involvement, policy, funding, etc.). Many items are available to download.

http://www.nectac.org/topics/atech/bibliography.asp

Simplified Technology

Look beyond the categories for older children and you'll find some great resources on this site. The handouts, fact sheets, links and vendor information are all applicable to young children.

http://www.lburkhart.com/

Simple Technology Encourages Independence in Play and Communication for Infants and Toddlers With Disabilities

This site provides a clear, concise summary of the benefits of assistive technology. Geared for parents and teachers, it includes examples of how technology can increase opportunities to communicate, play, learn, and grow.

http://www.circ.uab.edu/spages/cburktxt.htm

Synthesis on the Use of Assistive Technology With Infants and Toddlers (Birth Through Age Two)

Using examples and illustrations drawn from professionals and parents throughout the country, this report synthesizes the many ways in which assistive technology is enhancing opportunities for infants and toddlers with disabilities to learn and grow in home and community settings. The emphasis on natural environments makes this a unique and informative resource.

http://www.air.org/TECHIDEAS/Final%20Report.pdf

Tots 'n Tech (TnT) Research Institute

TnT is an interuniversity collaboration between Thomas Jefferson University and Arizona State University. A major component of the TnT's mission is to produce new knowledge and information about assistive technology (AT) use and practices and, specifically, about the ways in which AT may optimize children''s development and learning.

http://tnt.asu.edu/

Web-Based and Distance Education Training Resources

Interested in technology applications (e.g., distance education, listservs, chat rooms, etc.)? This compilation offers lots of examples, including online courses. Click on "NECTAC Online Workshop on Web-Based Training Demonstration" (at http://www.NECTAC.org/pubs/titlelist.asp#wbt) to discover a wealth of articles, checklists, and resources. You can also visit the following site for additional Web-based and distance education training resources.

http://www.NECTAC.org/topics/personnel/onlinetrngResources.asp

chapter
7

Indirect Supports

• • • • • •

Chapter 8

DEC Recommended Practices: Policies, Procedures, and Systems Change

· · · · · · · · · ·

Introduction
· · · · · · · · · · · · ·

Gloria Harbin and Christine Salisbury

Research on the development of organizations and public policy indicates that an adequate infrastructure increases the likelihood that recommended practices will be used to deliver services and supports to young children and their families. When quality practices are used consistently, it is more likely that children and their families will experience positive outcomes. The interdependent relationships among structure, services, supports, and outcomes are consistent with ecological theories of development (e.g., Bronfenbrenner, 1976; Gallimore, Weisner, Kaufman, & Bernheimer, 1989). These theories suggest that a child's development is influenced not only by the family, neighborhood, subculture, and community, but by the systems of services and supports that serve them as well (Bronfenbrenner, 1976).

The organizational structure, use of resources, policies, and program procedures are important elements of the infrastructure that provide the necessary foundation at the local, state, and federal levels for use of all the DEC Recommended Practices. For this infrastructure to be effective in facilitating the use of recommended practices, there must be coherence and alignment among the various elements. For example, the infrastructure will be stronger and more effective if the policies require the use of recommended practices, the administrative structure facilitates their use, and the funding and reimbursement mechanisms also are designed to promote the use of recommended practices.

A single agency, program, or provider often cannot meet the diverse needs of children with disabilities and their families. The need for an integrated system of services

Focus group members: Gwen Beegle, Barbara Bowman, Michael Conn-Powers, Carl J. Dunst, Jim Gallagher, Corrine Garland, Gloria Harbin, George Jesien, Penny Milburn, Sharon Rosenkoetter, Sarah Rule, Christine Salisbury, and Sharon Walsh

and supports creates challenges and adds complexity to the delivery of services (Salisbury, Crawford, Marlowe & Husband, 2003). The Practices contained in this chapter are designed to assist readers in the development of an adequate infrastructure that supports and integrates the Recommended Practices listed in the other chapters. This chapter also contains suggestions for the processes to be used in developing infrastructure supports. The concepts and processes used in this chapter are consistent with those developed by Senge (1990) and others who have recognized the need in organizations for decisions to be made collaboratively and for individuals to view themselves as active participants and life-long learners.

Since most infrastructures at the state and community level do not conform to all of the Recommended Practices in this book, this chapter also provides suggestions for changing public policies and systems so that improvements can be made in the structure and operation of organizations that deliver services and supports to children and their families. Constructive systems change requires leadership that is effective and that operates from a comprehensive plan developed through the collaborative partnerships of those involved with and affected by the changes of the organization.

Guiding Principles

chapter

8

Following are descriptions of the guiding principles related to the Recommended Practices in this chapter.

Families and Professionals Shape Policy at the Federal, State, and Local Levels

Everyone participating in the delivery of early intervention/early childhood special education services and supports can and should contribute in some way to developing policies that reflect recommended practices and improving service systems (Senge, 1990). The Recommended Practices in this strand echo the need for each person to educate him- or herself about the policy process and to take an active role in that process.

Public Policies Promote the Use of Recommended Practices

Public policy is defined as the rules and standards that are established in order to allocate scarce public resources to meet a particular social need (Gallagher, Harbin, Eckland, & Clifford, 1994). Policy includes documents, mechanisms, and processes. Policy documents include legislation, executive orders, rules and regulations, program guidelines, official memos, and interagency agreements. Policy documents exist at the federal, state, and local levels. For example, IDEA is an example of federal legislation, and there are federal regulations to further specify the requirements of the legislation. There is also state legislation with accompanying regulations: state special education regulations are an example. At the local level, there are local school board policies and individual program policies. Examples of ways that policy is communicated and implemented include the use of pilots and demonstration projects, use of requests for proposals (RFPs) to direct actions and resources, interagency planning agreements, and training and technical assistance initiatives. Policy evolves through three stages: (1) policy development occurs when the documents are being crafted; (2) policy approval occurs when the written policies receive official sanction and adoption; and (3) policy implementation occurs when the policies are implemented and used.

Program Policies and Administration Promote Family Participation in Decision Making, the Use of Recommended Practices, and Interagency and Interdisciplinary Collaboration

Practices in the three areas of (1) family participation in decision making; (2) promoting the use of Recommended Practices; and (3) interagency and interdisciplinary collaboration describe how programs should operate to ensure that children and families receive the services and supports they need. Appropriate implementation of these practices will make certain that services are flexible and responsive to the diverse needs of children and families, coordinated within and among organizations, and implemented by qualified personnel. In organizations implementing Recommended Practices, partnerships and participatory decision making are evident in the development, delivery, and evaluation of program policies and administration (Hayden, Frederick, & Smith, 2003). Program plans developed in such organizations represent an integrated, comprehensive array of services and supports designed to be implemented in inclusive and natural contexts. Mechanisms exist within these organizations to allow for the development of flexible service delivery approaches and regular self-assessment, program evaluation, and subsequent revision of services and supports based upon evidence of how well these approaches are meeting the needs of children and families.

Appropriate implementation of these practices will make certain that services are flexible and responsive to the diverse needs of children and families. . . .

Program Policies, Administration, and Leadership Promote Program Evaluation and Systems Change Efforts

Practices in this area describe the structure and work of organizations, as well as the results of effective leadership within these organizations. A leader is anyone who engages in the work of leadership. Leadership requires the redistribution of power and authority, leads to constructive change, and involves the promotion of inquiry and learning among all individuals in the organization (Hargreaves & Fullan, 1998;

Lambert, 1998). The work of effective leaders is grounded in their ability to develop effective partnerships; to align policies, structures, and practices to promote change; and to cultivate a culture within their organizations that not only supports, but encourages, data-informed decision making and change (Salisbury & McGregor, 2002).

Systemic change requires that the interdependence of key components of the system be addressed simultaneously, and impediments to change be understood. Systems change efforts can be designed to improve efficiency and effectiveness, or to alter more deeply the fundamental ways in which the overall system and its components are conceived, organized, and delivered. These changes often involve a fundamental revision in values, goals, structures, and roles within organizations (Cuban, 1996; Elmore, 1997; Fullan, 1991). Effective leaders guide the substantive changes within organizations and support the "reculturing" necessary to sustain those changes and to produce positive outcomes for children, families, and staff.

Research on large-scale systemic change affirms the essential role of leadership in guiding change efforts and the importance of collaborative, data-based, supported decision making (Roach, Salisbury, & McGregor, 2002). Recent research also suggests that organizational change involving inquiry about issues of importance to practitioners can help promote and sustain changes in services, structure, and policies (Salisbury & McGregor, 2002). Such inquiry often leads to changes in the procedures, structures, and/or design of services in ways that promote the use of Recommended Practices. Adoption and use of the Recommended Practices ensure that services are responsive, that families use them, and that they change as the needs of children and families change.

Conclusion

The Recommended Practices in this chapter can enhance the quality of early intervention/early childhood special education services. (An administrator's checklist for reflecting on these Recommended Practices is provided in Chapter 12.) Several conclusions can be drawn from field experiences and the research literature:

- There is clear wisdom in the use of participatory decision-making processes for developing and maintaining quality early childhood intervention programs.
- The capacity of state and local systems to deliver coordinated, comprehensive services to children and families rests, in large part, on the knowledge of policy makers, administrators, practitioners, and parents about what constitutes effective and Recommended Practices.
- At the state level, adoption and utilization of the Practices in this chapter implies a willingness to scrutinize current structures, policies, and practices within and across departments; adopt changes in the structure of divisions/departments to reflect integrated functions; and develop new professional practice standards.

chapter
8

- Local and program level adoption of the Recommended Practices would be evident in how teams are constituted and how they function; the location, content, and nature of services and supports; and the way in which planning processes and documents are used to stimulate a culture of inquiry and change.

- Optimizing the participation and inclusion of individuals from within and outside the organization helps ensure that the outcomes are viewed as meaningful and appropriate to the needs of those involved.

References

Bronfenbrenner, U. (1976). Ecology of the family as a context for human development: Research perspectives. *Developmental Psychology, 22,* 723-742.

Cuban, L. (1996). Myths about changing schools and the case of special education. *Remedial and Special Education, 17*(2), 75-82.

Elmore, R. F. (1997). Organizational models of social program implementation. *Public Policy, 26*(2), 185-228.

Fullan, M. (1991). *The new meaning of educational change.* New York: Teachers College Press.

Gallagher, J., Harbin, G., Eckland, J., & Clifford, R. (1994). State diversity and policy implementation: Infants and toddlers. In L. J. Johnson, R. J. Gallagher, M. J. LaMontagne, J. B. Jordan, J. J. Gallagher, P. L. Hutinger, & M. B. Karnes (Eds.), *Meeting early intervention challenges* (pp. 235-250). Baltimore: Paul H. Brookes.

Gallimore, R., Weisner, T. S., Kaufman, S. Z., & Bernheimer, L. P. (1989). The social construction of eco-cultural niches: Family accommodation of developmentally delayed children. *American Journal on Mental Retardation, 94*(3), 216-230.

Hargreaves, A., & Fullan, M. (1998). *What's worth fighting for out there?* New York: Teachers College Press.

Hayden, P., Frederick, L., & Smith, B. (2003). *A road map for facilitating collaborative teams.* Longmont, CO: Sopris West.

Lambert, L. (1998). *Building leadership capacity in schools.* Alexandria, VA: Association for Supervision and Curriculum Development (ASCD).

Roach, V., Salisbury, C. L, & McGregor, G. (2002). Applications of a policy framework to evaluate and promote large scale change. *Exceptional Children, 68*(4), 451-464.

Salisbury, C. L., Crawford, W., Marlowe, D., & Husband, P. (2003). Integrating education and human service plans: The Interagency Planning and Support Project. *Journal of Early Intervention, 26*(1), 59-75.

Salisbury, C., & McGregor, G. (2002). The administrative climate and context of inclusive elementary schools. *Exceptional Children, 68*(2), 259-274.

Senge, P. M. (1990). *The fifth discipline.* New York: Currency Doubleday.

chapter

8

DEC Recommended Practices and Examples: Policies, Procedures, and Systems Change

Families and professionals shape policy at the national, state, and local levels.

PS1. Families and professionals educate themselves about public policies and the policy development process and contexts (laws, regulations, etc.), and the key players at the federal, state, and local levels and advocate for consistent federal, state, and local policies that reflect recommended practices.

Example:

- *Families and professionals attend workshops on "How a Bill Becomes a Law" and other advocacy topics.*

PS2. Families and professionals participate in advocacy and public policy making in a variety of ways including: public awareness, creating coalitions, participating in task forces that revise or develop policies, and creating a unified community vision for children and families.

Example:

- *Families and professionals participate on committees and task forces.*

PS3. Families and professionals use and translate research data to educate themselves, the public, and decision makers about the importance of services provided in accordance with recommended practices.

Example:

- *The team of family members and professionals develops one-page fact sheets for policy makers and editorials and press releases for newspapers that explain, in layman's terms, the evidence underlying their policy recommendations (e.g., the efficacy of inclusion for young children and the cost-effectiveness of quality early intervention).*

PS4. Families and professionals analyze and explore policy options and the possible consequences of those options.

Example:

- *Teams of families and professionals identify policy barriers to their community vision for inclusive services, such as a lack of inclusive programs in public schools and a policy that prohibits schools from contracting with local child care or Head Start centers in order to serve children in inclusive settings. Teams develop options for solving the problem and provide pros and cons for each option.*

Public policies promote the use of Recommended Practices.

PS5. State and local policies and procedures are in compliance with federal policies (who, what, when, and where, the "musts" and the "shoulds") as well as recommended practices (e.g., identification for services is based on the educational needs of the child, not on cognitive referencing or the availability of resources).

Examples:

- *IDEA requires that all eligible children with disabilities or developmental delays receive special education and related services; therefore, the state or district may not restrict services to just a portion of the population, such as children with mental retardation.*

- *The state sets expectations and supports for districts to use recommended practices such as the NAEYC Developmentally Appropriate Practice guidelines and the DEC Recommended Practices.*

PS6. Public policies require an adequate infrastructure for appropriate services based on recommended practices (e.g., administration, funding, salaries, staffing, personnel standards, training, and leadership development, research and program evaluation, model or pilot programs, and technical assistance).

Example:

- *The state guidelines provide resources and expectations for funding, salaries, staffing standards and patterns, and staff development opportunities that reflect national recommendations such as those from NAEYC and DEC.*

PS7. Public policies provide for sufficient, alternative, flexible fiscal and administrative requirements that facilitate: (a) the effective use of natural and inclusive settings, (b) interagency coordination at the "systems" level, and (c) interdisciplinary collaboration at the "direct-service" level (Medicaid waivers, child care subsidies, blended funding, itinerant services, etc.).

Examples:

- *State Medicaid policies allow for reimbursement of services in the home and in natural inclusive environments such as child care.*

- *Financial policies support local interagency committees meeting regularly to ensure that children and families are receiving the supports they need and that resources are shared and not duplicated, funding across various funding streams is blended in settings resulting in inclusion, and specialized personnel are able to provide itinerant services across agencies.*

- *Personnel job descriptions allow for the commitment of time and effort to these activities and meetings and families are reimbursed for their participation in these meetings.*

chapter

8

. . . .

PS8. Public policies reflect family support principles across all systems of services, birth through 5 (e.g., providing service coordination for children birth-5 rather than just birth-2, etc.), including strategies that help to ensure participation of traditionally underrepresented families.

Examples:

- *State guidelines promote the continuance of service coordination for children after they turn three and are served in IDEA preschool programs in public schools.*
- *Local policies reimburse families for participating in planning meetings.*

. . . .

PS9. Public policies create a system of appropriate learning opportunities and environments that take advantage of community resources and inclusive or natural learning environments, not just traditional disability or school-based programs.

Example:

- *Local and state policies allow flexible funding across programs and resource sharing. For instance, public schools and local child care centers develop agreements for the schools to purchase slots in the child care centers and provide special services on an itinerant basis to the children with IEPs in those inclusive settings.*

. . . .

PS10. Public polices are examined and revised as needed to ensure that they reflect diversity.

Example:

- *The state conducts an annual survey of families to assess their satisfaction with services. Information is used to evaluate policies and procedures.*

. . . .

PS11. Public policies require periodic review and revision of policies based upon systematic evaluation of data regarding needs and outcomes.

Example:

- *The state and local programs conduct an annual evaluation of services, child outcomes, and parent satisfaction. State and local policies are revised based on the evaluation data, such as changing policies to promote more parent participation.*

Program policies and administration promote family participation in decision making.

. . . .

PS12. When creating program policies and procedures, strategies are employed to capture family and community voices and to support the active and meaningful participation of families and community groups, including those that are traditionally underrepresented.

Examples:

- *Periodic family and community forums and surveys are conducted to obtain input on program policies and procedures, share information, and to collect satisfaction data.*

- *Programs establish policy teams that are comprised of administrators, direct service staff, community providers, and family members. All policies are developed/revised by these teams based on data collected through evaluation procedures.*

PS13. Program policies create a participatory decision-making process of all stakeholders including individuals with disabilities. Training in teaming is provided as needed.

PS14. Program policies ensure that families understand their rights including conflict resolution, confidentiality, and other matters.

Examples:

- *Program policy requires that teachers ask newly enrolled families if they understand the materials and information they have received about their rights as family members. If the families do not, teachers, other professionals, and parents meet with the families to discuss, answer questions, and give examples in formats that are culturally and linguistically appropriate and matched to the needs of caregivers.*

- *Service coordinators provide families with information about their rights in accessible formats.*

PS15. Program policies are examined and revised as needed to ensure that they reflect and respect the diversity of children, families, and personnel.

Example:

- *Families, the policy team, and community members are asked to review and comment on the responsiveness of policies and practices to community needs.*

PS16. Program policies are provided in sufficient detail and formats so that all stakeholders understand what the policy means.

Examples:

- *The policy team and other stakeholders are asked to review and comment on the clarity of materials that explain policies.*

- *Materials explaining policies related to family rights and participation are written in language that family members say they understand, and are offered with verbal explanation.*

- *Families' rights are described in videos that are available for them to borrow.*

chapter

8

. . . .

PS17. Program policies require a family-centered approach in all decisions and phases of service delivery (system entry, assessment procedures, Individualized Family Service Plan (IFSP)/Individualized Education Program (IEP), intervention, transition, etc.) including presenting families with flexible and individualized options for the location, timing and types of services, supports, and resources that are not disruptive of family life.

. . . .

PS18. Program policies provide for the dissemination of information about program initiatives and outcomes to stakeholders.

Program policies and administration promote the use of Recommended Practices.

. . . .

PS19. Program policies establish accountability systems that provide resources, supports, and clear action steps to ensure compliance with regulations and to ensure that recommended practices are adopted, utilized, maintained, and evaluated; resulting in high quality services.

Example:

- *Periodically the policy team reviews program audit data and conducts a program assessment related to Recommended Practices.*

. . . .

PS20. Program policies reflect recommended practices including personnel standards, child-staff ratios, group size, caseloads, safety, assistive technology, and EI/ECSE services and practices. Incentives, training, and technical assistance to promote the use of recommended practices in all settings are provided.

Example:

- *The policy team obtains copies of current recommended practices related to personnel and practice guidelines [e.g., DEC, NAEYC, Head Start], conducts a program assessment related to the guidelines, and provides training related to identified needs.*

. . . .

PS21. Program policies support the provision of services in inclusive or natural learning environments (i.e., places in which typical children participate, such as the home or community settings, public and private preschools, child care, recreation groups, etc.). Strategies are used to overcome challenges to inclusion.

Examples:

- *Programs develop interagency collaboration teams comprised of staff and family members to address attitudes, concerns, training needs, resource sharing, specialized supports, transportation, and other policy and belief challenges.*

- *Teams visit successful inclusive programs to observe their practices and learn new strategies.*

. . . .

PS22. Program policies ensure that the IFSP/IEP is used on a regular and frequent basis to determine the type and amounts of services, the location of services, and the desired outcomes.

. . . .

PS23. Program policies provide clear job descriptions and provide for personnel competencies and ongoing staff development, technical assistance, supervision, and evaluation to inform and improve the skills of practitioners and administrators.

. . . .

PS24. Program policies ensure that family supports, service coordination, transitions, and other practices occur in response to child and family needs rather than being determined by the age of the child (e.g., b-2, 3-5).

Example:

- *Programs continue service coordination across infant-toddler and preschool programs as appropriate and determined by the IFSP/IEP teams.*

. . . .

PS25. Program policies ensure that multiple instructional models are available to meet the individual needs of children (e.g., less structure to more structure, child-driven to teacher-driven, peer mediated to teacher mediated, etc.).

. . . .

PS26. Administrators provide for a supportive work environment (e.g., hiring and retention policies, compensation and benefits, safety, workspace, etc.).

Examples:

- *Administrators use recognition of excellence and career ladders.*

- *Policies ensure the health and safety of staff, and compensation and benefit packages are considered a top priority for resource allocation.*

. . . .

PS27. Program coordinators/supervisors have training in early childhood education, early intervention, early childhood special education, and supervision.

. . . .

PS28. Administrators are affiliated with professional early childhood/early childhood special education organizations and encourage staff to maintain their affiliations. Continuing education, such as staff attendance at meetings and conferences, to enhance professional growth is supported.

chapter

8

Program policies and administration promote interagency and interdisciplinary collaboration.

. . . .

PS29. Program policies include structures and mechanisms such as job descriptions, planning time, training, and resources for teaming resulting in meaningful participation for on-going coordination among professionals, families, and programs related to service delivery including transition.

Examples:

- *Time is included in job descriptions for participation in planning meetings among professionals working with the same family.*

- *Staff and families identify common training and informational needs. Programs share resources to obtain quality training, hold discussion groups, and plan changes to improve service delivery.*

. . . .

PS30. Program policies facilitate and provide for comprehensive and coordinated systems of services through interagency collaboration by clearly delineating the components, activities, and responsibilities of all agencies (e.g., joint policies across agencies; collaborative planning on a system, child, and family basis; shared forms and plans; etc.).

Example:

- *Head Start, child care, and public school programs create a collaborative planning team. This interagency team develops a written agreement stipulating that Head Start and child care will allocate a percentage of openings for children with disabilities as inclusive placement options for the public school. The public school will reimburse for these openings and provide itinerant specialized personnel to consult with Head Start and child care staff. All three programs write program policies that describe and support these arrangements.*

. . . .

PS31. Program policies result in families and professionals from different disciplines working as a team developing and implementing IFSPs/IEPs that integrate their expertise into common goals.

Example:

- *Policies require that all staff and consultants representing the services and supports indicated on the child's IFSP/IEP meet regularly with the child's family to discuss plans for addressing the interdisciplinary needs of the child. Expertise is transferred/shared across disciplines and with the family so that all the therapists and teachers do not need to work directly with the child and family (i.e., transdisciplinary service delivery).*

chapter

8

Program policies, administration, and leadership promote program evaluation and systems change efforts.

PS32. Policies, structures, and practices are aligned to promote systems change.

Examples:

- *Program policies require the use of child-focused practices; provide the staffing, environment, and training related to the practices; and evaluate whether the practices are used appropriately.*

- *Program policies provide organizational, structural, regular monitoring, and training/coaching support to ensure implementation of recommended practices.*

PS33. A shared vision (of all stakeholders), clear values/beliefs, and an understanding of the culture and context to be changed guide efforts to restructure and reform systems. Decisions about what to change result from regular analysis and evaluation of discrepancies among the vision, beliefs, knowledge, and current practices.

Example:

- *The program ensures that a stakeholder planning group, including parents, staff, and leadership, develops a written vision for the program as well as a statement of values and beliefs. At least annually, data related to these statements are collected (e.g., child outcomes, parent satisfaction). If the data are in conflict with the statements, the group decides whether the statements should be revised or the practices must change to ensure outcomes that are in line with the vision and beliefs.*

PS34. Assessment of the interests, issues, and priorities of constituent groups guides the selection and direction of leadership and systems change strategies.

Example:

- *Program policies establish a systematic process to collect data to identify interests, inform decisions, and prioritize actions to be taken.*

PS35. Leadership and systems change efforts produce positive outcomes for children, families, and communities that are responsive to their needs. Evaluation data are used to ensure: (a) service utilization; (b) more efficient and effective supports for children, families, and staff; and (c) appropriate systems change, leadership and strategies.

Example:

- *The program conducts an annual evaluation and uses the data to identify areas of the program and services that receive improvement.*

chapter

8

. . . .

PS36. Leadership capacity, risk taking, and shared decision making among professionals and families at all levels of the organization are cultivated.

Example:

- *Family members and staff are encouraged by program leadership to assume leadership roles, participate in decisions, and to try new approaches.*

. . . .

PS37. Leadership and systems change efforts include attention to: timely job-embedded professional development, funding, program evaluation, accountability, governance, program accreditation, curriculum, and naturalistic instruction/supports.

Example:

- *Annual program evaluation data are used to plan professional development opportunities related to areas of unsatisfactory outcomes for children or families.*

. . . .

PS38. Leadership and systems change efforts rely on strong relationships and collaboration within and across systems: between consumer and system, across systems that deal with children and families, among components within a system, and among professionals from diverse disciplines.

Examples:

- *Programs have internal planning groups involving parents, staff of various disciplines, and leadership.*

- *Programs participate in interagency and community groups that include other systems (e.g., mental health) and programs in the community.*

. . . .

PS39. Leadership is committed and willing to change organizational structures (e.g., staffing, schedules, teaming) to be responsive to individual needs.

Example:

- *As a result of annual program evaluation data that indicate families are dissatisfied with the amount of involvement they have in their child's instruction, the program leadership provides for flexibility in staff schedules allowing them to work more closely with families.*

. . . .

PS40. Change is institutionalized through the development of coordinated management and accountability systems.

Example:

- *Program policies require an annual review of data that leads to continuous program improvement.*

PS41. Resources are provided for program evaluation that occurs along established time points, incorporating appropriate measurable indicators of progress including child and family outcomes and preferences.

Example:

- *Policies ensure that financial and staff resources are scheduled and available for quarterly data collection that is used in the annual program evaluation. Staff are trained in the use of appropriate data collection procedures.*

PS42. Program evaluation is comprehensive, is multidimensional, and incorporates a variety of methods for assessing the progress and outcomes of change. Evaluation efforts take into account differing cultural, contextual, demographic, and experiential perspectives including those of parents and individuals with disabilities.

Examples:

- *The annual program evaluation is directed by a team of administrative staff, direct service staff, and family members that represents diversity of culture, language, experience, and other demographic characteristics of the children and families served by the program.*

- *Evaluation data are collected in a variety of ways such as surveys, individual interviews, and focus groups.*

PS43. Program policies delineate all components of service delivery and provide for tracking and evaluation of all components, including child and family outcomes, to ensure that recommended practices are implemented as intended.

chapter

8

Policies, Procedures, and Systems Change Glossary

Accountability systems. A set of evaluation policies and procedures that are implemented to ensure that practices are in place and the goals are achieved.

Assessment. The process of collecting information, ideally from multiple sources and means, for making informed decisions for individuals, families, and programs.

Assistive technology. Any item, piece of equipment, or product, whether acquired commercially, off-the-shelf, modified, or customized, that is used to increase, maintain, or improve the functional capabilities of individuals with disabilities.

IDEA. The Individuals with Disabilities Education Act. IDEA is the major federal education law providing funding for early intervention and education services and rights and protections for children with disabilities birth to 21 and their families.

Individualized family services plan/individualized education program (IFSP/IEP). The written individualized plans for children with disabilities required under IDEA. Individualized Family Services Plans are for children ages birth to 3, while Individualized Education Programs (IEPs) are for children ages three and older.

Infrastructure. Policies, procedures, and organizational structure that guide all programmatic, fiscal, personnel, and administrative decisions.

Interagency collaboration. Cooperative activities between/among agencies or programs.

Natural learning environments. Settings in which children without disabilities spend time. Common places include the home, child care programs, family daycare homes, and in community settings (e.g., stores, barber's shops, doctor's offices, parks, etc.) and programs (e.g., children's hour at the library, gymnastics classes, etc.) available to all children in the society. Activities and routines may need to be adapted to ensure that children with disabilities are able to be integral members of the activity or routine.

Organizational structures. Definable units and/or processes around which personnel and practices are organized. Examples include the configuration of staff into teams, the schedules used to organize the flow of services; the administrative units that comprise an organization (e.g., offices, regions, buildings, programs); and/or an interagency council that provides an organizational structure for multiple agencies and programs to work together.

Public policy. The rules and standards that are established in order to allocate scarce public resources to meet a particular social need. Policy includes documents, mechanisms, and processes.

Stakeholders. People or representatives of groups of people who will be affected by a decision or practice.

Systems change. An approach to both program and system improvement that focuses on: (1) the development and interrelationship of all the main components of the program or system simultaneously; and (2) understanding the culture of the program or system as a basis for changing the system.

Policy, Procedures, and Systems Change Resources

Checklists and Measures

An Integrated Early Childhood System: A Guiding Rubric
G. L. Harbin (2004)

This instrument assesses 11 important service system components. Those using the tool can decide if their system is functioning at one of four levels, from "beginning" to "exceptional." This tool can serve as a guide to facilitate taking a system to the next level of quality.

> http://www.fpg.unc.edu/~beacons/tools

Interagency Agreement Rating Scale
G. L. Harbin (1990)

This scale is used to judge the completeness and adequacy of interagency agreements. It has been used with both state- and local-level agreements.

> http://www.fpg.unc.edu/~beacons/tools

Community Capacity Index: Promoting Quality Services
G. L. Harbin & D. Shaw (2000)

This tool is designed to be completed by community leaders (e.g., government, business, media). The purpose of the tool is to assess the level of the commitment of, and support from, the broader community for quality services for young children.

> http://www.fpg.unc.edu/~beacons/tools

Print Materials

America's Babies: The Zero to Three Policy Center Data Book
C. Oser & J. Cohen (2003)

America's Babies was developed to provide policymakers and writers with complete statistics on children from birth to 3 years in the U.S. In addition to demographic information, data on the quality of child health and well-being, family and economic factors, early education and child care, effects of violence and trauma, and how the U.S. compares with other countries are included.

> Zero to Three
> P.O. Box 960
> Herndon, VA 20172
> Phone: (800) 899-4301
> FAX: (703) 661-1501
> Web: http://www.zerotothree.org/ztt_bookstore.html

Blueprint for Action: Achieving Center-Based Change Through Staff Development
P. Jorde-Bloom, M. Sheerer, & J. Britz (1991)

This handbook is designed by directors of child care centers, and it provides a guide for program analysis and action. It presents a comprehensive method for analyzing

chapter

8

different program components to increase quality and effectiveness. It will help identify common organizational problems and select appropriate strategies for implementing and institutionalizing change.

> New Horizons
> P.O. Box 863
> Lake Forest, IL 60045
> Phone: (708) 295-2968

Collaboration Handbook: Creating, Sustaining, and Enjoying the Journey
M. Winer & K. Ray (1994)

Supports for interpersonal, organizational, and community collaboration are offered in this resource via case examples, activities, tools, and resources. It also offers thoughtful strategies for overcoming obstacles to collaboration, including trust, conflict, decision making, and change.

> Amherst H. Wilder Foundation Publishing Center
> 919 Lafond Avenue
> St. Paul, MN 55104
> Phone: (800) 274-6024
> E-mail: books@wilder.org

Essential Allies: Families as Advisors
E. S. Jeppson & J. Thomas (1995)

Developed to "help leaders bridge the gap between past training and new expectations of collaboration and partnership with families," this publication succeeds in a big way. It has lots of very practical information, illustrations, and resources for supporting family involvement in advisory and leadership roles, including training. Two related publications from the same organization (*Families as Advisors: A Training Guide for Collaboration* and *Words of Advice: A Guidebook for Families Serving as Advisors*) are also excellent resources.

> Institute for Family-Centered Care
> 7900 Wisconsin Avenue, Suite 405
> Bethesda, MD 20814
> Phone: (301) 652-0281
> FAX: (301) 652-0186
> Web: http://www.familycenteredcare.org/resources-frame.html
> E-mail: institute@iffcc.org

Family Involvement in Policy Making
N. M. Koroloff, R. W. Hunter, & L. Gordon (1995)

This monograph summarizes the findings of Families in Action, a five-year project to learn from the experiences of parents and other family members of children with emotional disorders who served as members of policy-making boards, committee, and other policy-related bodies. Lessons learned from families and the project are offered, along with measures and other project-related materials.

Portland State University
Research and Training Center on Family Support and Children's Mental Health
Regional Research Institute for Human Services
P.O. Box 751
Portland, OR 97207-0751
Phone: (503) 725-4175
FAX: (503) 725-4180
Web: http://www.rtc.pdx.edu/
E-mail: rtcpubs@rri.pdx.edu

Handbook for Ethical Policy Making

North Carolina Institute for Policy Studies (1992)

The original purpose of this handbook was to provide appropriate information that can be used by policy boards in the development and writing of guidelines for implementation of Part C. The vignettes, examples, and ideas provided, however, could easily be modified for use in assisting diverse preservice and inservice audiences to appreciate the complexities of the key issues in family-centered policy design.

FPG Child Development Institute
Publications Office
CB #8185
University of North Carolina
Chapel Hill, NC 27599-8185
Phone: (919) 966-4221
FAX: (919) 966-0862
Web: http://www.fpg.unc.edu
E-mail: pubs@mail.fpg.unc.edu

IDEA Requirements for Preschoolers With Disabilities: IDEA Early Childhood Policy and Practice Guide

S. Walsh, B. J. Smith, & R. C. Taylor (2000)

The purpose of this guide from the Division for Early Childhood (DEC) is to assist early childhood educators, administrators, and parents interpret and understand what IDEA requires for young children with disabilities, birth to five, and their families.

Council for Exceptional Children (CEC)
1110 North Glebe Road
Suite 300
Arlington, VA 22201-5704
Phone: (888) CEC-SPED
FAX: (703) 264-9494

The Leadership Challenge (3rd Ed.)

J. Kouzes & B. Posner (2002)

Using evidence and experiences from around the world, the authors provide practical guidance on how to lead, creating shared vision, collaboration, and change. (San Francisco: Jossey-Bass)

chapter

8

Leadership in Early Care and Education
S. L. Kagan & B. T. Bowman (Eds.) (1997)
> This book puts forth a definition of the multiple components of quality early childhood leadership. This book attempts to fuse relevant practical and theoretical ideas about leadership, and to identify leadership needs and how to address those needs. The authors sought the input of many diverse individuals to reflect the many facets of leadership.

> > National Association for the Education of Young Children (NAEYC)
> > P.O. Box 932569
> > Atlanta, GA 31193
> > Phone: (866) 623-9248
> > FAX: (770) 442-9742
> > Web: http://www.naeyc.org/
> > E-mail: naeyc@pbd.com

Leading in a Culture of Change
M. Fullan (2001)
> Author M. Fullan is recognized as an international authority on educational reform and systems change. In this book, he offers new and seasoned leaders' insights into the dynamics of change and presents a unique and imaginative approach for navigating the intricacies of the change process. Examples show how leaders in all types of organizations can accomplish their goals and provide effective leadership. (San Francisco: Jossey-Bass)

Learning to Lead: Effective Leadership Skills for Teachers of Young Children
D. Sullivan (2003)
> The purpose of this book is for individuals to examine their own potential as a leader, and their own roles in the leadership process. The book also points out the important day-to-day leadership actions of those who teach and care for young children. Finally, the book explores what it takes to "create a village to raise a child," and that each person has an important role in creating that village. (St. Paul, MN: Red Leaf Press)

Making Room at the Table
E. S. Jeppson, J. Thomas, A. Markward, J. A. Kelly, G. Koser, & D. Diehl (1997)
> Information and materials for conducting training designed to foster family involvement in the advisory and decision-making roles are offered in this publication. The content is relevant, current, and research-based. The format and activities reflect principles of adult learning, and all materials are clearly written.

> > Family Resource Coalition of America
> > 20 North Wacker Drive, Suite 1100
> > Chicago, IL 60606
> > Phone: (312) 338-0900
> > Web: http://www.familysupportamerica.org
> > E-mail: frca@frca.org

chapter
8

Managing Change Through Innovation
G. Smale (1998)

This book is based on the Managing Change and Innovation Programme of the National Institute for Social Work in the UK. This book addresses the often-asked question, "How do we change practice?" The ideas presented in this book are the result of studying both the successful and unsuccessful instances of adopting innovative practices. (London: The Stationery Office)

The New Meaning of Educational Change
M. Fullan (2001)

The book is organized around three themes: understanding educational change, change at the local level, and change at the regional and national level. Information to help policymakers avoid past mistakes and select promising practices is included. (New York: Teachers College Press)

Path to Excellence: A Blueprint for Developing High-Quality Comprehensive Service Systems
G. L. Harbin, N. L. Gardener, & I. Rodriquez (2004)

This handbook uses the lessons learned from ten years of research in communities with exemplary aspects of service delivery. The handbook presents a blueprint for community programs who are attempting to improve or evaluate resources.

FPG Child Development Institute
Publications Office
CB #8185
University of North Carolina
Chapel Hill, NC 27599-8185
Phone: (919) 966-4221
FAX: (919) 843-5784
Web: http://www.fpg.unc.edu/~beacons/pathtoexcellence
E-mail: pubs@mail.fpg.unc.edu

Reframing Organizations: Artistry, Choice, and Leadership
L. G. Bolman & T. E. Deal (2003)

This book was developed for teachers and professionals who want to become better leaders. It is designed to look through the eyes of both teachers and principals, and is filled with words of wisdom in trying to be a change agent within the public schools. Information about using four organizational frames is presented: political, human resource, structural, and symbolic. (San Francisco: Jossey-Bass)

A Roadmap for Facilitating Collaborative Teams
P. Hayden, L. Frederick, & B. J. Smith (2003)

This manual provides reasons and resources for creating collaborative teams to promote meaningful change in local early childhood systems. It was developed based on research on effective practice related to systems change and teaming/collaboration. Strategies, activities, reproducible forms, guidance, and encouragement are all offered as resources for the collaborative planning journey. (Longmont, CO: Sopris West)

What's Best for Infants and Young Children?
L. Brault & F. Chasen (Eds.) (2001)
> This guide provides a resource for families, professionals, policymakers, and others who are interested in improving services and programs for infants and young children in their community or state. Self-assessments and examples of recommended practice can be used for program evaluation, teaching, or training.

> Infant Development Association of California
> P.O. Box 189550
> Sacramento, CA 95818-9550
> Phone: (916) 453-8801
> Web: http://www.idaofcal.org (Click on "Order a Guide.")
> E-mail: idaofcal@softcom.net

What's Worth Fighting for Out There?
A. Hargreaves & M. Fullan (1998)
This book provides administrators, educators, parents, and governments with many basic, but excellent, ideas and guidelines about creating relationships between the school and the public. It also presents some thoughts to lead businesses to play active roles in associating with schools. Although the exemplified scenarios of this book are based on the Canadian public education, the scenarios and guidelines offered could assist with change in many kinds of systems. (New York: Teachers College Press)

Videotapes

Gone Through Any Changes Lately?
Center for Family and Infant Interaction and JFK Partners, University of Colorado Health Sciences Center (1998)
> The Slinky® video! This 4-1/2 minute video helps people consider past, current, or future changes through the humorous metaphor of a favorite childhood toy. Used to start a meeting or enliven a discussion, this video can help any group address changing roles, policies, or practices in a positive way.

> Western Media Products
> P.O. Box 591
> Denver, CO 80201
> Phone: (800) 232-8902
> Web: www.media-products.com

Web Sites

Addressing the Needs of Latino Children

Latinos are the fastest growing ethnic group in the U.S. today. Nationally, Latino parents have participated at lower rates in early childhood education and early intervention services than parents from other racial and ethnic backgrounds. This Web site describes the linguistically and culturally relevant practices that state administrators reported were recommended or being used by early education and intervention programs that enroll Latino children and families.

http://www.fpg.unc.edu/~nuestros/pdfs/NNExecSummary.pdf

Administrator's Essentials: Creating Policies and Procedures that Support Recommended Practices in Early Intervention/Early Childhood Special Education (EI/ECSE)

This checklist of DEC's Recommended Practices can be used by administrators to reflect on their policies, procedures, and supports for young children and families. It can also be a tool to identify and monitor progress in making targeted changes.

http://www.dec-sped.org/pdf/recommendedpractices/adminessen.pdf

An Administrator's Guide to Preschool Inclusion

This guide was developed to help administrators who are responsible for setting up, monitoring, supporting, and maintaining inclusive programs for preschool children with and without disabilities. It delineates barriers and roadblocks, while offering strategies, supports, and illustrations. One very useful feature is the section on collaboration and consultation.

http://www.fpg.unc.edu/~publicationsoffice/pdfs/AdmGuide.pdf

Assuring the Family's Role on the Early Intervention Team: Explaining Rights and Safeguards

A synthesis of innovative practices and ideas for explaining procedural safeguards to families are offered in this publication. It provides a step-by-step model and useful information and practices for administrators, providers, or family members.

http://www.nectac.org/~pdfs/pubs/assuring.pdf

Consortium for Appropriate Dispute Resolution in Special Education (CADRE)

CADRE is a research and technical assistance center funded by OSEP to develop and provide information and resources related to mediation and other dispute resolution processes. At the CADRE Web site you'll find information on frequently asked questions (FAQ), benefits of mediation, locating a special education conflict resolution professional, and choosing a qualified mediator.

http://www.directionservice.org/cadre/index.cfm

Determining Policy Support for Inclusive Schools

The Consortium on Inclusive Schooling Practices, funded by the OSEP, developed this and other online products to help build the systemic capacity of state and local agencies to provide inclusive educational services. Resources blend research and practical examples and include extensive references.

http://www.inclusiveschools.org/DPSFIS.pdf

chapter

8

IDEA Practices

The most informative and popular sections of the IDEA Practices Web site, "Law & Regulations" and "Professional Development Resources," are available through the Council for Exceptional Children (CEC). This site has materials for implementing IDEA, including IDEA law and regulations as well as the IDEA Partnership products and online resources.

http://www.ideapractices.org/

Part C Updates: Fifth in a Series of Updates on Selected Aspects of the Early Intervention Program for Infants and Toddlers with Disabilities, Part C of IDEA

Information on the policies and practices of the states and jurisdictions that participate in Part C can be a resource to guide policymakers and administrators. This compilation includes a range of materials on implementation of Part C services (e.g., definitions, managed care activity, age focus, etc.) and a copy of the IDEA Amendments of 1997.

http://www.nectac.org/~pdfs/partcupdates.pdf

Procedural Safeguards and Complaint Resolution Under IDEA

Clear, straightforward information about procedural safeguards, mediation, conflict management, and dispute resolution in early intervention are provided by this Web site, as well as additional information and resources.

http://www.nectac.org/topics/procsafe/procsafe.asp

Results and Performance Accountability

Evaluating the impact of the policies and procedures of early intervention is an essential part of ensuring continuous improvement. This Web site offers a variety of resources and measures to support results-based decision making.

http://www.resultsaccountability.com/

The Results and Performance Accountability Implementation Guide: Questions and Answers About How to do the Work

If the "nuts and bolts" to help guide the performance accountability of your programs and policies is what you're looking for, you'll appreciate this Web site. It offers a practical "how to" guide with numerous examples (e.g., schematics, indicators, performance measures).

http://www.raguide.org

Section 619 Profile

Updated information on state policies, programs, and practices under the Preschool Grants Program (Section 619 of Part B) of the Individuals with Disabilities Education Act (IDEA) can be a valuable policy and systems resource. This compilation covers a range of topics including program administration, funding, education reform, charter and private schools, interagency coordination, personnel, transitions, programming, accreditation and monitoring, performance outcomes, public awareness, IFSPs, IEPs, family-centered services, and state preschool program data.

http://www.nectac.org/~pdfs/sec619_2003.pdf

Chapter 9

DEC Recommended Practices: Personnel Preparation

. . . .

Introduction

. . . .

Patricia S. Miller and Vicki D. Stayton

A critical element in the provision of quality services for young children with disabilities and their families is the preparation of qualified personnel to deliver those services (Rose & Smith, 1993; Winton & McCollum, 1997; Yates & Hains, 1997). Personnel preparation in EI/ECSE includes practices in both preservice and inservice education. This chapter presents practices that have been recommended by the field for the preparation of early childhood special educators to work with children with special needs birth through 5 years of age and their families.

In this chapter are Recommended Practices for the *delivery* or *process* of preservice and inservice education programs. Standards for *content* (i.e., knowledge and skills) of preparation programs can be found on the DEC Web site (www.dec-sped.org) (DEC, NAEYC, & ATE, 2000). The Recommended Practices (process) and standards (content) have been developed and validated separately, but should be considered together when developing, revising, or evaluating personnel preparation programs. The standards should be used to ensure that the content of a personnel training program is consistent with Recommended Practices in terms of how, when, and where services are provided to young children. The DEC Recommended Practices speak directly to how that content should be delivered in both preservice and inservice contexts. The DEC Recommended Practices in personnel preparation are built on the assumption that the content standards (DEC, NAEYC, & ATE, 2000) will define the knowledge and skills of the personnel training program.

Focus group members: Vivian Correa, Laurie Dinnebeil, Jeanette McCollum, Patricia S. Miller, Sarah Rule, Vicki D. Stayton, Amy Whitehead, and Barbara Wolfe

Early childhood special educators provide services in a variety of roles and settings. The early childhood special educator may work directly with children who have disabilities and their families or may work in a collaborative relationship with other professionals. Settings for service delivery include, but are not limited to, the home, public and private child care, Head Start, public and private school special classes and inclusive classes, hospital settings, specialized agency programs, and other community settings. Specialized areas of preparation for early childhood special educators include the development and implementation of intervention plans and strategies, in-depth competence in developing and conducting assessment procedures, competence in initiating and conducting interdisciplinary planning teams, coordinating interagency services for families, assessing family resources and needs, and serving as an advocate for children and families (DEC, NAEYC, & ATE, 2000). In addition, because of the increase of inclusive preschool settings, many early childhood special educators may be working with children without disabilities as well. As explained in the introduction to this book, the DEC Recommended Practices are designed to be used in developmentally appropriate environments. As such, the NAEYC guidelines for developmentally appropriate practices (Bredekamp & Copple, 1997) are an important foundation for the implementation of the DEC Recommended Practices.

Recommended Practices in personnel preparation for early childhood special education and intervention evolved significantly over the last decade of the 20th Century . . .

Recommended Practices in personnel preparation for early childhood special education and intervention evolved significantly over the last decade of the 20th Century despite the relative scarcity of data-based decisions guiding innovation and change. To a large extent, preservice and inservice preparation practices in EI/ECSE have been influenced more by policy, legislation, and philosophy than by empirical data (Snyder & McWilliam, 1999). However, there is a growing body of research on preservice training and consultation (Wesley, Buysse, & Keyes, 2000) that focuses on effective strategies for providing information and supporting practitioners in using that information. Much of this research has focused on the identification of training needs and preferences for formats, the application of adult learning principles to preservice and inservice settings, and the effects of different approaches to the application of practices in applied settings.

Guiding Principles

Both preservice and inservice preparation practices reflect several prominent principles of an inclusive philosophy toward direct services for children and families and toward preparing providers of those services. Over the last decade, Recommended Practices in professional preparation were characterized by: (1) greater participation of families in the planning and delivery of training activities; (2) an increase in the crossing of discipline boundaries to access appropriate preservice and inservice education and training; (3) greater emphasis on preservice and inservice educational opportunities that include students from both early childhood and early childhood special education together; (4) increasing interest in interdisciplinary collaboration among preservice faculty and inservice providers; and (5) support for family-centered preparation practices (Bredekamp, 1992; Bredekamp & Copple, 1997; Burton, 1992; Burton, Hains, Hanline, McLean, & McCormick, 1992; Buysse & Bailey, 1993; Kilgo & Bruder, 1997; LaMontagne, Danbom, & Buchanan, 1998; Miller, 1992; Smith, Miller, & Bredekamp, 1998).

The professional associations of the Division for Early Childhood (DEC) of the Council for Exceptional Children (CEC), the National Association for the Education of Young Children (NAEYC), and the Association of Teacher Educators (ATE) collaborated to produce sets of professional standards for licensure of educators. The standards incorporated the perspectives of both general and early childhood special education. In addition to a common core of knowledge needed by all teachers of young children (Hyson, 2003), the literature supports the need for specialized areas of skill and knowledge for professionals who work with young children who have disabilities and their families (Bailey, 1989; McCollum & Bailey, 1991; Odom & McEvoy, 1990; Rose & Smith, 1993; Winton & McCollum, 1997). The content in the areas of specialized skill and knowledge needed by those who work with children who have disabilities are described in the *Personnel Standards for Early Education and Early Intervention: Guidelines for Licensure in Early Childhood Special Education* (DEC, NAEYC, & ATE, 2000). See the DEC Web site (www.dec-sped.org) for this information or the book *DEC Personnel Preparation in Early Childhood Special Education: Implementing the DEC Recommended Practices* (Stayton, Miller, & Dinnebeil, 2003).

Professional practice standards have established inclusive services as critical to the development of young children with disabilities (Bredekamp, 1992; DEC, 2000; Odom & McLean, 1996; Strain, 1990). Inclusive services for children and families happen best when the preparation of service providers is inclusive of content and practices across essential disciplines (Able-Boone, Crais, & Downing, 2003; Bredekamp & Copple, 1997; Burton et al., 1992; Mellin & Winton, 2003; Miller, 1992). Trends in the field and support from the literature have led to a rapid growth in the development of interdisciplinary, or blended, teacher preparation programs designed to prepare teachers for inclusive education settings (Blanton, Griffin, Winn, & Pugach, 1997; Miller & Stayton, 1998, 1999). Teacher preparation programs that blend both early childhood education (ECE) and early childhood special education (ECSE) professional practice standards are recognized by the National Council for the

Accreditation of Teacher Education (NCATE) only if they include all DEC/CEC and NAEYC personnel standards (Hyson, 2003). Successful interdisciplinary teacher preparation programs prepare professionals who can select those strategies and practices from both ECE and ECSE that match the needs of a specific child and family (Kilgo et al., 1999; LaMontagne et al., 1998).

Organization of the Practices

The Recommended Practices in this chapter are organized into eight categories. Seven categories provide practices that are relevant for both preservice and inservice activities; the final category is unique to inservice. Categories for the organization of indicators of Recommended Practice in personnel preparation are: (1) family involvement; (2) interdisciplinary aspects; (3) design of learning activities; (4) cultural and linguistic diversity; (5) learning activities and evaluation; (6) field experiences; (7) characteristics and roles of faculty/trainers; and (8) inservice activities. Each category is headed by a statement that captures the essential elements of the Practices.

Definition of Terms

It is helpful to understand the definitions of a few key terms when reading the Practices. *Preservice* refers to postsecondary programs at the two-year, four-year, or graduate level that lead to entry-level preparation in the field of study and result in a degree and/or licensure in that field. *Inservice* means the process of providing ongoing professional development for professionals and paraeducators in a specific discipline with the outcome being enhanced professional practice. The term *student* refers to individuals enrolled in preservice programs. *Staff* refers to participants in inservice programs.

Conclusion

The Recommended Practices for the preparation of early childhood special educators provide guidance in the development, implementation, and evaluation of personnel preparation programs. These *process* practices and the *content* standards are found on the DEC Web site (www.dec-sped.org) and have been validated by the field as essential to professional preparation in EI/ECSE.

The reader is encouraged to use the following Recommended Practices as guidelines for the critical examination of personnel preparation programs. They include themes of cultural diversity, collaboration and partnerships, family-centered philosophy, and a belief in making research-based decisions in practice. Implementation of the Practices will enhance the knowledge and skills of those who work with or on behalf of young children with special needs and their families.

References

Able-Boone, H., Crais, E. R., & Downing, K. (2003). Preparation of early intervention practitioners for working with young children with low incidence disabilities. *Teacher Education and Special Education, 26*(1), 79-82.

Bailey, D. B. (1989). Issues and directions in preparing professionals to work with young handicapped children and their families. In J. Gallagher, P. Trohanis, & R. Clifford (Eds.), *Policy implementation and P.L. 99-457: Planning for young children with special needs* (pp. 97-132). Baltimore: Paul H. Brookes.

Blanton, L. P., Griffin, C. C., Winn, J. A., & Pugach, M. C. (1997). *Collaborative programs to prepare general and special educators.* Denver, CO: Love Publishing.

Bredekamp, S. (1992). The early childhood profession coming together. *Young Children, 47*(6), 36-39.

Bredekamp, S., & Copple, C. (1997). *Developmentally appropriate practice in early childhood programs* (Rev. ed.). Washington, DC: National Association for the Education of Young Children (NAEYC).

Burton, C. B. (1992). Defining family-centered education: Beliefs of public school child care and Head Start teachers. *Early Education and Development, 3,* 45-59.

Burton, C. B., Hains, A. H., Hanline, M. F., McLean, M., & McCormick, K. (1992). Early childhood intervention and education: The urgency of professional unification. *Topics in Early Childhood Special Education, 2*(4), 53-69.

Buysse, V., & Bailey, D. B. (1993). Behavioral and developmental outcomes in young children with disabilities in integrated and segregated settings: A review of comparative studies. *The Journal of Special Education, 26,* 434-461.

Division for Early Childhood (DEC). (2000). *Position statement on inclusion.* http://www.dec-sped.org/positionpapers.html

Division for Early Childhood (DEC), National Association for the Education of Young Children (NAEYC), & Association of Teacher Educators (ATE). (2000). *Personnel standards for early education and early intervention: Guidelines for licensure in early childhood special education.* http://www.dec-sped.org/positionpapers.html

Hyson, M. (Ed.). (2003). *Preparing early childhood professionals: NAEYC's standards for programs.* Washington, DC: National Association for the Education of Young Children (NAEYC).

Kilgo, J., & Bruder, M. B. (1997). Creating new visions in institutions of higher education: Interdisciplinary approaches to personnel preparation in early intervention. In P. J. Winton, J. A. McCollum, & C Catlett (Eds.), *Reforming personnel preparation in early intervention: Issues, models, and practical strategies* (pp. 81-101). Baltimore: Paul H. Brookes.

Kilgo, J., Johnson, L., LaMontagne, J., Stayton, V., Cook, M., & Cooper, C. (1999). Importance of practices: A national study of general and special early childhood educators. *Journal of Early Intervention, 22,* 294-305.

LaMontagne, M. J., Danbom, K., & Buchanan, M. (1998). Developmentally and individually appropriate practices. In L. J. Johnson, M. J. LaMontagne, P. M. Elgas, & A. M. Bauer (Eds.), *Early childhood education: Blending theory, blending practice* (pp. 83-109). Baltimore: Paul H. Brookes.

McCollum, J., & Bailey, D. (1991). Developing comprehensive personnel systems: Issues and alternatives. *Journal of Early Intervention, 12,* 195-211.

Mellin, A. E., & Winton, P. J. (2003). Interdisciplinary collaboration among early intervention faculty members. *Journal of Early Intervention, 25*(3), 173-188.

Miller, P. S. (1992). Segregated programs of teacher education in early childhood: Immoral and inefficient practice. *Topics in Early Childhood Special Education, 11*(4), 39-52.

Miller, P. S., & Stayton, V. D. (1998). Blended interdisciplinary teacher preparation in early education and intervention: A national study. *Topics in Early Childhood Special Education, 18*(1), 49-58.

Miller, P. S., & Stayton, V. D. (1999). Higher education culture—A fit or misfit with reform in teacher education? *Journal of Teacher Education, 50,* 290-302.

chapter

9

Odom, S. L., & McEvoy, M. A. (1990). Mainstreaming at the preschool level: Barriers and tasks for the field. *Topics in Early Childhood Special Education, 10*(2), 48-61.

Odom, S. L., & McLean, M. E. (1996*). Early intervention/early childhood special education: Recommended practices.* Austin, TX: Pro-Ed.

Rose, D. F., & Smith, B. J. (1993). Preschool mainstreaming: Attitude barriers and strategies for addressing them. *Young Children, 48,* 59-62.

Smith, B. J., Miller, P. S., & Bredekamp, S. (1998). Sharing responsibility: DEC-, NAEYC-, and Vygotsky-based practices for quality inclusion. *Young Exceptional Children, 2*(1), 11-21.

Snyder, P., & McWilliam, P. J. (1999). Evaluating the efficacy of case method instruction: Findings from preservice training in family-centered care. *Journal of Early Intervention, 22,* 114-125.

Stayton, V. D., Miller, P. S., & Dinnebeil, L. A. (Eds.). (2003). *DEC personnel preparation in early childhood special education: Implementing the DEC recommended practices.* Longmont, CO: Sopris West.

Strain, P. S. (1990). LRE for preschool children with handicaps: What we know, what we should be doing. *Journal of Early Intervention, 14,* 291-296.

Wesley, P. W., Buysse, V., & Keyes, L. (2000). Comfort zone revisited: Child characteristics and professional comfort with consultation. *Journal of Early Intervention, 23,* 106-115.

Winton, P. J., & McCollum, J. A. (1997). Ecological perspectives on personnel preparation: Rationale, framework, and guidelines for change. In P. J. Winton, J. A. McCollum, & C. Catlett (Eds.), *Reforming personnel preparation in early intervention* (pp. 81-101). Baltimore: Paul H. Brookes.

Yates, T., & Hains, A. H. (1997). State perspectives on meeting personnel challenges: Closing the gap between vision and reality. In P. J. Winton, J. A. McCollum, & C. Catlett (Eds.), *Reforming personnel preparation in early intervention* (pp. 27-52). Baltimore: Paul H. Brookes.

chapter

9

DEC Recommended Practices and Examples: Personnel Preparation

Families are involved in learning activities.

. . . .

PP1. Family involvement begins early and continues throughout all aspects of the preservice or inservice program (e.g., co-instructing, planning, evaluating, and providing field experiences).

Examples:

- *Family members who are serving as co-instructors meet weekly with the faculty instructor prior to and during the course to plan, conduct, and evaluate activities.*

- *The personnel preparation program has active participation of family members on the advisory committee.*

- *Students participate in family mentor projects.*

. . . .

PP2. Family participants in personnel training represent diversity in race, culture, and socioeconomic status.

Learning activities are interdisciplinary and interagency.

. . . .

PP3. Community agency and school personnel are involved in the preparation program.

Example:

- *Representatives from community agencies participate in the program by completing surveys, delivering guest lectures, and serving on the advisory committee and planning teams.*

. . . .

PP4. Preparation includes skill development in interagency collaboration.

Examples:

- *Students attend and observe local interagency meetings.*

- *The personnel preparation program includes course work on effective teaming, collaboration, and communication skills.*

chapter 9

PP5. Faculty and other personnel trainers within and across disciplines plan and teach together regularly.

Examples:

- *Courses are cross-listed and cotaught by faculty from diverse disciplines.*
- *Interdisciplinary teams of faculty meet frequently to plan and evaluate the preparation program.*

PP6. Students/staff participate in sequenced learning activities and field experiences with students and professionals from other disciplines to learn about their own and other discipline roles and to learn about teaming practices.

Examples:

- *Students participate in interdisciplinary seminars on issues and trends in the field.*
- *Students engage in interdisciplinary field work and teaming with students in related disciplines.*

Learning activities are systematically designed and sequenced.

PP7. Students receive preparation in the content and practice of their field (i.e., demonstrate skills and knowledge appropriate to the birth through 5 age group and special needs characteristics).

Examples:

- *Courses use DEC, NAEYC, and other recommended practices as essential texts in core courses.*
- *Students read and discuss current research literature in the field.*
- *Students are involved in practicum experiences in general and special early childhood classrooms or programs (birth through kindergarten or birth through 8).*

PP8. The program is based on recommended practices of the field including standards from accrediting agencies and professional associations.

Example:

- *Students compare and discuss professional standards.*

chapter
9

PP9. Recommended practices and professional standards are reviewed systematically and updated in the program periodically, reflecting the dynamic nature of the field.

Examples:

- *All members of the interdisciplinary faculty team are familiar with professional standards in related disciplines.*
- *Regular and formal reviews of professional standards occur with faculty teams.*

PP10. A written program philosophy is used as a basis for program structure and experiences, and is available to students and faculty.

Examples:

- *Students discuss and evaluate the program philosophy and implications for the curriculum in courses.*
- *The Interdisciplinary faculty planning team develops the program philosophy and shows how the philosophy is reflected in courses/training events.*

PP11. All learning activities across and within courses/modules/experiences are sequenced logically from initial knowledge acquisition to guided application and independent application.

PP12. Faculty and other personnel trainers use a variety of recommended and sequenced instructional strategies and methods.

Examples:

- *Information is provided in a variety of formats such as lectures, demonstrations, small group problem solving, and case studies.*
- *Program faculty use data-based decisions in selecting instructional strategies and methods and materials.*

PP13. Students/staff learn to apply instructional strategies in natural environments.

Example:

- *Students take methods courses in conjunction with related practicum experiences in natural environments.*

chapter

9

PP14. Faculty and other personnel trainers design learning experiences within courses and field placements that teach students to be reflective and to engage in systematic processes of reflection and self-knowledge acquisition.

Examples:

- *Students keep learning journals in courses and field experiences and receive regular feedback from instructors.*

- *Students observe their own practice by way of video or other means.*

Learning activities include the study of cultural and linguistic diversity.

PP15. Students/staff participate in activities in which they increase their knowledge of their own culture and heritage, learn that they are a member of different cultures and recognize intragroup and intergroup differences among members of different cultures.

Example:

- *Staff and students conduct research into their own and other cultures.*

PP16. Students/staff participate in activities in which they systematically learn about and from various cultural and linguistic groups in ways that are not stereotypic.

Example:

- *Students develop case studies in work with families of different cultural and linguistic backgrounds as part of extensive field work.*

PP17. Students/staff participate in activities in which they acknowledge their own biases and recognize their own culture as being one of many which have equal validity.

Example:

- *Courses and learning experiences include activities (e.g., videos, role plays, case studies) in which students/staff confront their biases and values.*

PP18. Learning experiences consistently engage students in activities in which they learn how culture, ethnicity, language, and socioeconomic status influence early childhood development and practices.

Example:

- *Field work involves planning, implementing, and evaluating activities for children and with families from diverse backgrounds.*

chapter

9

PP19. Students/staff participate in activities in which they learn to develop and implement intervention strategies that are congruous with and respectful of the beliefs, values, and traditions, as well as the preferred/dominant language, of families from varying cultural and linguistic groups.

Example:

- *Students/staff develop group case studies that involve assessment and planning of culturally sensitive, family-centered interventions.*

PP20. Students/staff participate in activities in which they learn to recognize the potential "power" differential that may exist between them and the families they serve and learn about issues that may be of concern to specific groups (e.g., racism and prejudice).

Examples:

- *Activities such as videos on racism and prejudices are included in course work.*

- *Students/staff develop a resource file of antibias curricula materials.*

PP21. Students/staff participate in activities in which they learn to respect the dignity and the right to privacy of the children and families they serve.

Examples:

- *Students discuss reasons for rights to privacy, and the ethical and professional responsibilities involved.*

- *Students are taught laws, regulations, and precedent-setting court cases mandating privacy and confidentiality.*

chapter 9

PP22. Students/staff participate in activities in which they learn to balance between supporting the unique cultural and linguistic patterns of families and communities and preparing children to meet societal expectations and to find a meaningful place in American society.

Examples:

- *A family panel that includes recent immigrants shares their experiences with students.*

- *Faculty use books, case studies, and videos to highlight key issues and set the stage for serious conversation.*

Learning activities and evaluation procedures are designed to meet the needs of students and staff.

. . . .

PP23. Content is integrated in unified learning experiences across related disciplines.

Examples:

- *Students take courses and engage in field experiences with students in related discipline programs.*

- *Interdisciplinary faculty meet to review each others' syllabi, and identify courses that can be cross-listed.*

. . . .

PP24. Students/staff have choices about how to learn and to be evaluated.

Examples:

- *Courses offer choices in projects, reading materials, and field sites, allowing for differences in student needs and interests.*

- *Students select from several options of evaluation methods for their work.*

. . . .

PP25. Students/staff access, read, and engage in discussion about current literature and research in the field.

Examples:

- *All courses and other learning experiences are grounded in current research from the field.*

- *Students are encouraged to debate and address issues in the literature.*

. . . .

PP26. The program incorporates various levels and types of evaluation, involving faculty, students, and family members in assessing predetermined course and program outcomes.

Examples:

- *The annual evaluation of the program includes a variety of methods including surveys; focus groups; and interviews with families, students, faculty, and practitioners.*

- *The annual evaluation of the program includes gathering information from families concerning their experiences with students.*

- *Program graduates and employers of graduates provide regular, systematic feedback.*

PP27. Students/staff acquire knowledge and skills needed to effectively consult with other professionals.

Examples:

- *Students observe effective consultation practices in their field experiences.*
- *The program includes content and practice in the areas of consultation with other professionals and with parents.*

PP28. Faculty and other personnel trainers deliver learning activities or other trainings to help teachers supervise paraeducators and volunteers.

Examples:

- *Courses include readings, discussions, and skill development for working with paraeducators.*
- *Practitioners meet with students to discuss effective ways of working with paraeducators (e.g., hiring, delegating, evaluating).*

Field experiences are systematically designed and supervised.

PP29. Field experiences offer opportunities to practice performance competencies of the discipline.

Examples:

- *Students are placed in settings where they are given opportunities to plan, implement, and evaluate Recommended Practices.*
- *Field experience sites are selected using Recommended Practices as the guidelines.*
- *Students are evaluated on performance competencies in natural environments.*

PP30. Field experiences are diverse and are matched to student/staff needs, experiences, and interests.

PP31. Field experiences occur in a variety of community-based settings in which children with and without disabilities and their families receive EI/ECSE services, including natural environments and inclusive programs.

Example:

- *Students practice in home-, school-, and other community-based settings.*

. . . .

PP32. Field experiences in homes are planned in collaboration with the family.

Examples:

- *All students participate in supervised home visiting experiences.*

- *Families participate in the formative and summative evaluation of students participating in home-based services.*

. . . .

PP33. Field experiences occur in high quality settings that reflect recommended practices in the field.

Examples:

- *Faculty evaluate how programs use Recommended Practices when selecting field placements.*

- *Field experience sites are reviewed on a regular basis.*

. . . .

PP34. Field experiences are jointly supervised by faculty and site personnel with experience and licensure in the field.

Examples:

- *All supervisors are licensed in the areas of supervision (e.g., early childhood special education).*

- *Faculty and site personnel use consistent supervision methods and meet regularly to plan and evaluate methods used.*

. . . .

PP35. Field experiences begin early, are sequenced, and provide opportunities for students to provide direct and indirect services to children and to families.

Examples:

- *Field experiences accompany early orientation courses following admission to the program, are sequenced within the curriculum, and reflect increasing responsibility and intensity of work.*

- *Each student has opportunities to actively implement intervention strategies and consultation strategies for children and families as part of his or her sequenced field experience plan.*

. . . .

PP36. Field experiences include multiple methods of supervision, including on-site modeling, coaching, feedback, and technological methods.

PP37. Community providers, cooperating teachers, and program faculty receive support and guidance from each other.

Examples:

- *Meetings are held prior to placement of students to discuss supervision models, expectations, and evaluation procedures.*
- *Cooperating teachers and other field personnel receive acknowledgment for their work.*

PP38. Field experiences include standards for professional and ethical behavior for students in the program.

Examples:

- *Standards for professional conduct and ethical behavior are discussed with the students and related written documents are provided to students and field personnel.*
- *Standards for professional conduct and ethical behavior are modeled by program faculty and by on-site staff.*

PP39. Field experiences offer experiences with children and families of diverse racial, cultural, linguistic, and socioeconomic backgrounds.

Faculty and other personnel trainers are qualified and well-prepared for their role in personnel preparation.

PP40. Faculty and other personnel trainers show commitment to improved services for community schools, agencies, and families.

Examples:

- *Faculty are involved in community activities such as local interagency teams, collaboratives, and professional affiliates.*
- *Faculty members work with local schools through various professional development activities.*
- *Faculty members establish relationships with community providers and participate in action research planning teams in schools.*

PP41. Faculty and other personnel trainers have a strong knowledge base, and are credentialed and experienced in working with young children who have disabilities.

PP42. Faculty and other personnel trainers represent diversity in race, culture, gender, language, and other underrepresented groups.

PP43. Faculty and other personnel trainers participate regularly in experiences that build their knowledge and improve their pedagogical practices.

Examples:

- *Faculty attend professional development activities on an ongoing basis.*
- *Faculty demonstrate improved practices through professional development plans.*

PP44. Faculty and other personnel trainers model recommended practices in the field.

Examples:

- *Faculty model for students the practices desired in early childhood special education with children and families.*
- *A faculty team examines the literature in college teaching and identifies needed revisions and practices of excellence by faculty.*

PP45. Faculty and other personnel trainers produce professional products that contribute to the knowledge of the field.

Examples:

- *Faculty members engage in dissemination of professional knowledge in a variety of ways (e.g., presentations at meetings; local presentations of advocacy; action research, and published papers, books, and manuals).*
- *Faculty members collaborate with students to conduct research related to practices in the field.*

PP46. Faculty and other personnel trainers have knowledge of content and issues in related disciplines.

Examples:

- *Faculty members serve on interdisciplinary planning teams and seek knowledge from those in different disciplines.*
- *Faculty members coplan and coteach with faculty from related disciplines.*

PP47. Faculty and other personnel trainers translate content in effective ways to meet individual needs of students.

Examples:

- *Faculty members work together to identify and translate issues from related disciplines for inclusion in course material.*
- *Faculty from related disciplines develop and present modules in each others' courses.*

PP48. Faculty and other personnel trainers model collaboration with others and have successful interpersonal skills.

Examples:

- *Faculty members coteach courses with colleagues from the same or other related disciplines and model communication about issues in class together.*

- *Faculty members use reflective teaching strategies to model for their students.*

PP49. Faculty and other personnel trainers mentor students and other faculty.

Examples:

- *Faculty members show a personal interest in the development of their students by holding regular individual and small group conferences to discuss skill and knowledge development.*

- *Faculty members invite students to participate in research with them.*

PP50. Faculty and other personnel trainers serve in leadership and advocacy roles in their community and profession.

Examples:

- *Faculty members are officers in local, state, and national professional associations.*

- *Faculty members advocate for children and families with school boards, state legislatures, and national groups.*

- *Faculty members serve as advisors to student groups.*

PP51. Faculty and other personnel trainers translate current research into practice in teaching and supervision.

PP52. Faculty and other personnel trainers who teach methods courses also supervise field experiences and act as mentors in field experiences.

PP53. Faculty and other personnel trainers use appropriate, research-based preservice and inservice instructional strategies.

PP54. Faculty and other personnel trainers promote practitioner-action research.

Examples:

- *Faculty engage in action research with colleagues, students, and community practitioners.*

- *Students conduct action research projects in conjunction with methods courses and field work.*

. . . .

PP55. Faculty and other personnel trainers participate as learners and coconstructors of knowledge.

Examples:

- *Faculty members demonstrate reflective practices in decision making with their students.*

- *Faculty members view themselves as learners and participate with students in debates, individual learning activities, action research, and other projects.*

Professional development (inservice) activities are systematically designed and implemented.

. . . .

PP56. The curriculum is available in a variety of delivery formats to match the needs of participants.

Examples:

- *The context of training and of the participant work environment are considered when selecting training materials and methods.*

- *Videos, online delivery, mail, telephone, face-to-face meetings, and other electronic and written methods are part of inservice options.*

. . . .

PP57. Practitioners maintain and expand their skills and knowledge through training that is linked to credits for licensure or other formal credentials.

Examples:

- *The training program is consistent with the state's Comprehensive System of Personnel Development (CSPD) objectives and reflects the needs of the community, region, or state.*

- *The program offers a range of discipline-specific CEU or licensure credits or provides cross-discipline credits.*

. . . .

PP58. The program promotes worksite support by colleagues and administrators for implementing new practices.

Example:

- *Program trainers provide coaching and mentoring on-site for participants.*

chapter
9

. . . .

PP59. Administrators ensure that training is accessible to participants financially and according to location and schedules.

Examples:

- *Program planners write grants to state or federal agencies to support professional development.*

- *Faculty members deliver the training on-site, through electronic means, or in a regionally selected facility accessible to participants.*

. . . .

PP60. Personnel trainers provide follow-up within service delivery contexts.

Example:

- *Faculty members provide coaching, modeling, and feedback on-site.*

. . . .

PP61. Training involves teams of participants (e.g., general early childhood teachers, early childhood special educators, paraeducators, therapists).

Examples:

- *Inservice participants are encouraged to attend training with a team of professionals and families with whom they work.*

- *Teams of participants engage in authentic projects and assignments.*

. . . .

PP62. The program emphasizes meaningful practical content and experiences based on expressed needs of participants.

. . . .

PP63. Teachers and staff from early education programs and community child care centers are provided with knowledge and skills relative to the inclusion of young children with disabilities.

Examples:

- *Inservice programs include general early childhood and early childhood special education professionals from the same community and encourage collaborative projects.*

- *Itinerant teachers attend the same workshops and inservice trainings as the staff from the community-based program.*

. . . .

PP64. Administrators support ongoing professional development plans.

chapter 9

. . . .

PP65. Paraeducators participate in training opportunities that allow for continuing development of skills and knowledge (i.e., tiered or leveled training).

Examples:

- *Paraeducator training is aligned with existing state credentialing or licensure standards.*

- *The state or lead agency develops a career lattice or pathway system to allow paraeducators to move from one level of the profession to the next.*

. . . .

PP66. Paraeducators have opportunities for increased job independence based on more training.

Examples:

- *Written and formal policies are in place to link job responsibility and salary to levels of training and documented expertise.*

- *Programs employ appropriate levels of supervision to support paraeducators' increased levels of job independence.*

Note: These Recommended Practices relate to the *process* of personnel preparation. They should be used in conjunction with the DEC standards for the *content* of personnel preparation found on the DEC Web site (www.dec-sped.org/ positionpapers.html).

Personnel Preparation Glossary

Accrediting agencies. Entities at the national or regional level through which higher education teacher education programs (e.g., National Council for the Accreditation of Teacher Education) or colleges/universities (e.g., Southern Association of Colleges and Schools) acquire approval based on specific criteria and a prescribed process.

Coaching. An ongoing, interactive, reciprocal process between a coach and a learner in which the coach supports the learner in applying knowledge and skills when working with children birth through 5 with disabilities/developmental delays and their families. Coaching promotes self-observation and self-correction through a series of conversations and reflections.

Co-instructing. Two or more faculty members/professional development specialists jointly planning, teaching/training, and evaluating courses/inservice activities.

Curriculum. A planned, sequenced program of study based on knowledge, skills, and disposition standards/competencies.

Delivery formats. The means by which the curriculum is delivered (e.g., face-to-face, interactive television, Web-based).

Disciplines. A branch of knowledge, service, or teaching. In early intervention and early childhood special education, individuals from multiple professional disciplines provide services. (Among these are early childhood education, early childhood special education, speech-language pathology, physical therapy, occupational therapy, etc.).

Field experiences. Application of skills in ECSE settings prior to student teaching or its equivalent.

Inservice. The process of providing ongoing professional development for professionals and paraeducators in a specific discipline with the outcome being enhanced professional practice.

Instructional strategies. Methods used to facilitate the acquisition of knowledge, skills, and dispositions. Methods are matched to learning outcomes with more passive methods employed to convey knowledge (e.g., lectures, discussions, media) and more interactive methods used to support the acquisition of skills and dispositions (e.g., role plays, simulations, case studies).

Interagency collaboration. Cooperative activities between/among agencies or programs.

Modeling. An instructional strategy in which skills are demonstrated (e.g., use of prompts, use of reinforcement, storytelling).

Performance competencies. The knowledge, skills, and dispositions that guide the curriculum and identify what program completers must know and be able to do.

Practitioner-action research. Research conducted by ECSE providers in an applied setting (e.g., home-based early intervention, preschool classroom) for the purpose of answering a question(s) specific to the program.

chapter 9

Preservice. Postsecondary programs at the two-year, four-year, or graduate level that lead to entry-level preparation in the field of study and result in a degree and/or licensure in that field.

Professional associations. Membership organizations on the national and state level that provide various member services and leadership/advocacy for the respective discipline(s) represented by the organization (e.g., Division for Early Childhood of the Council for Exceptional Children, National Association for the Education of Young Children, American Physical Therapy Association).

Reflection. Systematic and ongoing review, critical analysis, application, and synthesis of knowledge, skills, and dispositions specific to working with children birth through 5 with disabilities/developmental delays and their families.

Personnel Preparation Resources

Position Statements

"Division for Early Childhood (DEC) Position Statement on Personnel Standards for Early Education and Early Intervention"

"DEC Personnel Standards for Early Education and Early Intervention: Guidelines for Licensure in Early Childhood Special Education"
The DEC position statements are found on the DEC Web site at http://www.dec-sped.org. Click on "Position Statements."

Print Materials

101 Ways to Make Training Active
M. Silberman & K. Lawson (1995)
   This extensive collection of active learning techniques offers specific suggestions on how to organize and conduct lively training sessions for any subject. From team building to stimulating discussions to prompting questions, developing skills, inviting feedback, and promoting application, readers will discover inventive, proven strategies to make training sessions unforgettable. (Somerset, NJ: Wiley)

Active Training: A Handbook of Techniques, Designs, Case Examples, and Tips (2nd ed.)
M. Silberman (1998)
   Serving both the novice trainer and the seasoned professional, this useful handbook shows how to effectively design and conduct active, experientially based training programs in private and public sector organizations. Active training techniques are illustrated by more than 200 real-life designs and case examples culled from more than 35 training topics, including such diverse subject matter as project management, team building, selling skills, and stress management. (San Francisco: Jossey-Bass/Pfeiffer)

Adult Learning Methods: A Guide for Effective Instruction (3rd ed.)
M. W. Galbraith (Ed.) (2004)
   Individuals who seek a clearly written guide to understanding and facilitating adult learning will enjoy discovering this book. Part One ("Understanding and Facilitating Adult Learning") addresses the characteristics of a good teacher, understanding adults as learners, philosophical and teaching style orientations and designing instruction. The 14 chapters of Part Two ("Methods and Techniques") describe in detail an array of methods and techniques to use in actual instruction (e.g., selecting methods, critical thinking techniques, distance learning).

   Krieger Publishing Company
   P.O. Box 9542
   Melbourne, FL 32902
   Phone: (321) 724-9542
   Web: http://www.krieger-publishing.com/

chapter **9**

The Art of Teaching Adults: How to Become an Exceptional Instructor and Facilitator
P. Renner (1994)

> In step-by-step detail, this book describes dozens of fresh approaches to such time-honored techniques as group discussions, case studies, role playing, small group tasks, individual assignments, field projects, learning journals, and yes, even lecturing. The chapter on "asking beautiful questions" should be required reading for all new faculty members and trainers.

> Training Associates
> Site 720, 999 West Broadway
> Vancouver, BC Canada V5Z 1K5
> Phone: (604) 732-4552
> FAX: (604) 738-4080
> Web: http://www.peter-renner.com

By Design: Family-Centered, Interdisciplinary Preservice Training in Early Intervention
A. Whitehead, B. Ulanski, B. Swedeen, R. Sprague, G. Yellen-Shiring, A. Fruchtman, C. Pomije, & P. Rosin (1998)

> This guide for faculty and trainers was developed by the Family-Centered Interdisciplinary Training Project in Early Intervention. It describes strategies used to stimulate, support, and evaluate learning by students from different disciplines (e.g., seminars, team activities, family mentor experience, community placement, supervision). All materials for replicating these strategies are included, along with evaluation data from the project to guide implementation.

> The Waisman Center
> Early Intervention Program
> 1500 Highland Avenue, Room S101G
> Madison, WI 53705
> Phone: (608) 265-2544
> Web: http://www.waisman.wisc.edu/birthto3/products.html
> E-mail: sanders@waisman.wisc.edu

Coaching Families and Colleagues in Early Childhood
B. E. Hanft, D. D. Rush, & M. L. Shelden (2004)

> Coaching is offered, through this book, as an effective strategy for supporting other professionals and families in the work of early intervention. Readers will learn about essential qualities such as objectivity and adaptability; cultivate communication skills such as observing, listening, and planning; consider key issues, such as ensuring administrative support; and reinforce what they learn with engaging anecdotes, reflection questions, points to remember, and practical forms. (Baltimore: Paul H. Brookes)

Creating Patient and Family Faculty Programs
B. Blaylock, E. Ahmann, & B. H. Johnson (2002)

> Many examples are shared that explain how to engage and support the participation of families, especially those of children with disabilities, in the undergraduate and graduate classrooms for preparing teachers, therapists, and medical doctors.

chapter
9

Professionals discuss the value of family contributions during staff development exercises and tell exactly what they learned from listening to patient and family stories. Highlights of more than 50 different programs make this a valuable resource for staff supervisors, directors, or faculty members.

Institute for Family-Centered Care
7900 Wisconsin Avenue, Suite 405
Bethesda, MD 20814
Phone: (301) 652-0281
FAX: (301) 652-0186
Web: http://www.familycenteredcare.org/resources-frame.html
E-mail: institute@iffcc.org

Creative Training Techniques Handbook: Tips, Tactics, and How-Tos for Delivering Effective Training (3rd ed.)
R.W. Pike (2003)

This key resource focuses on delivering professional development results, not just training. All the basics are covered—how to tap into learners' motivation, customizing for the specific audience, great presentation techniques, and creative activities. Chapters address topics that range from assessment and presentation techniques to eLearning. Consult this resource to obtain a wealth of ideas that support education as a process, not an event.

HRD Press, Inc.
22 Amherst Road
Amherst, MA 01002-9709
Phone: (800) 822-2801
Web: http://www.hrdpress.com

Design Considerations for State TA Systems
P. Trohanis (2001)

The three parts of this publication (foundations, workbook, selected readings) offer readers a combination of knowledge, firsthand implementation experiences, guidance, discussion tools, and worksheets. The publication can serve as a planning resource for state officials, helping them think strategically about the coherent design and effective operation of their technical assistance (TA) systems.

NECTAC (National Early Childhood Technical Assistance Center)
CB #8040
University of North Carolina
Chapel Hill, NC 27599-8040
Phone: (919) 962-2001
FAX : (919) 966-7463
Web: http://www.nectac.org
E-mail: nectac@unc.edu

chapter
9

Discussion as a Way of Teaching: Tools and Techniques for Democratic Classrooms
S. D. Brookfield & S. Preskill (1999)
> Stimulating good discussions is often one of the more difficult tasks of teaching and training. This book offers a wealth of information and strategies for planning, conducting, and evaluating lively dialogs. (San Francisco: Jossey-Bass)

Early Childhood Workshops That Work: The Essential Guide to Successful Training and Workshops
N. P. Alexander (2000)
> Good training results from the instructor's skill, knowledge, and the ability to plan a session based on both what participants want and need. This resource is a comprehensive guide that illustrates how to design, organize, conduct, and evaluate workshops and training seminars. Tips, guidance, inside information, examples, and sections on troubleshooting make this a very practical resource. (Beltsville, MD: Gryphon House)

Lives in Progress: Case Stories in Early Intervention
P. J. McWilliam & Invited Contributors (2000)
> This thought-provoking book uses the case method of instruction to give students (preservice) and participants (inservice) the opportunity to practice the problem-solving and decision-making skills they need on the job. The book includes 20 "unsolved" case stories based on actual work experiences of early interventionists across the United States. These can be used to develop skills for listening, advocacy, understanding diverse points of view, and collaborative action planning. A companion *Instructor's Guide*, featuring teaching notes and other supplemental materials, is available upon request to instructors. (Baltimore: Paul H. Brookes)

DEC Personnel Preparation in Early Childhood Special Education: Implementing the DEC Recommended Practices
V. D. Stayton, P. S. Miller, & L. A. Dinnebeil (Eds.) (2003)
> This book offers guidance to early childhood and early childhood special education programs that want to reflect the DEC Recommended Practices in their student preparation. What to teach and how to teach it are described in chapters on family participation in personnel preparation, cultural and linguistic diversity, interdisciplinary and interagency collaboration, and quality field experiences. Examples of model programs, extensive references, self-assessment checklists, and action planning forms make this a very useful resource. (Longmont, CO: Sopris West)

Preparing Early Childhood Professionals: NAEYC's Standards for Programs
M. Hyson (2003)
> This single volume summarizes the NAEYC's latest standards for higher education programs seeking NCATE accreditation at the Initial Licensure (four- and five-year) and Advanced (master's and doctorate) levels and for associate degree programs. Standards materials from the Council for Exceptional Children (CEC) Division for Early Childhood (DEC) and the National Board for Professional Teaching Standards (NBPTS) also are included.

National Association for the Education of Young Children (NAEYC)
P.O. Box 932569
Atlanta, GA 31193
Phone: (866) 623-9248
FAX : (770) 442-9742
Web: http://www.naeyc.org/
E-mail: naeyc@pbd.com

Tapping Potential: Community College Students and America's Teacher Recruitment Challenge
Recruiting New Teachers (2002)

Recommendations are given from results found in a nationwide study that evaluated the potential of community colleges to address teacher shortages across the nation. The report includes program highlights from six effective programs; a state-by-state overview; and information specific to community colleges, four-year institutions, policymakers, and funders that support and strengthen programs for teachers in community colleges.

Recruiting New Teachers
385 Concord Avenue, Suite #103
Belmont, MA 02478
Phone: (617) 489-6000
FAX: (617) 489-6005
Web: http://www.rnt.org/
E-mail: rnt@rnt.org

Teaching With Your Mouth Shut
D. L. Finkel (2000)

Finkel outlines the joys and the difficulties of helping students connect with their most powerful and enduring teacher, themselves. The author offers a variety of approaches to support teachers and trainers in designing learner-centered experiences to lead them to the discovery of the conceptual material. (Portsmouth, NH: Boynton/Cook)

Tools for Teaching
B. G. Davis (2001)

From designing and offering a new course to tackling the problems of burnout or stagnation, *Tools for Teaching* provides adult educators with the information they need to improve and revitalize their courses. This is a rich compendium of tested strategies and suggestions, organized according to 49 teaching tools (e.g., personalizing the large lecture class, motivating students). This is an easy-to-use, practical, and very helpful resource. (San Francisco: Wiley and Sons)

What Every Special Educator Must Know: Ethics, Standards, and Guidelines for Special Educators (5th ed.)
Council for Exceptional Children (CEC) (2003)

This is a core library resource for faculty who are developing curricula and seeking accreditation, as well as for state policymakers who are evaluating their state

chapter 9

licensure requirements. This book provides a common core of standards for all beginning special education professionals, as well as standards in various specialization areas, including early childhood special education.

> Council for Exceptional Children (CEC)
> P.O. Box 79026, Dept. K80827
> Baltimore, MD 21279-0026
> Phone: (888) 232-7733
> Web: http://www.cec.sped.org

The Winning Trainer: Winning Ways to Involve People in Learning
J. E. Eitington (1996)

> With its extensive appendices available for reproducing (120+ pages), this book presents engaging and dynamic techniques that involve learners in the learning process, increasing retention and understanding. Sections on getting things started (icebreakers, openers),using small groups effectively, role playing, games, exercises, puzzles, case method, evaluation, and transfer will have application in both preservice and inservice settings. There's even a chapter called "If you must lecture . . . ," describing how to make this instructional approach as effective as possible. The spiral-bound format allows easy photocopying of exercises, measures, and activities. (Woburn, MA: Butterworth-Heinemann)

Web Sites

Center to Inform Personnel Preparation Policy and Practice in Early Intervention and Preschool Education

> This project Web site includes resources that are related to: (1) the certification and licensing requirements for personnel working with infants, toddlers, and preschoolers who have special needs and their families; (2) the quality of training programs that prepare these professionals; and (3) the supply and demand of professionals representing all disciplines that provide both early childhood special education and early intervention services.

> http://www.uconnced.org/personal%20prep/personalprephome.htm

Center on Personnel Studies in Special Education (COPSSE)

> COPSSE is supported by a cooperative agreement between the U.S. Department of Education, Office of Special Education Programs (OSEP), and the University of Florida. The project Web site has resources related to the four guiding questions of their research: (1) What characterizes efficient and effective practice in initial preparation as measured by beginning teacher quality and retention? (2) How do school and district context influence beginning teacher quality and retention? (3) How does state policy context affect the shortage of qualified special education teachers? and (4) How does policy context affect the content and process of teacher education?

> http://www.copsse.org/

chapter

9

Center for Research on Education, Diversity, and Excellence (CREDE)
CREDE offers a wide range of multimedia products (e.g., interactive CD-ROMs, videos, online directories), print publications, and a useful Web site for practitioners, researchers, and parents.

http://www.crede.ucsc.edu

Clearinghouse for Special Education Teaching Cases
The Clearinghouse is an outgrowth of a project designed to develop, evaluate (field test), and nationally disseminate teaching cases to aid in the preservice and inservice preparation of teachers who work with children and youth with disabilities and their families. Fifty-four teaching cases have been written by trained case writers who interviewed classroom teachers from all over the United States as informants for the cases. Each case has been field tested, includes questions for discussion, and is cross-referenced with expected areas of teacher competence designated by the Council for Exceptional Children (CEC).

http://cases.coedu.usf.edu

Diversity Within Unity: Essential Principles for Teaching and Learning in a Multicultural Society
A consensus panel of interdisciplinary scholars worked over a four-year period to determine what we know from research and experience about education and diversity. This online publication summarizes their findings, which are delineated as 12 major principles. From the findings, the authors developed a checklist for assessing the extent to which any institution or environment is consistent with the principles.

http://www.educ.washington.edu/coetestwebsite/pdf/DiversityUnity.pdf

Does Diversity Make a Difference? Three Research Studies on Diversity in College Classrooms
The studies presented here strongly support the proposition that practices such as race-sensitive admissions lead to expanded educational possibilities and better educational outcomes for all students, regardless of race or ethnic origin. Along with results of the studies, this site includes a measure ("Faculty Classroom Diversity Questionnaire") for assessing the extent to which any course/program reflects culturally competent practices.

http://www.acenet.edu/programs/caree/diversity.cfm

A Guide to Distance Learning for Early Childhood Students in North Carolina
D. Torrence, S. Powell, & S. Doig (May 2002)
This helpful resource guide is designed to help technology neophytes to successfully complete an Internet-based college course. It provides useful information about: the basics of distance learning; purchasing and using a computer; registering for a distance learning course; financial aid sources; resources for accessing adaptive technology; and online resources to support distance education. It also features a reference list of common distance learning and computer terms. While some of the information is specific to North Carolina, most is generic enough to apply in any state.

http://www.fpg.unc.edu/~contact/distancelearningtools.cfm

chapter
9

Multimedia Educational Resource for Learning and Online Teaching (MERLOT)
MERLOT is a resource designed primarily for faculty and students of higher education. Links to online learning materials are collected here along with annotations such as peer reviews and assignments. Materials range from syllabi to online exercises and assignments.

http://www.merlot.org/

National Clearinghouse for Paraeducator Resources
The nation's nearly 500,000 paraeducators represent a promising source of prospective new teachers, at once more representative of and more rooted in the communities in which they serve. The Clearinghouse offers resources for supporting the professional development of this segment of the early childhood workforce.

http://www.usc.edu/dept/education/CMMR/Clearinghouse.html

Online Workshop for Web-Based Training Demonstration
Take a "beach retreat" and "dive into a sea of information" on the Web-based training. This site captures the components of an interactive, facilitated online workshop designed by the National Early Childhood Technical Assistance Center (NECTAC) for its technical assistance audiences. Content, activities, and resources are organized in six sessions (e.g., "Introduction to Web-Based Training (WBT)"; "WBT Toolkit"). These materials increase understanding, enhance confidence, and support motivation to undertake WBT efforts.

http://www.nectac.org/~wbtdemo/

Paraeducator Issues
Recommendations for paraeducator competencies and training, indicators, mentoring, and other key issues are discussed on this site.

http://www.wa.nea.org/Prf_Dv/PARA_ED/PARA.HTM

Quality on the Line: Benchmarks for Success in Internet-Based Distance Education
The Institute for Higher Education Policy released this publication in 2000, offering tangible measures of quality in distance education.

http://www.ihep.com/Pubs/PDF/Quality.pdf

Reforming Personnel Preparation in Early Intervention: Issues, Models, and Practical Strategies
P. J. Winton, J. A. McCollum, & C Catlett (Eds.) (1997)
Organized by content and process, this online book includes techniques and resources that appeal to both seasoned and novice faculty, trainers, and planners. Sections address ecosystemic perspectives, critical components of personnel preparation, strategies for applying Recommended Practices to key content areas, and models of exemplary practice. Sample chapter titles include: "Needs Assessment and Evaluation in Early Intervention Personnel Preparation"; "Follow-Up Strategies";

"Supervision, Mentoring and Coaching"; "Distance Learning in Early Intervention Personnel Preparation"; and "Designing and Implementing Innovative, Interdisciplinary Practica." This book is available to download in its entirety, or chapter-by-chapter.

http://www.fpg.unc.edu/~scpp/pages/reforming_book.cfm

Study of Personnel Needs in Special Education (SPeNSE)

SPeNSE addresses concerns about nationwide shortages in the number of personnel serving students with disabilities and the need for improvement in the qualifications of those employed. This Web site provides information about key findings on the quality of the workforce nationally, within each geographic region, and within and across personnel categories.

http://ferdig.coe.ufl.edu/spense

Teaching and Learning on the Web

Hundreds of examples of how the Web is being used to support learning is what this site offers. The searchable collection includes sites that range from courses delivered entirely via the Web to courses that offer specific activities related to a class assignment and class support materials.

http://www.mcli.dist.maricopa.edu/tl

Teaching for Inclusion: Diversity in the College Classroom

This free, reproducible resource is designed to provide college teachers with an easy-to-use source of ideas and teaching techniques to help create instructional environments that are welcoming to and supportive of culturally diverse students. Sections on the importance of campus diversity, inclusive teaching, evaluations, and grading offer examples that can be applied on any campus.

http://ctl.unc.edu/tfitoc.html

Technology and Early Childhood Professional Education: A Policy Discussion

This report provides a summary of the presentations and discussions held at a July 2002 meeting hosted by the Education Commission of the States and the KnowledgeWorks Foundation. It concludes with ten recommendations that promote the use of technology to better prepare early childhood professionals.

http://www.kwfdn.org/Resources/tech_report_jul02

Web-Based and Distance Education Training Resources

Interested in technology applications (e.g., distance education, listservs, chat rooms, etc.)? This compilation offers lots of examples, including online courses, articles, checklists, and distance education resources.

http://www.NECTAC.org/topics/personnel/onlinetrngResources.asp

Notes

Chapter 10

Real-Life Experiences: Tips for Using the DEC Recommended Practices

. . . .

Linda Askew, Barbara J. Smith, Linda Frederick, Heidi Heissenbuttel, and Gail Whitman

"It's important for everyone to understand the 'big picture'—using the Recommended Practices will improve what we do with children and families!"

"While the process was sometimes difficult and time consuming, it was well worth while."

"It's important not to get impatient."

"We built trust and relationships that we have never had."

"We needed to develop an accountability system for preschool and there were many Recommended Practices that addressed that need. This effort helped us develop that system."

Two Denver, Colorado area early childhood programs partnered with DEC and the University of Colorado–Denver from 2001–2004 to use the DEC Recommended Practices and document what worked and what didn't. This initiative was possible through a grant from the U.S. Department of Education, Office of Special Education Programs (OSEP), and was called Bridging the Gap (BTG). Both of the programs—the preschool program of the Douglas County School District and Sewall Child Development Center, a community-based nonprofit program serving children birth to 5—use an inclusive model for serving young children with and without disabilities and their families and share a commitment to quality programming.

Douglas County School District (serving a county approximately 25 miles south of Denver) serves an area of 860 square miles that has experienced an average 58% annual population growth for the past six years. The Douglas County School District places a strong emphasis on continuous quality improvement and has implemented several research-based and nationally known models of service delivery. The preschool program uses a model of inclusive services with a lead early childhood education teacher and teams of specialists (e.g., therapists, early childhood special educators, etc.) that fully participate in all classroom planning and implementation activities. All children with disabilities are included in the regular preschool program.

Sewall Child Development Center is an urban, inner city program in the Denver metro area that provides comprehensive services for young children with disabilities, including contracted services from the Denver Public Schools and through programs such as Head Start, child care, a home visitors program, an infant program, consultative outreach, an inclusive preschool, and a diagnostic/evaluation program. Sewall Child Development Center is a leader in the community, participating in numerous state initiatives and programs. Like Douglas County School District, Sewall places a high value on quality programming, evident in the high-quality ratings their program receives. The on-site Sewall preschool program incorporates early childhood special educators and related services personnel as part of the staff-child ratio in daily planning and programming.

This chapter briefly summarizes these programs' "stories" and describes some "lessons learned" from using the DEC Recommended Practices to improve services and outcomes for young children with disabilities and their families.

Telling Their Story:
Douglas County School District (Douglas County) and Sewall Child Development Center (Sewall)

Because of their reputations for striving for high-quality programming and their willingness to try innovations, the two programs' Early Childhood Coordinators were asked by the Bridging the Gap (BTG) project staff if they would be interested in helping the project and DEC learn strategies for using the DEC Recommended Practices in "real life." This reputation for quality was important because, as noted in previous chapters, the DEC Recommended Practices assume a foundation of high-quality, developmentally appropriate practices for all children and then build upon this foundation by including the specialized practices for children with disabilities.

The two programs agreed and, in the fall of 2001, the project began. Building on previous research and work with the DEC Recommended Practices, the BTG staff adopted the "direct services" practice strands (i.e., Assessment, Child-Focused Practices, Family-Based Practices, Interdisciplinary Models, and Technology Applications) and the "indirect supports" strands for those services (i.e., Policies, Procedures, and Systems Change; and Personnel Preparation) (see the introduction of this book and Figure 1). Thus, the BTG staff suggested that the two sites establish two teams each: a Systems Change Team to implement the Practices related to indirect supports, and a Direct Services Team to implement the direct services Practices. These teams and their composition are described in the following sections.

Figure 1.

DEC'S Recommended Practices

Direct Services Strands: Assessment, Child-Focused Practices, Family-Based Practices, Interdisciplinary Models, Technology Applications

Indirect Supports Strands: Policies, Procedures, Systems Change, and Personnel Preparation

Policies, Procedures, and Systems Change

Assessment
Child-Focused Practices
Family-Based Practices
Interdisciplinary Models
Technology Applications

Personnel Preparation

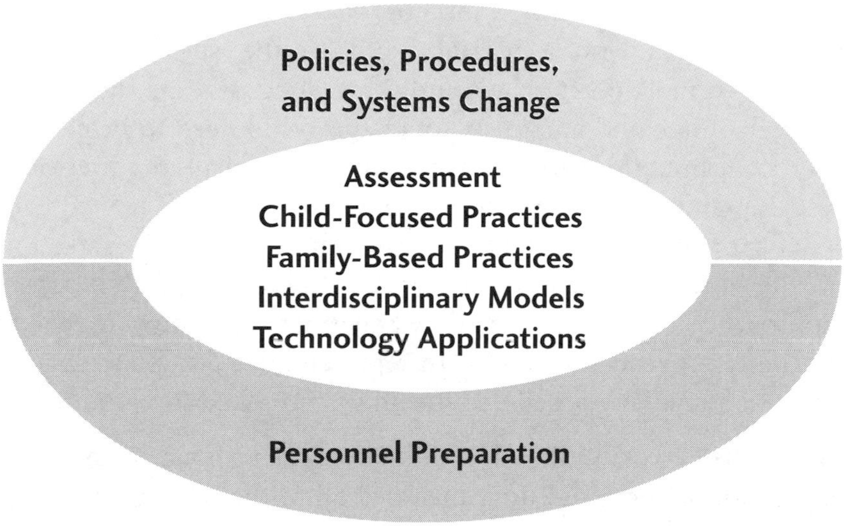

Getting Started

The Early Childhood Coordinators of both sites expressed enthusiasm for trying something new for program improvement, and for improving and documenting children's outcomes. The Early Childhood Coordinators took steps to garner the support of administration leadership. First, they *designed a plan* for using the Recommended Practices. This plan was aided by BTG staff who proposed a model of implementation based on previous work (Hayden, Frederick, & Smith, 2003). As mentioned previously, the plan included establishing two teams: (1) a Direct Services Team comprised of direct services personnel, family members, and representation from administration to address the direct services strands and the practical applications in the service delivery setting; and (2) a Systems Change Team comprised of coordinators, directors, parents, and representation from the direct services staff to address the two indirect supports strands and provide leadership at the system level (i.e., policies/procedures and resources needed to improve the program and services). The two sites selected for their Direct Services Team classroom personnel who, while not working together previously, had, as individuals, exhibited high-quality approaches to children and families. (As noted previously, the DEC Recommended Practices assume a *foundation of quality programming* that can be built upon to specifically and effectively address the needs of children with disabilities.)

Second, the Early Childhood Coordinators *met with their appropriate upper-level administration personnel* to explain the effort, show the link between the DEC Recommended Practices and the goal/mission of their respective organizations, and to solicit their ideas about how the Recommended Practices effort could meet current needs. These meetings accomplished two important goals: (1) leadership buy-in and support, and (2) leadership awareness of the initiative and the time and resources it would require.

Third, the Early Childhood Coordinators *met with other people key to improving services (stakeholders)* who would be important to the success of implementing the Recommended Practices: teachers and other direct services staff; parents; staff development personnel; and administrators who would need to be closely involved such as other coordinators, special education and curriculum directors, etc. This step involved explaining: (1) the Recommended Practices and related evidence base; (2) the benefits of such an effort; and (3) the importance of the stakeholders' participation in the initiative. The Coordinators used two strategies for recruiting members: they approached individuals who they believed would bring knowledge and enthusiasm to the effort, and they met with representative groups (e.g., all the elementary principals at a regularly scheduled meeting) and asked for volunteers.

Finally, the Early Childhood Coordinators each convened an *orientation meeting* of the stakeholders. These meetings included all of the people who had agreed to consider participating in the effort. The meetings had the following purposes:

- Acquaint the stakeholders with the DEC Recommended Practices;
- Describe how the Practices could be used to improve the program and outcomes;
- Orient the stakeholders to the early childhood program, jargon, and terms;
- Confirm who would be willing to participate on one of the teams; and
- Outline a plan for managing the logistics of the teams including schedules for monthly meetings (of two to three hours each), format for action planning, facilitation, and timelines.

chapter

10

Getting Started, Building Support

Are you willing to take the lead and take risks?

Do you have administrative support?

Are there plans to have the Teams share decision making so that people who will be affected (i.e., stakeholders) will understand, have input into, and feel ownership of the changes being made?

Are all of the key people involved?

Are the Teams as small as possible and yet have key stakeholder groups represented?

Persevere and expect frustration. Does everyone understand what they have control over and what they don't? Do the best you can.

Are there plans to share the load (i.e., take some activities to other ongoing groups)?

Following is a brief summary or "story" of each of the two sites' approaches to implementing the DEC Recommended Practices.

Douglas County: Systems Change Team

The two Coordinators in the Douglas County School District for early childhood education and early childhood special education met with the BTG staff and mapped out a timeframe for getting started and for contacting key stakeholders within the district. Then in the summer of 2001, the Coordinators met with the Assistant Superintendent and the Director of Special Education. In this meeting they explained the initiative, the DEC Recommended Practices, and the research base for the Practices. They described how the use of the Recommended Practices could benefit services to young children in Douglas County as well as the resources that might be needed, including team members' time. They then described who they thought should be on the Systems Change Team and asked for support from the Assistant Superintendent in the form of issuing invitations and encouragement to some of the key people the Coordinators sought (e.g., curriculum administrators, staff development personnel, principals). She agreed to the initiative and to provide the support needed. The Director of Special Education was asked to serve on the Team, and he agreed to serve and to support the effort.

Over the next few weeks, the Coordinators invited potential Systems Change Team members to participate. They invited key stakeholders: administrators (e.g., curriculum, special education); principals; staff development personnel; families; etc. To their surprise, many people volunteered once they heard of the project. Indeed, two or three people represented each stakeholder group.

chapter

10

In August 2001, the potential Systems Change Team members attended an orientation meeting. Nearly 30 people attended! At this meeting, the Coordinators and the BTG staff gave overviews of:

- The DEC Recommended Practices
- The Bridging the Gap project
- The Douglas County preschool program, teams, etc.
- The role and responsibilities of the Team and members
- The plan for implementation (i.e., two teams, self-assessing on the Recommended Practices, developing and implementing action plans, and re-assessing at the end of the year)
- Logistics (e.g., team membership and responsibilities, frequency and schedule of team meetings, taking minutes, expectations, etc.)

A professional group facilitator was provided for this orientation meeting. At this first meeting, the Team identified the strengths, weaknesses, opportunities, and threats (SWOT) (Hayden, Frederick, & Smith, 2003) of the preschool program and areas of focus to address in the project. Examples of each were: strengths—enthusiastic personnel; weaknesses—lack of program evaluation system; opportunities—BTG project; and threats—shrinking resources. Based upon this initial analysis of their focus areas, the Team began to develop a vision/goal statement to provide direction for the initiative (see Figure 2 for the agenda of the orientation meeting).

Defining a Vision/Desired Result

Has the Team agreed on the purpose and desired result of using the DEC Recommended Practices?

Will the vision/desired result help everyone stay focused?

Can the vision/desired result be used to measure progress?

Is everyone on the same page (i.e., does everyone have the same understanding of terminology, need, etc.)?

Is there ample opportunity to change the vision statement as the needs of the Team or program priorities change?

Have the DEC Recommended Practices been used to build upon a baseline of quality work concerning current issues (e.g., a child currently enrolled, a systems challenge)?

Has everyone kept the DEC Recommended Practices in view so as not to veer off course?

Figure 2

Douglas County Systems Change Team Orientation
August 14, 2001 — University Center at Chaparral

Session Outcomes The Team will have:
1. A common understanding of the Bridging the Gap project and how this project will support Douglas County in establishing/increasing the infusion of early childhood into the district's strategic plan and initiatives related to standards
2. An awareness of their role as a team, including ground rules for how they will operate over the coming year and a schedule for their meetings
3. An initial analysis based on team member perceptions of Douglas County strengths, weaknesses, opportunities, and threats related to quality early childhood services as defined by DEC Recommended Practices
4 One or more identified priorities for the Team's initial focus/direction over the coming year
5. A sense of team and increased capacity to work as a team
6. A plan for next steps including: (a) outcomes for the next team meeting, and (b) follow-up needed

Agenda

Time	Activity
8:00	Session registration and materials review (coffee, etc. available)
8:30	Welcome and opening remarks
8:45	Session overview and get-acquainted activity
9:30	Bridging the Gap project overview
10:00	Break
10:15	Bridging the Gap project overview cont'd
10:45	Background on Douglas County participation in Bridging the Gap
11:00	Debrief on what we have heard
11:30	Lunch (after lunch, sit with "new" people)
12:15	Strengths, weaknesses, opportunities (including Bridging the Gap), and Threats
1:00	Small group activity to determine direction/focus
1:45	Break
2:00	Team ground rules
2:30	Team logistics
3:00	Wrap-up and next steps
3:30	Evaluating our time together
3:45	Closing remarks - Douglas County personnel
4:00	Adjourn

chapter
10

Following this orientation meeting, the Systems Change Team met two more times. The Team used the forms in the *DEC Recommended Practices Program Assessment* book (Hemmeter et al., 2001) to self-assess on the practices in the Policies, Procedures, and Systems Change strand (see Chapter 8) and the Personnel Preparation strand (see Chapter 9). Using the results from the self-assessment, the Team refined the original focus areas. The final focus areas were: (1) develop a data system for accountability; (2) improve transition to kindergarten with a continuum of DAP practices; (3) provide training in DAP and Recommended Practices for all staff with equity in staff development opportunities between ECE and ECSE personnel (ECE personnel in Colorado school districts are typically not hired as certificated employees, thus, they do not receive the same benefits, salary, and training as ECSE personnel who are hired as certificated employees); and (4) increase awareness of and better align the preschool program with the overall school district's goals and initiatives. Action planning began on the identified practices within the focus areas. An action plan was developed for each focus area and related Recommended Practices, and a work group assigned to each (see Figure 3 for a sample "Action Planning Form"). Chapter 11 gives details on the self-assessment process and action planning.

Figure 3

ACTION PLANNING FORM

Date ....

Objective/Focus Area ....

Team/Work Group Members ....

....

Purpose Statement ....

....

Practices to be Addressed	Action Steps to be Taken	Timelines & Persons Responsible	Resources & Supports Needed	Indicators of Success	Status/Date Completed

Team Meetings

Date .... Present .... Notes ....

Date .... Present .... Notes ....

Date .... Present .... Notes ....

However, during the first three months, several members missed meetings and there seemed to be confusion concerning purpose and a lack of ownership. The Coordinators and BTG staff met to reevaluate the effort and decided that the Team was too large to promote ownership and understanding. It was decided that each stakeholder group should have only one representative and the person who had indicated the most interest in each group was invited to remain on the Team. (The others were thanked and it was explained to them that the Team needed to be smaller and that they would continue to receive all minutes from the subsequent meetings.)

Following this paring down of the Team, the eight-member Systems Change Team was much more efficient and membership was consistent from meeting to meeting.

The new Team met every month (two to three hours each time), implementing the action plans and the related DEC Recommended Practices.

At the end of the second year, the Team reassessed on the identified Recommended Practices and found they had improved on all of them. In addition, improvement was noted in other strand practices as well. The Team found that many of the Practices related to those in other strands (i.e., there was crossover from one set of practices to another). They updated their action plans and reported that they had achieved their goals on all their action plans. (See Figures 4A, 4B, 4C, and 4D for sample completed action plans. Note that the updated plans show the successful completion of all the goals and activities.)

At the end of the second year, the Team reassessed on the identified Recommended Practices and found they had improved on all of them.

At the end of the project period, the Team made several specific recommendations for using the Recommended Practices, which are reflected in the "lessons learned" later in this chapter. One overall recommendation made was for a closer tie to the Direct Services Team. While the Direct Services Team had a representative on the Systems Change Team and any policy barriers they identified were brought to the Systems Change Team, to be addressed, both teams felt the coordination of the two teams was not strong enough. Second, the Team recommended that programs realize and plan for the time commitment this process requires. The Team reported that the process was invaluable for overriding some systems barriers (as evident in the action plans in Figures 4A-4D), raising the awareness of the preschool program throughout the District, and using the DEC Recommended Practices.

Figure 4A

ACTION PLANNING FORM

Date 4/03 Update

Objective/Focus Area Alignment, Awareness, and Transition

Team/Work Group Members Mary, Mark, John

Purpose Statement Alignment of the preschool program with the overall district initiatives to ensure awareness and appreciation of the program and effective transition to kindergarten by families, children, and staff

Practices to be Addressed	Action Steps to be Taken	Timelines & Persons Responsible	Resources & Supports Needed	Indicators of Success	Status/Date Completed
PS29	Data gathered from building principals regarding feedback on target areas	By 10-02; Mark	Survey format	Survey completed for analysis	Completed 10/02
PS29	Data gathered regarding process and efficiency relative to transition processes, preschool-K	John Gail	Subgroups developed; input meetings occur	Data gathered from multiple sources for analysis	Completed 11/02
PS6-PS7	General Fund budget adjustments considered relative to funding preschool programming	John, Patsy, Fiscal Services	Meetings to discuss	Thorough discussion occurs and recommendations made	Completed; All changes made; all stakeholders agree to changes- 4/03 Completed 4/03
PS33	Board of Education policies and procedures developed regarding preschool retention	John, Gail, Liz, RDs, Caplan and Earnest	Policy/procedures development	Policy/procedures in place	

Figure 4B

ACTION PLANNING FORM

Date 4/03 Update

Objective/Focus Area Staff Development

Team/Work Group Members Becky, Liz, Christy

Purpose Statement "BRT" (Building Resource Team/Teacher) for Preschool Program

Practices to be Addressed	Action Steps to be Taken	Timelines & Persons Responsible	Resources & Supports Needed	Indicators of Success	Status/Date Completed
PS29	Need for BRT (Building Resource Team/Teacher) in the preschools	Liz & Gail— 9/02	funded by District and part funded by a grant	Accomplished— 2 teachers appointed as BRTs	8/02
PS20	Staff awareness of new position	Ongoing— Liz & Gail	Flier & e-mail	BRTs contacted by teams— ongoing	completed in 11/02—but ongoing process
	Job responsibilities of the position clarified ... use school BRT model (template)	Liz & Gail— to be completed in Jan. '03	Follow model and report out (evaluations)	List out responsibilities given to staff by 12/02— will be done in Jan.	
PS20	Create a District-funded source for continuation of BRT position	10/02–6/03 Liz & Gail	Documentation of the work being done and number of contacts made (Jill & Kerry)	Paid for by District Funding to continue '03–'04	Completed December '02

Figure 4C

ACTION PLANNING FORM

Date 4/03 Update

Objective/Focus Area Accountability

Team/Work Group Members Steering Committee, Bridging the Gap staff, Colorado Department of Education (CDE)

Purpose Statement Develop a data collection system to ensure accountability and effectiveness of the preschool program in promoting optimal outcomes for children

Practices to be Addressed	Action Steps to be Taken	Timelines & Persons Responsible	Resources & Supports Needed	Indicators of Success	Status/Date Completed
PS33, PS34, PS35, PS40, PS41, PS42, PS43	• obtain additional resources • assign staff and consultant • meet with CDE and others to design project/system • design components of the system • design instrumentation and procedures for collecting and analyzing data • pilot the system • refine system based on pilot • final data system designed and implemented • look at next steps and alignment with other district systems and rubrics	BTG—by 5/02 BTG—by 5/02 Gail, Liz, BTG Steering Committee, project staff, BTG CDE by 6/02 Steering Committee, project staff, BTG CDE by 8/02 DC schools, BTG project staff, CDE —9/02–5/03 Steering Committee, BTG project staff, DC, CDE by 7/03 DC, CDE, BTG project staff by 8/03	Grant from CDE; consultant from BTG	• grant • consultant assigned • meeting held • components designed • instruments and procedures designed • pilot data collected and analyzed • new data system in place	• grant obtained 9/02 • 4/8/02 • 4/02 • 9/02 • draft of child outcome data system: 7/02 • pilot started 11/02—completed • implement in all classrooms in 8/03

Figure 4D

ACTION PLANNING FORM

Date 4/03 Update

Objective/Focus Area Staff Development

Team/Work Group Members Liz, Becky, Christy

Purpose Statement Pay for regular ed staff for skills block & performance pay

Practices to be Addressed	Action Steps to be Taken	Timelines & Persons Responsible	Resources & Supports Needed	Indicators of Success	Status/Date Completed
PS23	Liz will meet with Staff Development Committee (District) to share concerns and brainstorm ideas	Jan. '03—Liz End of Jan. '03	Schedule time with Cathy & Robin	Better understanding of problem Equal pay for staff development opportunities for preschool regular ed staff	Jan. '03 Completed 4/03; will begin July 1, 2003
PP64	Meet with Performance Pay Committee to share concern about preschool regular ed staff not being able to participate		Meeting time	Regular ed preschool staff will be able to participate in District's performance pay plan	Completed 4/03; will begin July 1, 2003

Douglas County: Direct Services Team

In the fall of 2001, the Douglas County Coordinators held an orientation meeting for all the preschool teachers, teaching assistants, and related services personnel. The orientation included describing the DEC Recommended Practices, the BTG project, and the plan to have one classroom implement the direct services practices. Subsequently the Coordinators selected the Direct Services Team, composed of an early education teacher, early childhood special education teacher, a teaching assistant, and related services personnel. These individuals had not previously worked together, but were excited to participate. The Direct Services Team worked with the BTG staff to assess the direct services strands of the Recommended Practices. They met monthly with a BTG facilitator; self-assessed; prioritized the Practices for study; developed action plans for implementation in the classroom; and received ongoing support, mentoring, and coaching.

The Coordinators selected the Interdisciplinary Models strand (see Chapter 6) as the first area of focus for this team since they were working together for the first time. The Direct Services Team self-assessed on the practices in this strand (see Chapter 11 for the steps in assessment). Upon review of their self-assessment data, they chose to first improve their transdisciplinary practices (e.g., 17—"Team members engage in role release ... and role acceptance ... "; 18—"Team members use a transdisciplinary model to plan and deliver interventions"). They established three goals: (1) to work as a team using an additional child assessment instrument that would support joint curriculum planning; (2) to strengthen the communication system for team members

Assessing the Need

Does everyone understand the "big picture": that the DEC Recommended Practices will improve what they do for children and families?

Has the Team used the DEC Program Assessment procedures to identify practices that need improvement? (See Chapter 11 for more guidance and ideas on self-assessment.)

Has the Team decided how to begin the process (e.g., by a topic or activity the Team already is interested in, by practice strands)? (See Chapter 11.)

Has the Team used the program assessment process to gather and use data about current knowledge, skills, and use of practices to promote decision making based on facts, not opinions?

Has the Team used the program assessment process as a team rather than as individuals so that each team can establish common language and understanding? (If there is no team, individuals can self-assess their own knowledge and practices related to their work.)

Has the Team identified all the Recommended Practices that will support their areas of focus?

and families; and (3) to assess the degree to which the Team is using a transdisciplinary approach.

For the next several months, the Team and the BTG facilitator explored a variety of materials, resources, and strategies to meet their goals. In the spring, the Team continued with the Interdisciplinary Models strand and began work on the Assessment strand (see Chapter 3). They continued to use the program assessment process and to participate in action planning. Their procedures and forms were similar to those in Figures 3 and 4A-4D.

During the second year of the project, the Direct Services Team moved through the process more quickly—they were able to select a strand, self-assess, create an action plan, and implement the plan at a more rapid pace. They completed work on the Assessment strand, the Child-Focused Practices strand (see Chapter 4), and the Family-Based Practices strand (see Chapter 5). There were two contributing factors to this increase in speed and effectiveness. First, it seemed there was a "learning to learn" or "ah ha" phenomenon; once the Team completed the work on one strand, they had an understanding of the process and were able to be more efficient. Second, at the end of the first year, BTG staff began a series of workshops that were provided as the teams began working on a new strand. Each workshop addressed a new strand by presenting key concepts and evidence-based strategies. The self-assessment and the workshops were a useful combination for helping the Team determine priorities and strategies for implementation.

The Direct Services Team also began using a strategy to select one or two children in the classroom as the focus of their work. In this process, children were identified as needing additional support. The Team selected their priority area from the Program Assessment and developed or tried strategies from the selected strand that were relevant to the child's needs. Then the Team evaluated whether the strategies were working. The BTG staff was involved in facilitating implementation of the strategies in the classroom.

The Team's greatest success was their increased understanding of the transdisciplinary approach.

The Team's greatest success was their increased understanding of the transdisciplinary approach. They stated that: "We always understood the theoretical meaning of 'transdisciplinary,' but the 'feelings' are what make the relationships and the role release work. The Team has learned to step out of our roles (which kept us in a box) and now we have a philosophy of helping each other. This extends to little things (like washing off the tables) and that makes a big difference!"

At the conclusion of the project, the Team indicated that an outside facilitator, a champion or leader to keep the Team focused, and more administrative support from the district would be required for them to continue using the full model; however, what they learned would continue to be implemented. The Direct Services Team also

chapter
10

recommended that they build on their success by working with the Systems Change Team to develop a common goal and joint action plans.

Sewall: Systems Change Team

Because of their long history of striving for quality, leaders at Sewall were immediately interested in participating in the Bridging the Gap project. A series of meetings between BTG staff and the Sewall Program Director began in the 2000-2001 school year to conceptualize the most meaningful way to engage the Sewall community with DEC's Recommended Practices. In August 2001, approximately 40 staff members from Sewall were brought together for an orientation which had three purposes: (1) to meet each other (Sewall has many programs on- and off-site); (2) to learn about DEC and the Recommended Practices; and (3) to hear about the Bridging the Gap project. Volunteers for participating more fully with the BTG project were identified.

On September 14, 2001, the first meeting of the Sewall Systems Change Team was held with eight administrators and three parents present. Taking place only three days after the September 11 terrorist attacks, the group took time to reflect on the world situation. Then they shared their dreams for Sewall, including: increasing services by adding kindergarten, establishing similar programs across the state, receiving full funding, providing a healthy working environment, and creating a shining example of best practices. Individuals in the group self-assessed on the Policies, Procedures, and Systems Change strand practices (see Chapter 8). Ground rules were established and future (two-hour) meetings were scheduled.

Over the next two years, the Systems Change Team prioritized and worked on specific policies and procedures using the Recommended Practices. The team employed several different sources of data in order to understand the complexity of all the different components of Sewall, including their NAEYC Accreditation Survey, the Board of Director's proposed strategic plan, a high-impact planning process, and the *Early Childhood Environment Rating Scale* (Harms, Clifford, & Cryer, 1998). The Team chose to work on developing a holistic, systemic way of managing all the different programs at Sewall in order to be more proactive and less reactive (i.e., "in crisis mode") (e.g., PS32—"Policies, structures, and practices are aligned to promote systems change") and to better communicate with each other and with the outside community (i.e., PS16—Program policies are provided in sufficient detail and formats so that all stakeholders understand what the policy means.").

During the second year the Systems Change Team shifted their focus to finding meaningful ways to support and involve staff. They identified four Recommended Practices that they determined would best support their goals to provide a healthy work environment, identify and access personal and organizational supports to maintain emotional wellness, reduce staff stress, and increase staff participation (i.e., PS23—"Program policies provide clear job descriptions and provide for personnel competencies and ongoing staff development . . ."; PS38—"Leadership and systems change efforts rely on strong relationships and collaboration within and across systems

chapter 10

. . ."; PS26—"Administrators provide for a supportive work environment . . ."; PS37—"Leadership and systems change efforts include attention to timely job-embedded professional development, funding, program evaluation, accountability, governance, program accreditation, curriculum, and naturalistic instruction/supports.").

The Team used procedures and action plans similar to those in Figures 3 and 4A-4D. For example, one action plan reflected their goal to implement or improve efforts to provide reflective supervision, mentoring, and team facilitation, and increase ongoing educational/inservice opportunities to support emotional wellness. As a result of this focus, the Sewall Board of Directors, administrative staff, and program staff have significantly increased their awareness of the various roles of staff. After the project ended, they continued to identify strategies to increase staff input into decisions that are made on a variety of matters that influence both daily life and the future of Sewall.

Crafting the Action Plan

Does the action plan include a goal or purpose?

Are the Recommended Practices that were identified in the self-assessment process addressed and is their relationship to the goal listed on the plan?

Are there activities listed that address how the Practices will be implemented?

Are the resources (e.g., training, financial resources) that are needed to implement the Practices listed?

Are the timelines realistic?

Do all the team members understand the steps, timelines, and their tasks that will be needed to accomplish the action plan?

Does the action plan include both long-range (major impact) as well as short-range (that can be accomplished quickly) objectives and activities?

chapter
10

By the end of the project, evaluations and self-assessments of the Systems Change Team showed that the simple act of bringing staff, parents, and the Board of Directors together monthly had positive effects (e.g., joint and informed decision making) for the entire organization. The Systems Change Team became a catalyst for analysis and decision making as well as a structure for creating change. During a severe budget crunch in 2002, members of the Systems Change Team met weekly to produce a cost/benefit analysis of each program component for the Board of Directors. The Board was able to make budgetary decisions using the evidence-based findings of the Recommended Practices as part of their decision-making process.

Sewall: Direct Services Team

During the fall of 2001, the classroom team (Direct Services Team) was selected by the Early Childhood Program Coordinator and the BTG staff. The team was comprised of an early education teacher, early childhood special educator, a paraeducator, and related services staff. The Team participated in an orientation with the Systems Change Team (as described previously).

With the assistance of the BTG facilitator, the Team self-assessed on the Child-Focused Practices strand (see Chapter 4) and analyzed the data from the assessment. They selected child-focused practices because, as they explained, that "topic is our strength but it's also the most important for our work." They decided to focus on data collection, peer interactions, and play because they could interrelate these three practices that they considered important goals for their classroom (e.g., C23—"Peer-mediated strategies are used to promote social and communicative behavior."; C14—"Data-based decisions are used to make modifications in the practices …"; C4—"Play routines are structured to promote interaction, communication, and learning …").

The Team participated in action planning using similar forms and procedures as described for the other teams. They outlined several strategies, such as collecting data on child interactions, using a buddy system, making changes to the curriculum by better utilizing the thematic approach, and making changes in the length of center time activities. To check their progress and to analyze peer interactions, the Team specificed that the target classroom be videotaped.

During the next several months, the BTG facilitator met with the Team and facilitated their work toward meeting their priorities on the action plan. Everyone viewed and discussed the videotape. There was a great deal of momentum. Then, as the Team was in the middle of their work, Sewall experienced several significant challenges. Changes in funding resulted in several budget cuts. These cuts reduced staff resources, increasing the work load on all staff. In addition, a new Executive Director was hired. The Team expressed feelings of being overwhelmed and had less time to incorporate changes into their already hectic schedule. As a result, the Team, the Early Childhood Coordinator, and the BTG facilitator restructured the staff development time and adopted a more hands-on approach. In addition, the Coordinator and the BTG facilitator met with the new Executive Director to acquaint her with the DEC Recommended Practices and invite her participation in the BTG activities.

Concurrently, BTG began holding workshops for the Direct Services Teams from both sites on topics selected by the Teams. All of the Sewall staff had an opportunity to participate in the workshops. These workshops created a springboard for generating ideas for the Team to try in the classrooms.

During the second year of the project, due to staff turnover, the original team was no longer intact. The Coordinator met with staff and selected a new Direct Services Team and a new classroom for participation based on interest and availability of the team members. As with Douglas County, the Sewall Direct Services Team selected one child whose needs were addressed as the Team made decisions on which practices to prioritize and what strategies would be implemented.

For the next year, and with this child in mind, the Team worked through the Child-Focused Practices (see Chapter 4), Family-Based Practices (see Chapter 5), and Assessment strands (see Chapter 3) by completing the self-assessment, strand by strand. The workshops on each strand continued and the information was used to develop and refine action plans. The action planning process remained the method used to keep everyone on track. The hands-on approach of the BTG facilitator participating in the classroom activities and planning process provided the necessary ongoing support.

Using the Action Plan and Determining Next Steps

Does each team meet on a regular basis to update their action plan?

Are meetings structured around the action plan and is the action plan used as the meeting agenda?

Have the Teams considered using the action plan to record minutes of their meetings, and included spaces on the action plan for dates, team members present, and notes about decisions made during meetings?

Is the action plan form simple, easy-to-use, and does it minimize clerical work (see Figure 3)?

If the objectives were not achieved, does the appropriate team reflect on the process in order to determine why?

Are team efforts supported? Are there incentives for implementing the DEC Recommended Practices?

Is ongoing professional development provided to ensure that team members have the knowledge, skills, and attitudes needed to implement the change?

Did the Teams "keep it simple"?

If an outside facilitator was used in the beginning, has this role eventually transitioned to a within-group facilitation that will sustain the effort?

Do the Teams have a written plan to evaluate both the process as well as the outcomes?

Will a written report be shared at the end of each year that summarizes the progress and outcomes of the initiative? Will the report be shared with team members, other stakeholders, and program leadership?

Are there plans to expand the effort to other teams, other issues, etc?

Is there a plan for the next year?

chapter
10

By the end of the project, the Sewall Teams reported they had increased their knowledge and were better at implementing a variety of practices in the classroom. In fact, they were able to transfer the strategies they had learned to other settings. For example, one team member was instrumental in implementing a social skills program that she had learned about during the workshops into a classroom in which she worked at another location. The Teams agreed that the self-assessment was difficult, but that it helped them break tasks down and allowed them to clearly identify their strengths and areas of need.

Lessons Learned

Following is a summary of "lessons learned" in the process of adopting and using the DEC Recommended Practices. These lessons reflect the direct experiences of the BTG staff and the Systems Change and Direct Services Teams from both programs while implementing the DEC Recommended Practices. These lessons were gleaned from interviews with all participating teams and the administrators during the project evaluation, as well as from observations throughout the project period.

1. *Get support from "higher-ups" and other people key to success (i.e., stakeholders).* The initiative leadership (e.g., administrators, classroom teacher, Early Childhood Coordinator, personnel development professional) must enlist the support of the upper-level administrators and other stakeholders. Get assistance from "higher-ups" to help develop a plan, provide appropriate resources, and obtain additional time to work on the Practices (e.g., inservice time and/or regular planning time). Implementing the Practices requires time, energy, and commitment to quality services. The process will likely require at least two to three hours per month of meetings (more for learning new Practices and implementing procedures) for one to two years (however, once one strand of Practices is learned, the subsequent strand work will be accomplished in less time because the process will be familiar). This process should be a priority for staff development activities. All key stakeholders need to be informed of the initiative. Hold an orientation meeting and invite all stakeholders, even those who may not participate on the Teams that will implement the Practices.

2. If possible, *align this effort with other similar efforts of the agency* so that this process is not an "add-on" or "just another meeting." Show the alignment between the DEC Recommended Practices and the mission of the organization (e.g., better outcomes for children).

3. *Create "stakeholder" teams for making decisions together* (i.e., people who have a "stake" in services for young children). One team, the Systems Change Team of stakeholders, implements the indirect supports Recommended Practices strands: Policies, Procedures, and Systems Change (see Chapter 8) and Personnel Preparation (see Chapter 9). The second team of stakeholders, the Direct Services Team, implements the direct services Recommended Practices strands: Assessment (see Chapter 3), Child-Focused Practices (see Chapter 4), Family-Based Practices (see Chapter 5), Interdisciplinary Models (see Chapter

6), and Technology Applications (see Chapter 7). Begin with a Systems Change Team or administrative team. Then, once that Team is familiar with the process and is ready to support the Direct Services Team, establish the Direct Services Team. The Systems Change Team may need to establish policies and procedures to address challenges the Direct Services Team identifies as barriers to using the Recommended Practices. Telephones, faxes, computers, training opportunities, and time or child care costs for parent members to attend meetings are examples of resources the Direct Services Teams may need from the Systems Change Team.

4. *Tie the work of the Direct Services Team to overall performance expectations* so that team members can see the importance and relevance of the effort (e.g., regular reporting on their progress and how it is affecting services for children). To support the Team's efforts, provide them with the necessary:

- Time (e.g., scheduling, reduction in other responsibilities);
- Technology (e.g., computers, phone, fax machine);
- Other resources (e.g., stipends for family members so they can participate on the Team); and
- Ongoing training and technical assistance (TA) (to learn the Recommended Practices).

5. *Keep teams small and revisit membership as plans progress.* The core team members are the necessary stakeholders and those who want to be there (e.g., six to ten people). As each team's focus becomes clearer, the Team may decide that some individuals should be core members, versus others who might serve on an ad hoc basis or in work groups targeted to specific activities. The key is to try to have representation from the major leadership stakeholders (e.g., Coordinators, directors, parents, principals, Direct Services Team representative or Systems Change Team representative, etc.) without being too big and unwieldy.

6. *Establish a close relationship between the two Teams.* Have shared membership, joint meetings, and shared activities. Sharing action plans helps Systems Change and Direct Services Teams recognize the relationship between their actions. The Teams benefit from additional input and insight from those who have different roles/perspectives and who will promote working together on related activities. For example, if the Direct Services Team identifies and works on the Family-Based Practices strand, they may need the Systems Change Team to develop some training opportunities or flexible hours to work with families.

7. *Obtain local technical support.* Identify a technical assistance or staff development provider who typically works with the program to be part of the Direct Services Team and provide support to the Team. This person should understand the DEC Recommended Practices in order to provide support to the Team. The terminology and perspectives of the DEC Recommended Practices are often technical. It will be important to include someone on each team who is knowledgeable about the Practices and who can provide support in terms of applying the Practices to their work context. Teams may need support in identifying and/or maintaining priorities and identifying training needs. Direct Services Teams need to learn how to embed the Practices into what they already do.

chapter

10

8. *Use the self-assessment process as a reflective tool to examine beliefs, actual/current practice, and each others' understandings.* To learn, team members must share an understanding. A discussion about what a Practice should "look like" and how often it is seen in real life is an important learning process and has a high potential to generate commitment to action. Such discussion is also important for team members to agree on definitions for their particular situation. For instance, if the Practices refer to "administrators," to whom does this refer in a particular program? Or, a Systems Change Team might find that team members are operating with different perceptions of how to provide services in inclusive settings or natural learning environments. Teams will need to clarify definitions as they relate to their own settings, use the glossaries provided, and come to agreement about what a Practice should look like when fully implemented and whether they have achieved that level of performance.

9. *Provide a team facilitator.* This person organizes the meetings, ensures that meetings result in an updated action plan, helps everyone in the meeting feel valued and have an opportunity to voice their ideas, and keeps meetings on track. An outside facilitator is beneficial because he or she is a neutral party, and allows everyone to participate. Initially the facilitator may be more directive, such as providing an agenda before a team meeting and then writing up the meeting notes or minutes with the decisions made at the meeting. Over time, the facilitator may shift roles by helping the Team become more self-sufficient.

10. *Sustaining momentum requires at least one champion.* There should be at least one person who will keep each team on track and will persevere when faced with challenges. The champion is a person whose presence is perceived by team members as key to the initiative. This person has the respect of the group and has enough power and/or commitment to bring resources together for team benefit.

Sustaining the Process

A typical process to adopt and use the Recommended Practices as outlined in this chapter may look like that in Figure 5. However, timelines and specifics will depend on the circumstances of each program. For example, how a program implements the DEC Recommended Practices will be determined by the goals and challenges of the program, the objectives of the Systems Change Team, the number and scope of Direct Services Teams, and the size and resource capacity of the organization.

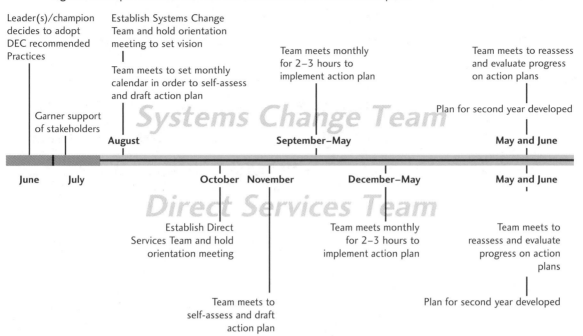

Figure 5. Sample Timeline for First-Year Recommended Practices Adoption

An ongoing challenge to any effort to adopt new practices or initiatives is sustaining the change and momentum over time. "Institutionalization," or sustaining the use of the DEC Recommended Practices and the process of self-assessment and skill improvement, can be achieved through systems changes. For example, make the use of the Recommended Practices a program-wide expectation; embed them into professional development plans and inservice training opportunities; provide financial resources for training/TA and mentors; develop accountability systems; and change job descriptions/responsibilities as needed (e.g., mentors, facilitators, allow for planning time, etc.). Link the Recommended Practices to ongoing program initiatives.

Promote the DEC Recommended Practices through state-wide initiatives that support the adoption of the Practices at the local level. For example, partner with state agencies and institutions of higher education. State agencies can provide incentive grants to programs to adopt the Recommended Practices and to use the process as outlined. Link the state's compliance monitoring and corrective action plans with remedies that are based on the Recommended Practices. Align the state's standards with the DEC Recommended Practices. Establish training and TA systems for early childhood programs and ensure that the trainers have expertise in the DEC Recommended Practices. States might highlight one or two programs that have undergone the process of adopting and using the Recommended Practices as models for other programs in the state. Provide CEUs or university credit for direct services personnel who participate in structured professional development activities to implement the Recommended Practices. Finally, state agency and higher education training initiatives for preservice and inservice training can be linked to the Recommended Practices.

chapter

10

"Once we got the hang of it, how to do the assessment, action plans, and adopt the practices, the strands were adopted much faster."

"We built a new understanding and appreciation of our program within the district."

References

Harms, T., Clifford, R. M., & Cryer, D. (1998). *The early childhood environment rating scale* (Rev. ed.). New York: Teachers College Press.

Hayden, P., Frederick, L., & Smith, B. J. (2003). *A road map for facilitating collaborative teams.* Longmont, CO: Sopris West.

Hemmeter, M. L., Joseph, G., Smith, B. J., & Sandall, S. R. (2001). *DEC recommended practices program assessment: Improving practices for young children with special needs and their families.* Longmont, CO: Sopris West.

Chapter 11

Using the DEC Recommended Practices for Program Assessment and Improvement

· · · · · · · · · ·

Mary Louise Hemmeter, Susan Sandall, and Barbara J. Smith

High-quality programs regularly evaluate their own performance. In fact, program evaluation is a DEC Recommended Practice (see Chapter 8). Comprehensive program evaluation can answer many questions and serve a number of purposes. Documentation of the use of Recommended Practices provides information that can be used to improve the program. The ultimate goal is improved outcomes for children and families.

The information in this chapter is based on four years of work assisting programs in adopting and using the DEC Recommended Practices. The project, called Bridging the Gap (BTG), is described in Chapter 10. In this chapter, we use the information from our work with community-based programs to provide a framework for using the DEC Recommended Practices for the purposes of program assessment and improvement. Specifically, we describe the steps involved in conducting program assessment and using information from program assessment to develop an action plan for program improvement. *Note:* Complete forms and instructions for assessing the extent to which a program or individual is using the DEC Recommended Practices can be found in the forthcoming book *DEC Recommended Practices: A Program Assessment Workbook* (Hemmeter, Smith, Sandall, & Askew, in preparation).

This chapter provides an overview of the assessment process and is organized as follows: (1) the relationship between the DEC Recommended Practices and the NAEYC Developmentally Appropriate Practice Guidelines (Bredekamp & Copple, 1997); (2) three different approaches to assessing use of the DEC Recommended Practices; and

---

We would like to acknowledge the contributions of Linda Askew, Linda Frederick, and Gail E. Joseph to our work in this area.

(3) two case studies that show how to connect program assessment and action planning for improving use of the Practices. Based on recommendations from program personnel, we have expanded in this edition the ways that programs can approach assessment. The primary goal is to help programs and individuals identify and use practices that have evidence from research and experience that they improve outcomes for children and families. Program assessment is appropriate for any type of program that provides services to infants, toddlers, and/or preschoolers with disabilities (e.g., Head Start, child care, public school preschools).

DEC Recommended Practices and NAEYC Developmentally Appropriate Practice Guidelines

The DEC Recommended Practices are designed to be used in the context of developmentally appropriate early childhood environments. As such, they generally do not include specific practices related to setting up developmentally appropriate classroom environments and/or choosing curricula. The National Association for the Education of Young Children (NAEYC) has published a set of Developmentally Appropriate Practice Guidelines (Bredekamp & Copple, 1997) for all early care and education settings. The DEC Recommended Practices build upon these guidelines by recommending more specialized practices for meeting the individualized needs of young children with disabilities and their families in the context of developmentally appropriate learning environments. Table 1 lists essential components of high-quality early childhood programs.

Table 1. Quality Early Childhood Programs

- Use the NAEYC Developmentally Appropriate Practice Guidelines (DAP) to design environments and curricula for all children
- Ensure that all legal guidelines are adhered to, including IDEA and ADA
- Implement the DEC Recommended Practices for individual children with disabilities and their families
- Integrate the NAEYC DAP Guidelines and the DEC Recommended Practices with standards and other quality improvement activities such as the NAEYC Program Accreditation Standards, State Program Standards or Benchmarks, and Head Start Performance Standards

---

The DEC Recommended Practices are complementary to and an essential extension of the NAEYC Developmentally Appropriate Practice (DAP) Guidelines. In some cases, a DEC Recommended Practice may build on a DAP Guideline by describing a more specialized approach to working with a child with a significant disability. Table 2 demonstrates how two DAP Guidelines describe a general approach for all children while associated DEC Recommended Practices describe how to individualize a specific activity or routine so that children with disabilities can participate in meaningful ways. In the first example in Table 2, the DAP Guideline stresses a balance between adult-initiated and child-initiated activities while the DEC Recommended Practice suggests that the extent to which the teacher directs an activity is based on the individual needs of the children. In the second example, the DAP Guideline suggests that transitions should not be regimented while the DEC Recommended Practice indicates that transitions may need to be more structured for some children with disabilities.

While most children in a classroom may function independently, a child with a significant disability may need more direct support from an adult or peer to engage meaningfully in an activity or routine.

While most children in a classroom may function independently, a child with a significant disability may need more direct support from an adult or peer to engage meaningfully in an activity or routine. The more direct involvement of the adult or peer should be faded as the child learns the skills and is able to participate more meaningfully in the activity or routine. Just as renowned theorist and educator Lev Vygotsky suggested scaffolding learning according to an individual child's needs (Smith, Miller, & Bredekamp, 1998), it is important to consider the NAEYC Guidelines and DEC Practices as representing a continuum of support from the least support to the most support (Grisham-Brown, Hemmeter, & Pretti-Frontczak, in press; LaMontagne, Danbom, & Buchanan, 1998; Smith & Bredekamp, 1998; Smith, Miller, & Bredekamp, 1998).

Table 2. Two examples of how DAP Guidelines (General) Compare to DEC Recommended Practices (Individualized)

Example 1

Developmentally Appropriate Practice Guideline (Bredekamp & Copple, 1997)
A balance of child-initiated and adult-initiated activity is provided. The amount of time spent in large group, teacher-initiated activity is limited.

DEC Recommended Practice PS25:
Program policies ensure that multiple instructional models are available to meet the individual needs of children (e.g., less structure to more structure, child-driven to teacher-driven, peer mediated to teacher mediated, etc.).

Example 2

Developmentally Appropriate Practice Guideline (Bredekamp & Copple, 1997)
Teachers conduct smooth and unregimented transitions between activities.

DEC Recommended Practice C3
Routines and transitions are structured to promote interaction, communication, and learning by being responsive to child behavior and using naturalistic time delay, interrupted chain procedure, transition-based teaching, and visual cue systems.

chapter

11

Self-Assessment and Program Improvement

The self-assessment and program improvement approach outlined in this chapter is based on the fundamental assumption that children with disabilities have a right to be involved in community-based settings and to receive the services and supports necessary to participate meaningfully in those settings. Meaningful participation is likely to require specialized instruction and supports as described in the DEC Recommended Practices. This chapter is designed to assist programs and professionals in providing the supports that are needed so children with disabilities can participate and learn in any setting.

Specifically, this section focuses on how to *assess use of the DEC Recommended Practices and how to make plans for program improvement.* First, when conducting a program assessment for the purposes of program improvement, it is important to use a team approach that includes direct services staff, administrators, and families. However, it is also possible that an individual teacher or direct services provider may choose to use the program assessment to improve his or her own classroom or practices. Second, information must be systematically collected from a variety of sources including observations, interviews with families, and review of program documents (e.g., program policies, handbook) in order to evaluate the program's or individual's implementation of Recommended Practices.

Following are descriptions of: (1) approaches for deciding where to begin with a program assessment; (2) sample forms that can be used to conduct the program assessment; and (3) information on using assessment data to develop an action plan for program improvement. *Note:* Throughout this section, we refer to and use forms that are also in the forthcoming book *DEC Recommended Practices: A Program Assessment Workbook* (Hemmeter et al., in preparation).

Where to Begin

There are at least three ways to begin a program assessment. Which approach to choose will depend on a variety of variables including: (1) the amount of time a program has to commit to the process; (2) what other program improvement activities are occurring concurrently; (3) the extent to which the program has or has not identified priority areas of need for improvement; and (4) other program priorities or needs related to issues such as funding, accreditation, and accountability.

Approach 1: Use the Complete Set of DEC Recommended Practices

The most comprehensive method is to assess the program using the complete set of DEC Recommended Practices. This approach provides a program with a comprehensive assessment of their strengths and needs related to services for young children with disabilities and their families. This method is especially useful for new programs or for programs that have the resources and incentives to conduct a program-wide assessment. Using the complete set of Practices could also be useful to a program in terms of identifying priority areas of need for professional development. Figure 1 provides a sample form for assessing use of the DEC Recommended Practices. This form allows for assessing the same Practice at two different times so that improvement over time can be recorded.

Figure 1

DEC Recommended Practices: Program Assessment Form

Date (Time 1): .... **Date (Time 2):** ....

Team Members ....

....

Purpose Statement ....

....

Practices	Observations		Status				
			Fully Implemented (2)	Partially Implemented (1)	Not Implemented (0)	N/A	D/K
		Time 1					
		Time 2					
		Time 1					
		Time 2					
		Time 1					
		Time 2					
		Time 1					
		Time 2					

Summary for Family-Based Practices

Total number of points obtained

Total number of items scored (exclude N/A and D/K)   _____

Total number of possible points (total # of items scored multiplied by 2)   _____

Percentage score (total # of points obtained divided by total # of possible points)   _____

List Practices (by indicator code) requiring improvement:

chapter

11

Aproach 2: Use a Specific Strand of the DEC Recommended Practices

We discovered through our experiences with community-based teams (see Chapter 10), that use of the complete set of Practices at one time can be overwhelming. Some programs may not have the resources to devote to a comprehensive assessment. An alternative method is to select a specific strand or set of strands (e.g., Child-Focused Practices, Family-Based Practices) and conduct a self-assessment and planning process related to these specific strands. Then, once the work on a strand is complete, another strand of Practices can be assessed and implemented.

A program might choose this method for a variety of reasons. First, the program may have identified a specific area of need through some other process (e.g., accreditation self-study, or program personnel are aware of ongoing program challenges). A program that is having teaming issues between classroom staff, related services staff, and administrators, for example, might choose to self-assess and plan using the Interdisciplinary Models Practices. Second, the program might identify either a single strand or a few strands of Practices based on strategic planning or funding priorities. For example, a school district might be encouraging programs to enhance their family involvement component. Consequently, a program might choose to self-assess using the Family-Based Practices strand. Or, a program that has an opportunity to apply for funding related to technology might choose to self-assess using the Technology Applications Practices. Finally, some strands might be used by entities other than direct services personnel. For example, the Personnel Preparation strand might be used by university faculty to assess their teacher training program, while a state agency might employ the Policies, Procedures, and Systems Change Practices. In this approach, the same sample assessment form (see Figure 1) could be used.

Approach 3: Use Subsets of the Recommended Practices Across Strands That Correspond to a Specific Program Activity

This method is based on the recognition that Practices across strands are interrelated and that many activities within early childhood programs require the staff to use Practices from multiple strands. This approach allows programs to effectively respond to practical, everyday challenges. For example, implementing embedded instruction requires the use of Practices related to how children's goals are identified (i.e., Interdisciplinary Models Assessment); how families are involved in selecting goals (i.e., Family-Based Practices); and determining the most effective instructional approaches (i.e., Child-Focused Practices).

If a program determines that they are not adequately addressing children's goals and objectives in the context of ongoing activities and routines in the classroom or play groups, for example, there is no single Recommended Practices strand that is comprehensive enough to fully improve their practices in that area. Thus, the best

chapter
11

approach to self-assessment in this case is to identify the Practices across strands that relate to that specific function or activity. We provide two examples of how to assess by program activity in order to assist programs in using a similar process to address needs that do not fit neatly within a single, specific strand (i.e., monitoring children's progress toward their goals, Table 3, and preventing and addressing challenging behaviors, Case Study 2).

Table 3. Practices Associated With "Monitoring Children's Progress Toward Their Goals"

**Practices *Across Strands* Related to
"Monitoring Children's Progress Toward Their Goals"**

I1. Families and professionals, including regular caregivers, work as team members in planning, delivering, and evaluating EI/ECSE services.

I2. All team members participate in the IEP/IFSP process.

A13. Professionals use multiple measures to assess child status, progress, and program impact and outcomes (e.g., developmental observations, criterion/curriculum-based, interviews, informed clinical opinion, and curriculum-compatible norm-referenced scales).

A16. Professionals seek information directly from families and other regular caregivers using materials and procedures that the families themselves can manage to design IFSP/IEP goals and activities.

A24. Professionals assess not only immediate mastery of a skill, but also whether the child can demonstrate the skill consistently across other settings and with other people.

A25. Professionals appraise the level of support that a child requires in order to perform a task.

A26. Professionals choose and use scales with sufficient item density to detect even small increments of progress (especially important for children with more severe disabilities).

A41. Professionals monitor child progress based on past performance as the referent rather than on group norms.

A44. Professionals and families conduct an ongoing (formative) review of the child's progress at least every 90 days in order to modify instructional and therapeutic strategies.

A45. Professionals and families assess and redesign outcomes to meet the ever changing needs of the child and family.

A46. Professionals and families assess the child's progress on a yearly (summative) basis to modify the child's goal-plan.

C14. Data-based decisions are used to make modifications in the practices. Child performance is monitored and data are collected to determine the impact of the practices on the child's progress, and monitoring must be feasible and useful within the child's environments (i.e., ongoing monitoring must be user friendly) and is used to make modifications of intervention if needed.

C16. Children's behavior is recognized, interpreted in context, and responded to contingently, and opportunities are provided for expansion or elaboration of child behavior by imitating the behavior, waiting for the child's responses, modeling, and prompting.

---

chapter

11

What to Do With Information Learned From Self Assessment

The information obtained from the self-assessment must be summarized so that the Team can determine priority needs related to staff development and other program improvement activities. The assessment information can be summarized in a number of different ways. For example, if the Team has self-assessed on the entire set of Recommended Practices, the Team might compare scores across strands to determine the area of most significant need. If, on the other hand, the Team self-assessed on a single strand or by an activity across strands, the Practices might be rank ordered to determine which Practices were most problematic for the program. Figure 2 provides a sample form that can be used to summarize assessment scores by strands so that the Team can then select priority strands and practices on which to work.

Once the assessment information is summarized, it is critical to develop an action plan that identifies not only the priority needs and related activities for addressing those needs but also the supports the Team will need to implement the activities and accomplish the identified goals. The Practices selected from the summary form can be transferred to an action planning form (see Figure 3 for a sample form). Then the Team can complete the action plan (see Chapter 10 for additional information on action planning).

Figure 2

DEC Recommended Practices: Program Assessment Summary Form

Date (Time 1): ....   **Date (Time 2):** ....

Team Members ....

....

Recommended Practices Strand	Total Points From "Program Assessment Form"		Percentage Score From "Program Assessment Form"		Practices Identified for Improvement From "Program Assessment Form"
	Time 1	Time 2	Time 1	Time 2	
Assessment					
Child-Focused Practices					
Family-Based Practices					
Interdisciplinary Models					
Technology Applications					
Policies, Procedures, and Systems Change					
Personnel Preparation					
Total # Across Strands					Total # of points obtained divided by total # of possible points

Figure 3

ACTION PLANNING FORM

Date ....

Objective/Focus Area ....

Team/Work Group Members ....
....

Purpose Statement ....
....

Practices to be Addressed	Action Steps to be Taken	Timelines & Persons Responsible	Resources & Supports Needed	Indicators of Success	Status/Date Completed

Team Meetings

Date .... Present .... Notes ....

Date .... Present .... Notes ....

Date .... Present .... Notes ....

The following questions can help guide programs in prioritizing their program improvement activities:

- Are there strands or practices that need improvement sooner than others?
- Does a practice represent a legal compliance issue?
- What changes would have the greatest impact?
- Is the implementation of some practices necessary for the implementation of other practices?
- Are there resources available to help support the implementation of some practices but not others?
- Are some practices related to other program improvement initiatives?

Case Studies

Two case studies follow: Case Study 1 demonstrates assessing by strand and Case Study 2 demonstrates assessing by activity (one program's approach to dealing with challenging behavior). In both case studies, the Team self-assesses on the Recommended Practices and then develops an action plan to address the needs identified as a result of the program self assessments.

Scoring the Program Assessment

Ratings are assigned to the individual Practices. The "Program Assessment Form" uses the following rating system:

Rating	Number of Points	Key
Fully Implemented	Two (2) points	The Practice is implemented consistently across children, families, teachers, time, and/or settings.
Partially Implemented	One (1) point	The Practice is not implemented consistently across children, families, teachers, time, and/or settings.
Not Implemented	Zero (0) points	The Practice is not currently implemented.
Not Applicable (N/A)	Not included in point total	The item is not relevant to the specific program (e.g., a classroom-based Practice might not be relevant if the program is a home-based program).
Don't Know (D/K)	Not included in point total	Don't know what the Practice means or if it is being implemented (i.e., cannot confidently address this particular practices implementation.)

Case Study 1: Assessing by Practices Strand

The county early childhood program decides to begin their program assessment by looking at all strands. The team completes all the strands of the program assessment form by observing and then discussing their observations, making notes about the Practices, and assigning a rating to each Practice (2 = Fully Implemented, 1 = Partially Implemented, 0 = Not Implemented, N/A = Not Applicable, D/K = Don't Know). They then transfer the ratings and information on Practices identified for improvement to the Summary Form and Graph for Percentage Scores Across Strands. They decide to begin working on the Family-Based Practices strand because their lowest score is on this strand and because their district has made working with families a high priority and is providing schools with extra resources to improve this aspect of their program. They then use the "Action Planning Form" to develop an action plan for these Practices. In subsequent meetings, the team updates their progress on the action plan. This program is going to reassess their progress in six months to determine if they need additional work on the Family-Based Practices or if they can move on to another strand of practices.

DEC Recommended Practices: Program Assessment Form by Strand

Date (Time 1): 9/5–9/10   **Date (Time 2):**

Team Members Marcia (lead teacher), Jose (speech/language), Sarah (PT), Lynn (early childhood special education teacher), Jill (Program Coordinator), Donna (parent)

Purpose Statement To improve our knowledge and practice related to families

Practices	Observations		Status				
			Fully Implemented (2)	Partially Implemented (1)	Not Implemented (0)	N/A	D/K
F1. Family members and professionals jointly develop appropriate family-identified outcomes.	Teachers and therapists come to IEP meetings with some ideas for goals and objectives based on an assessment and ask families to come with some as well. Together, we identify and prioritize goals and objectives.	Time 1	X				
		Time 2					
F2. Family members and professionals work together and share information routinely and collaboratively to achieve family-identified outcomes.	We collaborate with families and share information about their child and the program both informally and formally (e.g., quarterly progress reports, assessment results). We videotape children at the center and send the tape home for parents who can't come to visit. We could improve informed two-way communication.	Time 1		X			
		Time 2					
F3. Professionals fully and appropriately provide relevant information so parents can make informed choices and decisions.	We share information about parents' rights and options in a manner (e.g., written, video, conversation) and language that they are most comfortable with. Not sure they understand it.	Time 1		X			
		Time 2					
F4. Professionals use helping styles that promote shared family/professional responsibility in achieving family-identified outcomes.	We assist families in understanding their role in implementing the IFSP/IEP and teach them how they can work on the objectives within their daily routines and activities using matrices that are developed jointly with the families. We are responsive to families' suggested changes in the program.	Time 1	X				
		Time 2					
F5. Family/professionals' relationship building is accomplished in ways that are responsive to cultural, language, and other family characteristics.	We are responsive to all of our families and have everything translated into Spanish and provide translation services at every meeting. We have also hired a Spanish-speaking interventionist. However, only certain information has been translated for the Vietnamese families.	Time 1		X			
		Time 2					
F6. Practices, supports, and resources provide families with participatory experiences and opportunities promoting choice and decision making.	Meetings take place where parents find it most convenient. During home visits, we ensure that the family has all of the assistance they need to meet their priorities for the rest of the week.	Time 1	X				
		Time 2					
F7. Practices, supports, and resources support family participation in obtaining desired resources and supports to strengthen parenting competence and confidence.	"Parent Education Night" (once each month), electronic and paper newsletters, and our bulletin boards keep parents informed.	Time 1	X				
		Time 2					
F8. Intrafamily, informal, community, and formal supports and resources (e.g., respite care) are used to achieve desired outcomes.	We provide respite care for the parents of infants and toddlers once per week for three hours in the afternoon. We also work with families to identify supports within their families and communities.	Time 1	X				
		Time 2					

Practices	Observations		Status				
			Fully Implemented (2)	Partially Implemented (1)	Not Implemented (0)	N/A	D/K
F9. Supports and resources provide families with information, competency-enhancing experiences, and participatory opportunities to strengthen family functioning and promote parenting knowledge and skills.	We are thinking about starting "Dads' Nights," when the dads meet with a PT and MSW with their children and learn new skills.	Time 1			X		
		Time 2					
F10. Supports and resources are mobilized in ways that are supportive and do not disrupt family and community life.	We offer a flexible schedule for our parent training and support groups. We always ask families if they prefer to meet in their homes, at the center, or at a coffee shop. We also ask what day of the week and time of the day work best for them.	Time 1	X				
		Time 2					
F11. Resources and supports are provided in ways that are flexible, individualized (tailored to the child's and family's preferences and styles), and promote well-being.	Most supports are provided in similar ways for all families.	Time 1		X			
		Time 2					
F12. Resources and supports match each family member's identified priorities and preferences (e.g., mother's and father's priorities and preferences may be different).	Not sure if we do this—should we be asking mothers and dads separately what their priorities are?	Time 1					X
		Time 2					
F13. Practices, supports, and resources are responsive to the cultural, ethnic, racial, language, and socioeconomic characteristics and preferences of families and their communities.	Translation services are provided for really important meetings and documents (e.g., IEP meetings, Rights), but not all.	Time 1		X			
		Time 2					
F14. Practices, supports, and resources incorporate family beliefs and values into decisions, intervention plans, and resources and support mobilization.	Parents' concerns and desires are always solicited and considered for intervention planning. We accommodate all children's dietary restrictions. We do not discount parents' use of alternative treatments; instead we help them to collect data to evaluate their effectiveness.	Time 1	X				
		Time 2					
F15. Family and child strengths and assets are used as a basis for engaging families in participatory experiences supporting parenting competence and confidence.	Most of our experiences for families have focused on skills they want their children to learn instead of on their strengths.	Time 1		X			
		Time 2					
F16. Practices, supports, and resources build on existing parenting competence and confidence.	After parents have been in the program for a while, we ask them to mentor new parents. Support is provided to help parents generalize their existing skills to new situations.	Time 1	X				
		Time 2					
F17. Practices, supports, and resources promote the family's and professional's acquisition of new knowledge and skills to strengthen competence and confidence.	Our parent education network allows for speakers on topics parents and professionals want to learn more about. For example, last month, we held a training on the Picture Exchange System.	Time 1	X				
		Time 2					

Summary for Family-Based Practices

Total number of points obtained	24
Total number of items scored (exclude N/A and D/K)	16
Total number of possible points (total # of items scored multiplied by 2)	32
Percentage score (total # of points obtained divided by total # of possible points)	75%

List Practices (by indicator code) requiring improvement: F2, F3, F5, F9, F11, F12, F13, F15

DEC Recommended Practices: Program Assessment Form by Strand

Date (Time 1): 9/5–9/10   **Date (Time 2):** ....

Team Members Marcia (lead teacher), Jose (speech/language), Sarah (P.T.), Lynn (early childhood special education teacher), Jill (Program Coordinator), Donna (parent)

Recommended Practices Strand	Total Points From "Program Assessment Form"		Percentage Score From "Program Assessment Form"		Practices Identified for Improvement From "Program Assessment Form"
	Time 1	Time 2	Time 1	Time 2	
Assessment	74		80%		Families and professionals collaborate in planning and implementing assessment — A4, A5, A7, A8, A9, A10 Assessment provides useful information for intervention — A22, A24, A25
Child-Focused Practices	42		78%		Adults design environments to promote children's safety, active engagement, learning, participation, and membership — C3, C5, C8 Adults individualize and adapt practices for each child based on ongoing data to meet children's changing needs — C12, C14 Adults use systematic procedures within and across environments, activities, and routines to promote children's learning and participation – C17
Family-Based Practices	24		75%		Families and professionals share responsibilities and work collaboratively — F2, F3, F5 Practices strengthen family functioning — F9 Practices are individualized and flexible — F11, F12, F13 Practices are strengths- and assets-based — F15
Interdisciplinary Models	35		90%		Teams including family members make decisions and work together — I1, I3
Technology Applications	42		95%		Professionals utilize assistive technology in intervention programs with children — T2
Policies, Procedures, and Systems Change	78		91%		Program policies and administration promote family participation in decision making — PS12, PS13, PS15 Program policies and administration promote the use of Recommended Practices — PS19
Personnel Preparation	9		82%		Professionals development activities are systematically designed and implemented – PP65, PP66
Total # Across Strands	316		86%		Total # of points obtained divided by total # of possible points

chapter 11

DEC Recommended Practices: Graph for Percentage Scores Across Strands

Instructions: After completing the "Program Assessment Form" for each strand you wish to assess and the "Summary Form," plot scores by drawing a dot at the correct percentage for each strand. Connect the dots to compare your program across strands. Use a different colored ink to plot program scores at different times.

Date (Time 1): 9/5–9/10   **Date (Time 2):**

Team Members Marcia (lead teacher), Jose (speech/language), Sarah (PT), Lynn (early childhood special education teacher), Jill (Program Coordinator), Donna (parent)

Purpose Statement To improve our knowledge and practice related to families

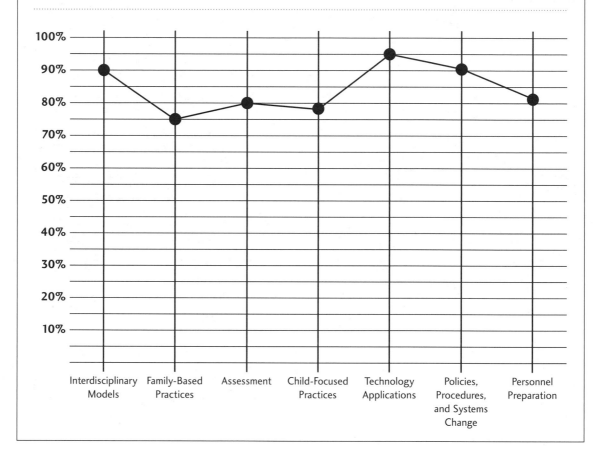

DEC Recommended Practices: Action Planning Form

Date 9/5–9/10

Objective/Focus Area Family-Based Practices

Team/Work Group Members Marcia (lead teacher), Jose (speech/language), Sarah (PT), Lynn (early childhood special education teacher), Jill (Program Coordinator), Donna (parent)

Purpose Statement To improve our knowledge and practice related to families

Practices to be Addressed	Action Steps to be Taken	Timelines & Persons Responsible	Resources & Supports Needed	Indicators of Success	Status/Date Completed
F2, F3, F5	1. Attend training on collaborating with families	By 9/30 — two interventionists/ Director	Financial support for interventionists and the Director to attend the training	Training attended at Regional DEC conference	9/25
	2. Report information back to team and develop next action steps	By 10/20 — see above		Skills from the training related to F2 implemented and data collected from parents indicating improvement	11/20
	3. Identify Vietnamese translator and translate materials	By 11/15 — Program Director	Funds to pay translator	Materials translated into Vietnamese	11/15
F9	Implement a "Dad's Night"	By November — all staff	Staff time, snacks	Dad's Night held	Held Nov. 15
F11, F12, F13	Obtain training and technical assistance on individualizing services: identify consultants and trainers, implement training	by 2/1 — all staff, but Coordinator takes lead	money for trainers and consultants & time for training	new skills implemented and rating on F11, F12, F13 improved	Still working on
F15	1. Generate a list of activities the children are really good at based on parent and teacher input	by 10/1 — teachers	Funding for trainings and child care if parents would like to leave their children at home	List generated	10/5
	2. Plan a training for staff and families on activities their children are strong on. Demonstrate how we can embed objectives into the activities.	by 10/15 — Director		Training on music and movement and on developing and implementing family-guided routines planned	10/15
	3. Conduct training	by 11/1 — parent, teacher, and therapist team		Training attended by 94% of families and all therapists and teachers. Parents and staff evaluate training positively	11/1

Team Meetings

Date 9/10 **Present** Marcia, Jose, Sarah, Lynn, Jill, Donna **Notes** developed action plan

Date 10/20 **Present** Marcia, Jose, Sarah, Lynn, Jill, Donna **Notes** updated action plan, reported on training, planned next training

Date 11/20 **Present** Marcia, Lynn, Jill, Donna **Notes** updated action plan, reported on training, Dad's Night

chapter

11

Case Study 2: Assessing by Program Activity

The Big Mountain Head Start Program staff recently conducted a needs assessment among all staff and identified challenging behavior and children's mental health as a high priority for professional development and training. The mental health consultants reported an increasing number of referrals from classroom staff about individual children with challenging behavior and other mental health needs. In addition, teachers expressed a need for training related to dealing with children with challenging behavior in the classroom. All staff feel like this is a high priority need as it is interfering with learning activities in the classroom. Because of the current emphasis on child outcomes, the program decides that they must address the problem behavior. The staff in each classroom work together to complete the Program Assessment related to preventing and addressing challenging behavior, and assign a rating to each Practice (2 = Fully Implemented, 1 = Partially Implemented, 0 = Not Implemented, N/A = Not Applicable, D/K = Don't Know). An example of one classroom's self-assessment is presented in this case study (see the "Program Assessment Form by Activity").

The Head Start Program has a Leadership Team that, among other tasks, plans professional development activities based on data and input from individual staff. The Leadership Team includes the following members: Macy Arnold (mental health consultant), Lester Gray (Director), Annie Corso (classroom teacher), Elsie Albers (Education Coordinator), Jim Sanchez (classroom assistant), and Cassie Brown (classroom teacher). After reviewing all of the completed Program Assessments related to preventing and addressing challenging behaviors, the Team identifies two major areas on which to focus training:

- Understanding the function of challenging behavior and how it is affected by factors in the environment
- The need for systematic approaches to teaching children social skills and appropriate behaviors

The Team also recognizes the need for program supports for teachers to use when they are having difficulty with an individual child. This information is used to develop an action plan (see the "Action Planning Form").

DEC Recommended Practices: Program Assessment Form by Activity

Date (Time 1): May 11   **Date (Time 2):**

Team Members Macy Arnold (mental health consultant), Lester Gray (Director), Annie Corso (classroom teacher), Elsie Albers (Education Coordinator), Jim Sanchez (classroom assistant), Cassie Brown (early childhood special education teacher)

Purpose Statement Our goal is to prevent challenging behavior by evaluating our environment and routines, teaching expectations, teaching appropriate social skills, and supporting emotional development; and to address persistently challenging behavior by focusing on the function of children's behavior and developing behavior support plans that lead to more socially appropriate behaviors across environments.

Practices	Observations		Fully Implemented (2)	Partially Implemented (1)	Not Implemented (0)	N/A	D/K
A20. Professionals assess the child's strengths and needs across all developmental and behavioral dimensions.	As part of our ongoing assessment, we use the AEPs but we don't directly assess children's behavior. We occasionally make notes about problem behaviors but we don't have a systematic way for collecting data on children's behavior	Time 1		X			
		Time 2					
A21. Families and professionals assess the presence and extent of atypical child behavior that may be a barrier to intervention and progress.	Sometimes when a child has lots of disruptive behaviors, we ask the mental health consultant to come and observe.	Time 1			X		
		Time 2					
A22. Professionals use functional analysis of behavior to assess the form and function of challenging behaviors.	Not really sure what this is	Time 1					X
		Time 2					
C1. Physical space and materials are structured and adapted to promote engagement, play, interaction, and learning by attending to children's preferences and interests, using novelty, using responsive toys, providing adequate amounts of materials, and using defined spaces.	We have spent a lot of time thinking about our classroom and making changes so that children know what to do and so that they play with lots of different things. We think that children have fun in our classroom and that they like to do lots of different things. But we still have some children who wander around the room and don't really do anything. We think they have attention deficit disorder maybe.	Time 1	X				
		Time 2					
C2. The social dimension of the environment is structured and adapted to promote engagement, interaction, communication, and learning by providing peer models, peer proximity, responsive adults, and imitative adults; and by expanding children's play and behavior.	We spend a lot of time playing with the kids and talking to them about what they are doing. We comment on children's play and we give them lots of really positive feedback. But we haven't really thought out using peers as models. Some of the children don't like to play with the children who have lots of aggressive behaviors.	Time 1		X			
		Time 2					
C3. Routines and transitions are structured to promote interaction, communication, and learning by being responsive to child behavior and using naturalistic time delay, interrupted chain procedure, transition-based teaching, and visual cue systems.	Our transitions are really rough sometimes. Children just don't follow directions. No matter what we do, they just don't seem to get it. We really need to figure out how to make these transitions work better. We have tried lots of different things but nothing seems to work.	Time 1			X		
		Time 2					

chapter 11

Practices	Observations		Status				
			Fully Implemented (2)	Partially Implemented (1)	Not Implemented (0)	N/A	D/K
C4. Play routines are structured to promote interaction, communication, and learning by defining roles for dramatic play, prompting engagement, prompting group friendship activities, and using specialized props.	Even though we do lots of things to teach social skills and we talk a lot about the importance of friendships we don't really teach social skills in any systematic way.	Time 1 Time 2			X		
C10. Interventionists facilitate children's engagement with their environment to encourage child-initiated learning that is not dependent on the adult's presence.	We have lots of problems with children not being involved in activities. Some children just don't seem to get it. They don't select activities during center and they won't sit during circle.	Time 1 Time 2		X			
C11. Environments are provided that foster positive relationships, including peer-peer, parent/caregiver-child, and parent-caregiver relationships.	We really work hard to create a positive atmosphere in our classroom. We try to be really positive with the children and to comment on the things that they do well and encourage the children to do that with each other. We try not to dwell on their mistakes or their problem behaviors. We are always telling parents about their child's accomplishments.	Time 1 Time 2	X				
C13. Practices target meaningful outcomes for the child that build upon the child's current skills and behavior and promote membership with others.	We have spent a lot of time assessing children and developing outcomes for them. However, we haven't really focused on social outcomes because we have been working so much on literacy and math. That has been a big push for our program.	Time 1 Time 2		X			
C15. Recommended practices are used to teach/promote whatever skills are necessary for children to function more completely, competently, adaptively, and independently in the child's natural environment. These skills should include teaching those that maximize participation and membership in home, school, and community environments—including those that are typical or similar to other persons' in that environment. Attention should be given to the breadth and sophistication of the child's skills.	Again, we have focused more on pre-academic skills and less on social skills. While we try to really teach each child in a way that they learn best, it is hard to do that with so many children with so many different skills. We also have focused on what children do at school and have not spent as much time thinking about their skills in other settings.	Time 1 Time 2		X			
C16. Children's behavior is recognized, interpreted in context, and responded to contingently, and opportunities are provided for expansion or elaboration of child behavior by imitating the behavior, waiting for the child's responses, modeling, and prompting.	We really try to respond to children's behavior so that we are teaching them new skills that are based on what they are interested in and what they are learning. We don't teach real direct because we think it is important to follow the child's lead and teach based on their interests.	Time 1 Time 2		X			
C18. Practices are used systematically, frequently, and consistently within and across environments (e.g., home, center, community) and across people (i.e., those who care for and interact regularly with the child).	We do a lot of teaching at school but we have not really done much in other environments. We try to share information with families but we don't know what they do with that information.	Time 1 Time 2		X			
C21. Consequences for children's behavior are structured to increase the complexity and duration of children's play, engagement, appropriate behavior, and learning by using differential reinforcement, response shaping, high-probability procedures (i.e., behavioral momentum), and correspondence training.	We don't really know what these procedures are.	Time 1 Time 2					X

Practices	Observations		Status				
			Fully Implemented (2)	Partially Implemented (1)	Not Implemented (0)	N/A	D/K
C22. Systematic naturalistic teaching procedures such as models, expansions, incidental teaching, mand-model procedure, and naturalistic time delay are used to promote acquisition and use of communication and social skills.	We do a lot of modeling and expansions but not the other things.	Time 1		X			
		Time 2					
C23. Peer-mediated strategies are used to promote social and communicative behavior.	We don't really do this.	Time 1			X		
		Time 2					
C24. Prompting and prompt fading procedures (e.g., modeling, graduated guidance, increasing assistance, time delay) are used to ensure acquisition and use of communicative, self-care, cognitive, and social skills.	We aren't sure about these.	Time 1					X
		Time 2					
C25. Specialized procedures (e.g., naturalistic strategies and prompt/prompt fading strategies) are embedded and distributed within and across activities.	We aren't sure about these.	Time 1					X
		Time 2					
C26. Recommended instructional strategies are used with sufficient fidelity, consistency, frequency, and intensity to ensure high levels of behavior occurring frequently.	We aren't sure about these.	Time 1					X
		Time 2					
C27. For problem behaviors, interventionists assess the behavior in context to identify its function, and then devise interventions that are comprehensive in that they make the behavior irrelevant (child's environment is modified so that problem behavior is unnecessary or precluded), inefficient (a more efficient replacement behavior is taught), and ineffective (i.e., reinforcement and other consequent events are used).	Sometimes our mental health person does this.	Time 1		X			
		Time 2					

Summary for Preventing and Addressing Challenging Behavior

Total number of points obtained	13
Total number of items scored (exclude N/A and D/K)	15
Total number of possible points (total # of items scored multiplied by 2)	30
Percentage score (total # of points obtained divided by total # of possible points)	43%

The Team identified the following practices as the highest priority: A20-A22, C3, C4, C21, C23. The Team will develop an action plan for these practices. Once this is accomplished, the Team will revise the action plan to address the following practices that need improvement: C2, C10, C13, C15, C16, C18, C22, C24, C25, C26, C27.

chapter
11

DEC Recommended Practices: Action Planning Form

Date May 15

Objective/Focus Area Challenging Behavior

Team/Work Group Members Macy Arnold (mental health consultant), Lester Gray (Director), Annie Corso (classroom teacher), Elsie Albers (Education Coordinator), Jim Sanchez (classroom assistant), Cassie Brown (early childhood special education teacher

Purpose Statement Our goal is to prevent challenging behavior by evaluating our environment and routines, teaching expectations, teaching appropriate social skills, and supporting emotional development; and to address persistently challenging behavior by focusing on the function of children's behavior and developing behavior support plans that lead to more socially appropriate behaviors across environments.

Practices to be Addressed	Action Steps to be Taken	Timelines & Persons Responsible	Resources & Supports Needed	Indicators of Success	Status/Date Completed
A20–A22	1. Obtain written information on functional analysis of behavior. 2. Obtain training on assessment related to understanding behavior and assessing social skills. 3. Obtain technical assistance to be provided in the classrooms.	By 9/30—Lester Gray	Financial support to attend training Identify trainer and provide financial support for technical assistance	1. PowerPoint presentation obtained. 2. Two teachers and Director attended training at regional DEC conference. 3. TA provider from county has visited classrooms twice. 4. We have learned how to do A20-22	9/1 9/25 10/15 3/15
C3	1. Assess current strengths and weaknesses during transition times. 2. Obtain information on use of visual schedules.	By 9/20—assess environment, Elsie Albers By 10/20—improve use of visual schedules or other supports.	Time for Elsie to observe classroom transitions and collect information Time to make visual schedules	1. Classroom observations completed. 2. Picture schedules completed for both classrooms.	9/20 10/5
C4	Obtain training on using play to promote social skills.	By 12/15—go to training	Resources to go to DEC Conference	Training obtained and using play to promote social skills. Learned strategies at the DEC Conference.	2/15
C21	1. Obtain and watch video on positive consequences. 2. Have technical assistance provider give feedback on use of positive consequences.	By 9/30—watch video By 10/30—obtain technical assistance	Financial support for cost of video Time and financial assistance for technical assistance	1. Video viewed and strategies learned. 2. Using consequences appropriately.	9/30 3/15
C23	1. Watch DEC video. 2. Learn strategies at DEC Conference	By 9/30—watch video By 12/15—attend conference	Cost of video Time and resources to attend conference	1. Video viewed. 2. Strategies implemented from video and conference.	9/30 3/15

Team Meetings

Date 5/15 **Present** Marcy, Lester, Annie, Elsie, Jim, Cassie **Notes** Developed action plan

Date 8/30 **Present** Marcy, Lester, Annie, Cassie **Notes** Planned TA on FAB (A20–A22)

Date 9/15 **Present** Marcy, Lester, Annie, Elsie, Jim, Cassie **Notes** Updated action plan and planned transition activities and how to get resources for DEC Conference attendance

Date 3/15 **Present** Marcy, Lester, Annie, Elsie, Jim, Cassie **Notes** reassessed (Time 2)

Conclusion

As previously indicated, it is optimal to work on all the practices and strands concurrently. However, it may not be feasible or possible for all programs to do so. We suggest that programs consider setting both short-term and long-term goals keeping in mind all the Practices. In addition, it is useful for programs to conduct ongoing program assessment and to make changes in their action plan as they accomplish goals or identify more pressing issues.

This chapter, in combination with Chapter 10, provides information on how to use the DEC Recommended Practices with a specific focus on improving services for young children with disabilities and their families. The information is flexible so that programs can assess their use of the Practices in a way that is consistent with their ongoing mission and priorities. A more complete description of the self-assessment and action planning process related to the DEC Recommended Practices, as well as observation instruments, summary forms, and action planning forms, can be found in the forthcoming book *DEC Recommended Practices: A Program Assessment Workbook* (Hemmeter, Smith, Sandall, & Askew, in press). Regardless of how a team or individual approaches the assessment process, it is important to remember that a high-quality program for young children with disabilities and their families will depend on the consistent and accurate implementation of all of the Recommended Practices.

References

Bredekamp, S., & Copple, C. (1997). *Developmentally appropriate practice in early childhood programs.* Washington, DC: National Association for the Education of Young Children (NAEYC).

Grisham-Brown, J. G., Hemmeter, M. L., & Pretti-Frontczak, K. (in press). *Blended practices for teaching young children in inclusive settings.* Baltimore: Paul H. Brookes.

Hemmeter, M. L., Smith, B. J., Sandall, S., & Askew, L. (in preparation). *DEC recommended practices: a program assessment workbook.*

LaMontagne, M. J., Danbom, K., & Buchanan, M. (1998). *Developmentally and individually appropriate practices.* In L. Johnson, M. LaMontagne, P. Elgas, & A. Bauer (Eds.), *Early childhood education: Blending theory, blending practice* (pp. 83-109). Baltimore: Paul H. Brookes.

Smith, B., & Bredekamp, S. (1998). In L. Johnson, M. LaMontagne, P. Elgas, & A. Bauer (Eds.), *Early childhood education: Blending theory, blending practice.* (Foreword). Baltimore: Paul H. Brookes.

Smith, B., Miller, P., & Bredekamp, S. (1998). Sharing responsibility: DEC-, NAEYC-, and Vygotsky-based practices for quality inclusion. *Young Exceptional Children, 2*(1), 11-20.

chapter

11

Notes

Chapter 12

Checklists for Family Members and Administrators

Mary Louise Hemmeter and Barbara J. Smith

As noted elsewhere in this book, DEC is committed to disseminating the DEC Recommended Practices in a variety of formats in order to address the specific needs of relevant consumers (e.g., parents, teachers, administrators, researchers). This book represents one of many products (both print and nonprint) that have been or will be produced based on the Recommended Practices. This chapter provides two collections of the Practices for family members and administrators, in checklist format. These checklists are offered as *examples* of ways that individuals or teams might use the Practices to examine programs (e.g., parents might use the "Parent Checklist" to determine if a program is a good match for their child) or for program assessment and improvement. Readers also are encouraged to design their own checklists or discussion guides that focus on their particular program development needs and concerns.

Administrator's Essentials: Creating Policies and Procedures That Support Recommended Practices in Early Intervention/Early Childhood Special Education (EI/ECSE)

The Recommended Practices identified in the Policies, Procedures, and Systems Change strand (see Chapter 8) were slightly modified and organized differently to put them into a checklist format. This checklist is appropriate for use by a variety of agencies and individuals who have responsibility for administering and/or supervising early childhood programs, including local program personnel, state departments of education, and lead agencies for infant and toddler programs. This checklist should be used in conjunction with the examples, resources, and glossary in Chapter 8.

Parent Checklist

. . . .

Parents and other family members often request guidance about what to look for or what to think about when selecting or working to improve their child's program of services and supports. For the purposes of this checklist, we identified and reworded some salient practices from all the DEC Recommended Practices related to the quality of programs for young children with disabilities and other special needs. This checklist was co-authored by a parent (Patricia S. Salcedo), reviewed by parents, and revised to incorporate terminology that would be familiar to families.

chapter
12

DEC Recommended Practices in Early Intervention/Early Childhood Special Education

Administrator's Essentials: Creating Policies and Procedures That Support Recommended Practices in Early Intervention/Early Childhood Special Education (EI/ECSE)

Barbara J. Smith

There is a link between program quality and child outcomes. Therefore, programs that employ best practices will positively impact the outcomes of children and families they serve. Implementing Recommended Practices in programs for young children with disabilities and their families requires administrative policies, procedures, and structures that support such practice. For instance, family-based services or services to children in natural settings might require flexible job descriptions and hours of work so that services can be provided in the home or community setting during hours convenient for the family or community program. Recommended Practices also require cutting-edge knowledge and skills through ongoing, job-related training and technical assistance supports. This richness of policies, procedures, and supports will occur only if administrators: (1) are knowledgeable of Recommended Practices in EI/ECSE; (2) share resources with other programs and agencies; and (3) engage in systems change and planning.

This checklist contains Recommended Practices from the Policies, Procedures, and Systems Change strand of *DEC Recommended Practices in Early Intervention/Early Childhood Special Education* (Sandall, Hemmeter, Smith & McLean, 2005; Sandall, McLean, & Smith, 2000) that give specific direction to administrators. However, administrators are encouraged to become familiar with all of the DEC Recommended Practices in order to appropriately serve young children with disabilities and their families.

Administrators, other professionals, and families shape policy at the national, state, and local levels that promotes the use of Recommended Practices in early intervention/early childhood special education. (PS1-PS11)

Examples/Notes:

Are these Practices evident in policy/procedure?   ❏ *Yes*   ❏ *Emerging*   ❏ *No*

Administrators ensure that they and their staff have the knowledge, training, and credentials necessary to implement the DEC Recommended Practices in early intervention/early childhood special education.

- Program coordinators/supervisors have training in early childhood education, early intervention, early childhood special education, and supervision (PS27).

Examples/Notes:

Is this Practice evident in policy/procedure?   ❏ *Yes*   ❏ *Emerging*   ❏ *No*

- Administrators are affiliated with professional early childhood/early childhood special education organizations and encourage staff to maintain their affiliations. Continuing education such as staff attendance at meetings and conferences to enhance professional growth is supported (PS28).

Examples/Notes:

Is this practice evident in policy/procedure?   ❏ *Yes*   ❏ *Emerging*   ❏ *No*

- Program policies provide clear job descriptions and provide for personnel competencies and ongoing staff development, technical assistance, supervision, and evaluation to inform and improve the skills of practitioners and administrators (PS23).

Examples/Notes:

Is this practice evident in policy/procedure?   ❏ *Yes*   ❏ *Emerging*   ❏ *No*

Program policies and administration promote families as partners in the planning and delivery of services, supports, and resources.

- When creating program policies and procedures, strategies are employed to capture family and community voices and to support the active and meaningful participation of families and community groups including those that are traditionally underrepresented (PS12).

  Examples/Notes:

  Is this practice evident in policy/procedure? ❑ *Yes*   ❑ *Emerging*   ❑ *No*

- Program policies create a participatory decision-making process of all stakeholders including individuals with disabilities. Training in teaming is provided as needed (PS13).

  Examples/Notes:

  Is this practice evident in policy/procedure? ❑ *Yes*   ❑ *Emerging*   ❑ *No*

- Program policies ensure that families understand their rights including conflict resolution, confidentiality, and other matters (PS14).

  Examples/Notes:

  Is this practice evident in policy/procedure? ❑ *Yes*   ❑ *Emerging*   ❑ *No*

- Program policies are examined and revised as needed to ensure that they reflect and respect the diversity of children, families, and personnel (PS15).

  Examples/Notes:

  Is this practice evident in policy/procedure? ❑ *Yes*   ❑ *Emerging*   ❑ *No*

chapter

12

reproducible

Permission to copy not required—distribution encouraged.

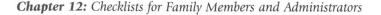

- Program policies are provided in sufficient detail and formats so that all stakeholders understand what the policy means (PS16).

  Examples/Notes:

  Is this practice evident in policy/procedure? ❑ *Yes* ❑ *Emerging* ❑ *No*

- Program policies require a family-centered approach in all decisions and phases of service delivery (system entry, assessment procedures, Individualized Family Service Plan (IFSP)/Individualized Education Program (IEP), intervention, transition, etc.) including presenting families with flexible and individualized options for the location, timing, and types of services, supports, and resources that are not disruptive of family life (PS17).

  Examples/Notes:

  Is this practice evident in policy/procedure? ❑ *Yes* ❑ *Emerging* ❑ *No*

- Program policies provide for the dissemination of information about program initiatives and outcomes to stakeholders (PS18).

  Examples/Notes:

  Is this practice evident in policy/procedure? ❑ *Yes* ❑ *Emerging* ❑ *No*

Program policies and administration promote the use of DEC's and other recommended practices.

- Program policies reflect recommended practices including personnel standards, child-staff ratios, group size, case loads, safety, assistive technology, and EI/ECSE services and practices. Incentives, training, and technical assistance to promote the use of recommended practices in all settings are provided (PS20).

  Examples/Notes:

  Is this practice evident in policy/procedure? ❑ *Yes* ❑ *Emerging* ❑ *No*

chapter

12

reproducible

- Program policies establish accountability systems that provide resources, supports, and clear action steps to ensure compliance with regulations and to ensure that recommended practices are adopted, utilized, maintained, and evaluated; resulting in high quality services (PS19).

  Examples/Notes:

  Is this practice evident in policy/procedure?   ❑ *Yes*   ❑ *Emerging*   ❑ *No*

- Program policies support the provision of services in inclusive or natural learning environments (places in which typical children participate such as the home or community settings, public and private preschools, child care, recreation groups, etc.). Strategies are used to overcome challenges to inclusion (PS21).

  Examples/Notes:

  Is this practice evident in policy/procedure?   ❑ *Yes*   ❑ *Emerging*   ❑ *No*

- Program policies ensure that the IFSP/IEP is used on a regular and frequent basis to determine the type and amounts of services, the location of services and the desired outcomes (PS22).

  Examples/Notes:

  Is this practice evident in policy/procedure?   ❑ *Yes*   ❑ *Emerging*   ❑ *No*

- Program policies ensure that family supports, service coordination, transitions, and other practices occur in response to child and family needs rather than being determined by the age of the child (e.g., b-2, 3-5). (PS24).

  Examples/Notes:

  Is this practice evident in policy/procedure?   ❑ *Yes*   ❑ *Emerging*   ❑ *No*

chapter 12

reproducible

Permission to copy not required—distribution encouraged.

- Program policies ensure that multiple instructional models are available to meet the individual needs of children (e.g., less structure to more structure, child-driven to teacher-driven, peer-mediated to teacher-mediated, etc.) (PS25).

  Examples/Notes:

  Is this practice evident in policy/procedure? ❏ *Yes* ❏ *Emerging* ❏ *No*

- Administrators provide for a supportive work environment (e.g., hiring and retention policies, compensation and benefits, safety, workspace, etc.) (PS26).

  Examples/Notes:

  Is this practice evident in policy/procedure? ❏ *Yes* ❏ *Emerging* ❏ *No*

Program policies and administration promote interagency and interdisciplinary collaboration.

- Program policies include structures and mechanisms such as job descriptions, planning time, training, and resources for teaming resulting in meaningful participation for on-going coordination among professionals, families, and programs related to service delivery including transition (PS29).

  Examples/Notes:

  Is this practice evident in policy/procedure? ❏ *Yes* ❏ *Emerging* ❏ *No*

- Program policies facilitate and provide for comprehensive and coordinated systems of services through interagency collaboration by clearly delineating the components, activities, and responsibilities of all agencies (e.g., joint policies across agencies; collaborative planning on a system, child, and family basis; shared forms and plans etc.) (PS30).

  Examples/Notes:

  Is this practice evident in policy/procedure? ❏ *Yes* ❏ *Emerging* ❏ *No*

chapter

12

reproducible

- Program policies result in families and professionals from different disciplines working as a team developing and implementing IFSPs/IEPs that integrate their expertise into common goals (PS31).

  Examples/Notes:

  Is this practice evident in policy/procedure?   ❏ *Yes*   ❏ *Emerging*   ❏ *No*

Program policies, administration, and leadership promote program evaluation and systems change efforts at the community level.

- A shared vision (of all stakeholders), clear values/beliefs, and an understanding of the culture and context to be changed guide efforts to restructure and reform systems. Decisions about what to change result from regular analysis and evaluation of discrepancies among the vision, beliefs, knowledge, and current practices. (PS33).

  Examples/Notes:

  Is this practice evident in policy/procedure?   ❏ *Yes*   ❏ *Emerging*   ❏ *No*

- Assessment of the interests, issues, and priorities of constituent groups guides the selection and direction of leadership and systems change strategies (PS34).

  Examples/Notes:

  Is this practice evident in policy/procedure?   *Yes*   *Emerging*   *No*

- Leadership and systems change efforts produce positive outcomes for children, families, and communities that are responsive to their needs. Evaluation data are used to ensure: (a) service utilization, (b) more efficient and effective supports for children, families, and staff, and (c) appropriate systems change leadership and strategies (PS35).

  Examples/Notes:

  Is this practice evident in policy/procedure?   ❏ *Yes*   ❏ *Emerging*   ❏ *No*

---

chapter

12

reproducible

Permission to copy not required—distribution encouraged.

- Leadership capacity, risk taking, and shared decision-making among professionals and families at all levels of the organization are cultivated. (PS36).

  Examples/Notes:

  Is this practice evident in policy/procedure? ❑ *Yes* ❑ *Emerging* ❑ *No*

- Leadership and systems change efforts include attention to: timely job-embedded professional development, funding, program evaluation, accountability, governance, program accreditation, curriculum and naturalistic instruction/supports (PS37).

  Examples/Notes:

  Is this practice evident in policy/procedure? ❑ *Yes* ❑ *Emerging* ❑ *No*

- Leadership and systems change efforts rely on strong relationships and collaboration within and across systems: between consumer and system, across systems that deal with children and families, among components within a system, and among professionals from diverse disciplines (PS38).

  Examples/Notes:

  Is this practice evident in policy/procedure? ❑ *Yes* ❑ *Emerging* ❑ *No*

- Leadership is committed and willing to change organizational structures (staffing, schedules, teaming) to be responsive to individual needs (PS39).

  Examples/Notes:

  Is this practice evident in policy/procedure? ❑ *Yes* ❑ *Emerging* ❑ *No*

chapter

12

reproducible

- Change is institutionalized through the development of coordinated management and accountability systems (PS40).

  Examples/Notes:

  Is this practice evident in policy/procedure? ❑ *Yes* ❑ *Emerging* ❑ *No*

- Resources are provided for program evaluation that occurs along established time points, incorporating appropriate measurable indicators of progress including child and family outcomes and preferences (PS41).

  Examples/Notes:

  Is this practice evident in policy/procedure? ❑ *Yes* ❑ *Emerging* ❑ *No*

- Program evaluation is comprehensive, is multi-dimensional, and incorporates a variety of methods for assessing the progress and outcomes of change. Evaluation efforts take into account differing cultural, contextual, demographic, and experiential perspectives including those of parents and of individuals with disabilities (PS42).

  Examples/Notes:

  Is this practice evident in policy/procedure? ❑ *Yes* ❑ *Emerging* ❑ *No*

- Policies, structures, and practices are aligned to promote systems change. Program policies delineate all components of service delivery and provide for tracking and evaluation of all components, including child and family outcomes, to ensure that recommended practices are implemented as intended (PS32, PS43).

  Examples/Notes:

  Is this practice evident in policy/procedure? ❑ *Yes* ❑ *Emerging* ❑ *No*

chapter

12

reproducible

Permission to copy not required—distribution encouraged.

References

Sandall, S., Hammeter, M. L., Smith, B. J., & McLean, M. E. (2005). *DEC Recommended Practices: A Comprehensive Guide for Practical Application* (2nd ed.). Longmont, CO: Sopris West.

Sandall, S., McLean, M. E., & Smith, B. J. (Ed.). (2000). *DEC recommended practices in early intervention/early childhood special education.* Longmont, CO: Sopris West.

Notes

This checklist is also available free of charge on the DEC Web site at http://www.dec-sped.org. For more information on *DEC Recommended Practices in Early Intervention/Early Childhood Special Education* contact:

Division for Early Childhood (DEC) of the Council for Exceptional Children (CEC)
634 Eddy Avenue
Missoula, MT 59812
Phone: (406) 243-5898
Fax: (406) 243-4730
Web: http://www.dec-sped.org
E-mail: dec@dec-sped.org

To order a copy of *DEC Recommended Practices in Early Intervention/Early Childhood Special Education* contact:

Sopris West
4093 Specialty Place
Longmont, CO 80504
Phone: (800) 547-6747
Fax: (888) 819-7767
Web: http://www.sopriswest.com

Disclaimer

Funding for this publication came in part from grants from the U.S. Department of Education (grant nos. H324M.000051 and H324D.980033). The contents of this checklist do not necessarily reflect the views or policies of the U.S. Department of Education or the University of Colorado at Denver.

IDEAs
that Work
Office of Special Education Programs

The Division for Early Childhood (DEC) assumes no liability or risk that may be incurred as a consequence, directly or indirectly, of the use and application of any of the contents of this material. DEC does not perform due diligence on advertisers or their products or services and cannot endorse or guarantee that their offerings are suitable or accurate.

chapter

12

reproducible

DEC Recommended Practices in Early Intervention/Early Childhood Special Education

Parent Checklist

Mary Louise Hemmeter and Patricia S. Salcedo

This checklist is designed to be used by parents to help evaluate programs for their young child with special needs. While this checklist is based on *DEC Recommended Practices in Early Intervention/Early Childhood Special Education* (Sandall, Hemmeter, Smith & McLean, 2005; Sandall, McLean, & Smith, 2000), it does not include all of the Recommended Practices. This checklist is meant to provide parents with a general overview of a program by highlighting some of the salient practices. Within the checklist, the term *service provider* is used to refer to child care providers, teachers, home visitors, therapists, classroom assistants, and others who work with children and families.

How does the program determine the strengths and needs of my child and family?

- ❑ My child's program provides me with a primary contact person and easy ways to contact that person.

- ❑ My family meets with my child's service providers to talk about how my child is doing, including both strengths and needs.

- ❑ My child's service providers know how important it is to talk with me about my child's interests, abilities, and needs in order to develop an effective program for my child.

- ❑ My family is asked about our resources, concerns, and priorities related to my child's development.

- ❑ My child's service providers work with me to determine my child's strengths and needs.

- ❑ My child's service providers work with me to gather information about my child in a variety of ways (e.g., observe my child in different settings, ask my permission for other agencies' and caregivers' information, interview us, test my child).

reproducible

How do service providers work together with me to meet the needs of my child?

❑ My family makes decisions and works together with my child's service providers with trust and open communication.

❑ My child's service providers from different fields (e.g., physical therapy, speech therapy) teach each other so that each provider can work on all of my child's goals.

❑ My child's services are based on his or her strengths and needs, involve all of the people who regularly care for him or her, and focus on his or her regular routines and activities throughout the day.

❑ My child's services are provided in ways that:
  • Decrease stress in our family;
  • Are flexible;
  • Meet my family's specific needs; and
  • Promote my family's sense of well-being.

❑ My child's services are responsive to my family's values and beliefs, and fit with our culture and home language.

❑ My child's service providers have included my extended family, friends, and community in helping me reach my goals for my child.

❑ My child's and family's services have increased our knowledge and confidence in parenting, decision-making, and our sense of control in meeting our child and family's needs.

How do my child's different environments support his/her learning?

❑ My child's environment is safe, child-friendly, and inviting (e.g., no sharp objects, interesting play areas, enough teachers).

❑ My child's environment contains interesting materials that are appropriate to his/her age and are adapted for his or her abilities, needs, and sense of independence.

❑ My child's environment contains materials that represent different cultures.

❑ My child's environment contains a variety of different types of activities (e.g., small group, large group, centers).

❑ My child's activities are designed for him or her to learn through play with materials, play with other children, and through interactions with adults.

❑ My child's service providers work together to help my child become more independent in all of the settings in which he or she participates, including at home, at school, and in the community.

chapter
12
reproducible

How do the service providers in my child's environments support my child's learning?

❑ The service providers give my child the level of support that meets his or her individual needs (e.g., physically assisting him or her, asking questions, providing models).

❑ The service providers use strategies and supports that relate to my priorities for my child and that I consider helpful.

❑ The service providers encourage the children around my child to help him or her and each other.

❑ The service providers work with my child in a way that focuses on his or her individual goals and objectives.

❑ The service providers try to prevent challenging behaviors by explaining rules, planning interesting activities for the children, decreasing the amount of time my child waits without having something to do, and modeling appropriate social skills.

❑ My child's service providers teach each other and all who work with my child to recognize and respond effectively to his or her cues and behavior.

❑ My child's service providers give me information about ways we can work on my child's goals during my family's typical daily routines and activities.

❑ My child's service providers choose technology that can be available in all the places where my child spends time (e.g., switches connected to toys, choice-making boards, computers) to help him or her learn new skills.

❑ If necessary, my child's service providers teach me how to use technology to access information.

What are the policies of the program, and how are they communicated to families?

❑ Program policies are shared with families in clear and understandable ways.

❑ Families are involved in the development of program policies.

❑ Program policies ensure that families are involved in all aspects of the program (e.g., assessment, curriculum development, professional development and evaluation).

❑ Program policies reflect and are sensitive to the diversity of children and families in the program.

❑ Program policies promote my family's active participation in all decisions and activities concerning my child.

❑ Program policies ensure that my child's program is based on the strengths and needs of my child and family.

❑ Program policies promote the provision of my child's services in our everyday settings and routines.

❑ Program policies promote programs working together to provide services and to support my family's transitions between programs.

chapter

12

reproducible

Permission to copy not required—distribution encouraged.

References

Sandall, S., Hemmeter, M. L., Smith, B. J., & McLean, M E. (2005). *DEC Recommended Practices: A Comprehensive Guide for Practical Application.* (2nd ed.). Longmont, CO: Sopris West.

Sandall, S., McLean, M., & Smith, B. J. (2000). *DEC recommended practices in early intervention/early childhood special education.* Longmont, CO: Sopris West.

Note

This checklist is also available free of charge on the DEC Web site at http://www.dec-sped.org. For more information on *DEC Recommended Practices in Early Intervention/Early Childhood Special Education* contact:

Division for Early Childhood (DEC) of the Council for Exceptional Children (CEC)
634 Eddy Avenue
Missoula, MT 59812
Phone: (406) 243-5898
Fax: (406) 243-4730
Web: http://www.dec-sped.org
E-mail: dec@dec-sped.org

To order a copy of *DEC Recommended Practices in Early Intervention/Early Childhood Special Education* contact:

Sopris West
4093 Specialty Place
Longmont, CO 80504
Phone: (800) 547-6747
Fax: (888) 819-7767
Web: http://www.sopriswest.com

Disclaimer

Funding for this publication came in part from grants from the U.S. Department of Education (grant nos. H324M.000051 and H324D.980033). The contents of this checklist do not necessarily reflect the views or policies of the U.S. Department of Education or the University of Colorado at Denver.

The Division for Early Childhood (DEC) assumes no liability or risk that may be incurred as a consequence, directly or indirectly, of the use and application of any of the contents of this material. DEC does not perform due diligence on advertisers or their products or services and cannot endorse or guarantee that their offerings are suitable or accurate.

chapter

12

reproducible

Concluding Thoughts

Susan Sandall, Mary E. McLean, Barbara J. Smith, and Mary Louise Hemmeter

The purpose of this book is to provide guidance to families and program personnel as they select, develop, implement, and evaluate services and supports for young children with disabilities and their families. In addition, the Recommended Practices offer useful guidelines for those who prepare the personnel who design and offer services and supports. The impact those individuals (e.g., teachers, therapists, service coordinators) have on families' lives is tremendous. In our focus groups, parents often shared stories about such individuals. "I'll never forget her," one mother said of her first service coordinator. One parent described her child's first home visit by saying, " . . . that was the biggest gift." Families also told us how important it was that these individuals be knowledgeable and work together with them.

Our aim in this book is to share the knowledge gained from the integration of the scientific literature with the experience and knowledge of researchers, parents, practitioners, administrators, and personnel trainers. This project has been a self-examination, undertaken by the field, of quality in early intervention/early childhood special education (EI/ECSE). The process was driven by our conviction that there is a link between high-quality programs and positive outcomes for children and families. The Recommended Practices identified from this process, when implemented in programs will, we believe, lead to improved child development and learning and enhanced family functioning.

The impact those individuals (e.g., teachers, therapists, service coordinators) have on families' lives is tremendous.

The DEC Recommended Practices are important. Yet, we know that they will continue to evolve as more scientific evidence is accumulated and as the field and society change. A professional organization must periodically examine the established practices in its professional discipline. With the participation of many, many DEC members and other colleagues we have undertaken such an examination.

Where do we go from here? Our analysis of the themes, practices, and findings derived from the research literature review and the focus groups continues. Throughout this book we've described products and training activities. DEC plans additional education activities. Efforts will focus on dissemination, training, and systems change to meet the promise of high-quality programs for young children with disabilities and their families.

To truly get to know the child, we must also get to know each other, not just as parents and professionals, but as people, too.

Parent Janice Fialka (2001) uses the metaphor of a dance to describe the time, energy, candor, and commitment that are necessary in early intervention/early childhood special education:

> *I believe that if parents and professionals are to be effective in creating marvelous opportunities for our children, then both sets of partners must carve out time to get to know each other's dreams, hopes, fears, constraints, and perspectives. We must take off our own sets of headphones and be willing to hear each other's music, with special attention to and inclusion of the parent's music and unique dance steps. To truly get to know the child, we must also get to know each other, not just as parents and professionals, but as people, too. This is hard work and takes patience, trust, and lots of getting to know each other. It is one of the most significant ways we can make a difference in the lives of our children.* (p. 27).

Reference

Fialka, J. (2001). The dance of partnership: Why do my feet hurt? *Young Exceptional Children, 4*(2), 21-27.

Appendices

● ● ● ● ● ●

Appendix A

Additional Acknowledgments

. . . .

DEC wishes to acknowledge and thank the following individuals for their contributions to the Recommended Practices project:

Literature Coders and Validators
. . . .

Melinda Ault
Meher Banajee
Cindy Bernheimer
Ted Bovey
Bill Brown
Debbie Bruns
P. Kay Nottingham Chaplin
Hsin-Ying Chou
Martha Cook
Leslie Craig-Unkerfer
Sharon Darling
Beth Delaney
Karen Diamond
Cyndi DiCarlo
Glen Dunlap
Sayaka Endo
Dennis Fell
Linda Flynn
Peggy Gallagher
Michael Gamel-McCormick

Mary Francis Hanline
Kathryn Haring
Mary Louise Hemmeter
Debra Reichert Hoge
Eva Horn
Mark Innocenti
Hazel Jones
Debra Judd
Michael Kelley
Jennifer Kilgo
Frank Kohler
Susan Kontos
Maggie LaMontagne
Karen La Paro
Antoinette Jardine Ledet
David Lovett
Bonnie McBride
Jeanette McCollum
Mary E. McLean
Leslie Munson

Samuel L. Odom
Melissa Olive
Jeff Oremland
Richard Roberts
Beth Rous
Diane Sainato
Susan Sandall
John Schuster
Ilene Schwartz
David Sexton
M'Lisa Shelden
Steve Stile
Phillip S. Strain
Bruce Thompson
Carole Torrey
Laura Vagianos
Margaret Werts
Ruth Wolery
Paul Yoder

Focus Groups

Members of Scientific Focus Groups

Members of these focus groups generated recommendations within a particular strand of practices. They are also listed within the strand chapters on which they worked.

Lynette Aytch	Corrine Garland	Jeanette McCollum
Isaura Barrera	Howard Goldstein	Penny Milburn
Gwen Beegle	Lourdes Gonzalez	Richard Roberts
Harriet Boone	Ann Hains	Sharon Rosenkoetter
Barbara Bowman	Marci Hanson	Sarah Rule
Darbi Breath	Eva Horn	Diane Sainato
Pip Campbell	Mark Innocenti	Barbara Schwartz
Michael Conn-Powers	Leslie Jackson	Daphne Thomas
Vivian Correa	George Jesien	Carol M. Trivette
Juliann Woods Cripe	Louise Kaczmarek	Sharon Walsh
Laurie Dinnebeil	Joan Karp	Amy Whitehead
Marilyn Espe-Sherwindt	John Killoran	Mark Wolery
Susan Fowler	Diana LaRocco	Barbara Wolfe
Lise Fox	Esther Leung	
Jim Gallagher	Gerry Mahoney	

Members of Stakeholder Focus Groups on Practices

Members of these focus groups represented family members, practitioners, and administrators and discussed and made recommendations related to practices across all strands.

Linda Brault	Andrea Knowlton	Bruce Orr
Darbi Breath	Jenny Lange	Mike Plotzker
Mary Jane Brotherson	Diana LaRocco	Karen Sullivan
Cyndi DiCarlo	Faye Manaster Eldar	Beth Swedeen
Amy Hicks	Bonnie McBride	Judy Swett
Ellen Hunt-Landry	Donna Miller	Deb Ziegler
Sharon Kilpatrick	Lorna Mullis	

appendix

A

Members of Stakeholder Focus Groups on Format

Members of these focus groups represented family members, practitioners, administrators, and personnel trainers and discussed and recommended best formats for the use and adoption of the DEC Recommended Practices.

Jane Amundson	Joe Hauth	Julie Newman
Mako Arai	Marian Hauth	Mele Olsen
Ellen Browning	Lauren Heller Kerstein	Linda O'Neil
Patricia Caro	Maureen Huguley	Amy Phillpott
Paula Caston	Lucinda Hundley	Ann Riall
Camille Catlett	Tracy Jirikowic	Helen Richards
Renee Charlifue-Smith	Gail Joseph	Linda Tuchman
Terry DeLeonardis	Maureen Kelly	Lizzie Waterson
Corrine Donley	Rita Lee	Fran Wegener
Stephanie Frazier	Desire Loeb-Guth	Amy Whitehead
Ann Hains	Julie Mack	
Kathy Hart	Mary Ann Marchel	

Members of Bridging the Gap Site Teams

Two programs in the Denver, Colorado, area established Systems Change and Direct Services Teams and implemented systematic procedures for adopting the DEC Recommended Practices in order to provide guidance on using the DEC Recommended Practices (see Chapter 10).

Sewall Child Development Center

Systems Change Team

Tiaja Dimas
Sandy Dimmick
Heidi Heissenbuttel
Kathleen King
Wendy Knoble
Cathy Kuffler
Heather Luehrs
Caroline McGregor Macaulay
Tina Myrsiades
Sue Okerson
Barbara Plous
Allen Rheem
Linda Roe
Alissa Rowland
Evelyn Sickle
Erica Stewart
Coleen Truax

Direct Services Team

Dana Choi
Wanda Figueroa-Rosario
Monica Hoffman
Sandy Kull
Becky Lower
Tina Myrsiades
Sue Okerson
Courtney Roy
Sarah Salazar
Kristian Slavick
Anne Tellez

appendix **A**

Douglas County School District

Systems Change Team

Becky Anderson
John Doherty
Liz Grams
Mark Harrell
Mary Johnson
Christy Kopp
Joan LiPuma
Gail Whitman

Direct Services Team

Becky Anderson
Pat Applebaum
Hilary Frazier
Nancy Friedel
Juli Graffeo
Celeste Hodges
Chris Melo
Frank Sanford
John Stanek
Gail Whitman

appendix

A

Appendix B

Selected Federal Laws and Resources Related to Children With Disabilities in Early Childhood Programs

· · · · · · · · · ·

The following information provides guidance on selected federal laws and how early childhood educators and families can work together to meet the needs of children with disabilities in early childhood programs. This information is taken in large part from a DEC/NAEYC brochure entitled "Including All Children: Children With Disabilities in Early Childhood Programs" (DEC & NAEYC, 2000).

What disability-related federal laws are important in meeting the needs of young children with disabilities?

· · · · · · · · · · · · · ·

There are three important federal disability laws that relate to early care and education for young children with disabilities. These laws promote inclusion to the fullest extent and civil rights for individuals with disabilities.

The Americans With Disabilities Act (ADA)

ADA is a federal civil rights law that prohibits discrimination against people who have disabilities. The Act states that people with disabilities are entitled to equal rights in employment; state and local public services; and public accommodations such as schools and early childhood programs, including child care centers, Head Start programs, and family daycare homes.

Section 504 of the Rehabilitation Act

Section 504 prohibits the discrimination against children and adults on the basis of a disability by any program or activity receiving federal financial assistance. These include any public or private preschool, child care center, Head Start/Early Head Start, or family daycare home that receives federal funds either directly or through a grant, loan, or contract.

The Individuals with Disabilities Education Act (IDEA)

IDEA requires states to provide early intervention and a free appropriate public education (FAPE) to eligible children with disabilities. There are three major provisions that apply to early childhood:

- Part B requires that a free appropriate public education be available for children with disabilities ages 3-21 years. Each eligible child receives services under a written Individualized Education Program (IEP).

- Section 619 of Part B authorizes grants to all states for services for children with disabilities ages 3-5 and for continuity of special education services for children moving out of Part C.

- Part C provides all states with grants for early intervention services for children from birth to 3 (and their families) who are: (1) developmentally delayed; (2) at a substantial risk of delay, due to diagnosed factors and conditions; or (3) at state discretion, those at risk due to other factors. Each family and child identified receives services under a written Individualized Family Service Plan (IFSP).

All three of these laws encourage the inclusion of children with disabilities in all early childhood settings. These laws can assist professionals in their continuing efforts to meet the individual needs of each child and family.

What should early childhood educators do to ensure that programs are meeting ADA, Section 504, and IDEA requirements?

For ADA and Section 504, assess the program's accessibility, policies, activities, and materials. Develop action plans to:

- Evaluate the recruitment, enrollment, and employment policies and procedures to make sure they are nondiscriminatory.

- Assess the physical accessibility of the setting. Rearranging furniture or installing a ramp or a handrail may be all that is required.

- Schedule time for staff to meet to develop ways the program includes children with disabilities and to evaluate progress in meeting their needs.

- Look for other ways to accommodate children, staff, and families with disabilities in the setting.

appendix B

For IDEA requirements, make sure to follow the activities and strategies of the Individualized Family Service Plan (IFSP) for infants, toddlers, and their families and the Individualized Education Program (IEP) for older children. Also, if you think a child in your care may have a disability or special need, talk with the family and provide them with contact information for the local school district or early intervention program for an IDEA evaluation.

Young children with disabilities who are eligible under IDEA have a right to services to meet their individual needs. Depending on the child's age, and your state's procedures, either the early intervention program or your local school district should respond to the parent's referral for evaluation. If the child is found eligible for IDEA services, an individualized education plan will be developed with the child's parent(s) and others to determine what services will be provided and where they will be delivered. If you are not involved in the development of the IFSP/IEP, ask for a copy and for training, if needed, to implement the plan.

How can early childhood educators work effectively with families?

Communication with the child's family is paramount. Find out what concerns they may have about their child's development as well as what the child is able to do in the home setting. Make sure that they understand the concerns you have about their child's development as well as your perceptions of the child's strengths.

As a person who spends time with the child, you are in an ideal position to assist the child and family in developing goals and plans to achieve those goals. Your involvement in this process is very important!

Where can I get help?

Help available:

1. Ask the families. Parents know their child better than anyone and may already be familiar with many resources for both services and support.
2. Ask your provider network. Many providers have experience in including children with disabilities.
3. Contact your local child care resource and referral program.
4. Contact your local school district and local early intervention program. They will likely know about training and technical assistance resources.
5. Contact state and local organizations whose members provide services to children with disabilities.

For more information:

ADA Information Line
U.S. Department of Justice
Phone: (800) 514-0301
TDD: (800) 514-0383
Web:
http://www.usdoj.gov/disabilities.htm

The Arc of the United States
1010 Wayne Avenue, Suite 650
Silver Spring, MD 20910
Phone: (800) 433-5255 or
(301) 565-3842
FAX: (301) 565-5342
Web: http://www.thearc.org
E-mail: info@thearc.org

*Architectural and Transportation Barriers
Compliance Board
(Access Board)*
Phone: (800) 872-2253 or
(202) 272-0080
FAX: (202) 272-0081
TDD: (800) 993-2822 or
(202) 272-0082
Web: http://www.access-board.gov
E-mail: info@access-board.gov

Child Care Law Center
221 Pine Street, 3rd Floor
San Francisco, CA 94104
Phone: (415) 394-7144
FAX: (415) 394-7140
Web: http://www.childcarelaw.org
E-mail: info@childcarelaw.org

IDEA Resources
Council for Exceptional Children (CEC)
1110 North Glebe Road, Suite 300
Arlington, VA 22201-5704
Phone: (888) CEC-SPED
Web: http://www.ideapractices.org

*National Early Childhood Technical
Assistance Center (NECTAC)*
Campus Box 8040
University of North Carolina
Chapel Hill, NC 27599-8040
Phone: (919) 962-2001
TDD: (919) 843-3269
FAX: (919) 966-7463
Web: http://www.nectac.org

*National Dissemination Center for
Children With Disabilities (NICHCY)*
P.O. Box 1492
Washington, DC 20013-1492
Phone: (800) 695-0285 (Voice/TTY)
FAX: (202) 884-8441
Web: http://www.nichcy.org
E-mail: nichcy@aed.org

*Office of Special Education Programs
(OSEP)*
U.S. Department of Education's Office of
Special Education and Rehabilitative
Services (OSERS)
U.S. Department of Education
400 Maryland Avenue, SW
Washington, DC 20202
Phone: (202) 205-5507
Web:
http://www.ed.gov/about/offices/list/
osers/osep/index.html

National Head Start Association
1651 Prince Street
Alexandria, VA 22314
Phone: (703) 739-0875
FAX: (703) 739-0878
Web: http://www.nhsa.org

appendix
B

Head Start Bureau
The Administration on Children, Youth, and Families
U.S. Department of Health and Human Services
370 L'Enfant Promenade, SW
Washington, DC 20447
Phone: (877) 696-6775
Web:
http://www.acf.hhs.gov/programs/hsb/

Child Care Bureau
The Administration on Children, Youth, and Families
U.S. Department of Health and Human Services
370 L'Enfant Promenade, SW
Washington, DC 20447
Phone: (202) 690-6782
FAX: (202) 690-5600
Web:
http://www.acf.hhs.gov/programs/ccb/

Rehabilitation Engineering and Assistive Technology Society of North America (RESNA)
1700 North Moore Street, Suite 1540
Arlington, VA 22209-1903
Phone: (703) 524-6686
TTY: (703) 524-6639
FAX: (703) 524-6630
Web: http://www.resna.org
E-mail: info@resna.org

The Division for Early Childhood (DEC) of the Council for Exceptional Children (CEC)
634 Eddy Avenue
Missoula, MT 59812
Phone: (406) 243-5898
FAX: (406) 243-4730
Web: http://www.dec-sped.org
E-mail: dec@dec-sped.org

National Association for the Education of Young Children (NAEYC)
1509 16th Street, NW
Washington, DC 20036-1426
Phone: (800) 424-2460 or
(202) 232-8777
Web: http://www.naeyc.org
E-mail: naeyc@naeyc.org

Reference

Division for Early Childhood (DEC) and National Association for the Education of Young Children (NAEYC). (2000). *Including all children: Children with disabilities in early childhood programs* [Brochure]. Washington, DC: National Association for the Education of Young Children (NAEYC). (To order the brochure, please contact NAEYC [address provided above]. Single copies are 50¢ each; 100+ are 13¢ each. NAEYC Order #514.)

appendix

B

Appendix C

List of DEC Position Statements and Concept Papers and DEC Code of Ethics

· · · · · · · · · ·

DEC develops and disseminates position statements and concept papers on issues of importance to the field. The development of position statements and concept papers involves: (1) a determination by the DEC Executive Board that the field would benefit from a DEC position and/or guidance on an issue; (2) input from members on a draft statement; and (3) final paper disseminated to the field as well as use for by the organization for guidance in future activities.

This Appendix includes:

1. A list of DEC Position Statements and Concept Papers
2. The DEC Code of Ethics

All of these documents can be found in their complete form on the DEC Web site at www.dec-sped.org.

Position Statements are brief, formal expressions that have been developed with input from DEC members, reviewed by subdivisions, and approved by the DEC Executive Board. These statements are usually one to two pages in length and address a specific topic or issue. DEC offers position statements on the following topics:

- Position Statement on Interventions for Challenging Behavior
- Position Statement on Developmental Delay as an Eligibility Category
- Position Statement on Responsiveness to Family Cultures, Values, and Languages
- Position Statement on Inclusion
- Position Statement on Personnel Standards for Early Education and Early Intervention
- Position Statement on Addressing Preventive Measures for Disabilities

Concept papers offer an in-depth discussion of a topic on which DEC has taken a position. Concept papers provide guidance for implementation and take into account best practices, research, philosophy, and other relevant issues. Concept papers are developed with input from DEC members, reviewed by subdivisions, and approved by the DEC Executive Board. DEC offers concept papers on the following topics:

- Concept Paper on Identification of and Intervention With Challenging Behavior
- Concept Paper on Developmental Delay as an Eligibility Category

Code of Ethics

Adopted: September 1996
Reaffirmed: April 1999

As members of the Division for Early Childhood (DEC) of the Council for Exceptional Children (CEC), we recognize that in our professional conduct we are faced with choices that call on us to determine right from wrong. Other choices, however, are not nearly as clear, forcing us to choose between competing priorities and to acknowledge the moral ambiguity of life. The following code of ethics is based on the Division's recognition of the critical role of conscience, not merely in preventing wrong, but in choosing among courses of action in order to act in the best interests of young children with special needs and their families and to support our professional colleagues.

As members of DEC, we acknowledge our responsibility to abide by high standards of performance and ethical conduct and we commit to:

1. Demonstrate the highest standards of personal integrity, truthfulness, and honesty in all our professional activities in order to inspire the confidence and trust of the public and those with whom we work;

2. Demonstrate our respect and concern for children and families, colleagues, and others with whom we work, honoring their beliefs, values, customs, and culture;

3. Demonstrate our respect for families in their task of nurturing their children and support them in achieving the outcomes they desire for themselves and their children;

4. Demonstrate, in our behavior and language, that we respect and appreciate the unique value and human potential of each child;

5. Strive for personal professional excellence, seeking new information, using new information and ideas, and responding openly to the suggestions of others;

6. Encourage the professional development of our colleagues and those seeking to enter fields related to early childhood special education, early intervention, and personnel preparation, offering guidance, assistance, support, and mentorship to others without the burden of professional competition;

7. Ensure that programs and services we provide are based on law as well as a current knowledge of and recommended practice in early childhood special education, early intervention, and personnel preparation;

8. Serve as an advocate for children with special needs and their families and for the professionals who serve them in our communities working with those who make the policy and programmatic decisions that enhance or depreciate the quality of their lives;

9. Oppose any discrimination because of race, color, religion, sex, sexual orientation, national origin, political affiliation, disability, age, or marital status in all aspects of personnel action and service delivery;

10. Protect the privacy and confidentiality of information regarding children and families, colleagues, and students; and

11. Reflect our commitment to the Division for Early Childhood and to its adopted policies and positions.

The Division for Early Childhood acknowledges with appreciation the National Association for the Education of Young Children, the American Society for Public Administration, and the Council for Exceptional Children, whose codes of conduct were helpful as we developed our own.

Division for Early Childhood
634 Eddy Avenue
Missoula, Montana 59812-6696
Phone: (406) 243-5898
Fax: (406) 243-4730
Email: dec@dec-sped.org
www.dec-sped.org

PERMISSION TO COPY NOT REQUIRED – DISTRIBUTION ENCOURAGED

Combined Glossary

· · · · · ·

Combined Glossary

Accountability systems. A set of evaluation policies and procedures that are implemented to ensure that practices are in place and the goals are achieved.

Accrediting agencies. Entities at the national or regional level through which higher education teacher education programs (e.g., National Council for the Accreditation of Teacher Education) or colleges/universities (e.g., Southern Association of Colleges and Schools) acquire approval based on specific criteria and a prescribed process.

Acquisition. The initial phase of learning. It refers to learning the basic requirements and movements of a skill or behavior; learning how to do something.

Active engagement. Children manipulating materials and/or interacting with others in ways that promote learning.

Assessment. The process of collecting information, ideally from multiple sources and means, for making informed decisions for individuals, families, and programs.

Assistive devices (or assistive technology). Any item, piece of equipment, or product system, whether acquired commercially, off-the-shelf, modified, or customized, that is used to increase, maintain, or improve functional capabilities of individuals with disabilities.

Authentic assessment. An assessment that examines naturally occurring skills in natural, everyday settings using the child's own toys and activities rather than from something external (e.g., a set of test questions).

Authentic measures. Materials that allow appraisal of functional, useful behavior in natural, routine circumstances.

Behavior. The actions people (children and adults) do; this term refers to both desirable or adaptive actions (e.g., speaking, playing with toys, interacting with peers) and undesirable or challenging actions (e.g., tantrums, aggression, self-injury).

Behavioral momentum. The theoretical principle underlying the effectiveness of the high-probability request procedure, often used as a synonym for the high-probability request procedure.

Coaching. An ongoing, interactive, reciprocal process between a coach and a learner in which the coach supports the learner in applying knowledge and skills when working with children birth through 5 with disabilities/developmental delays and their families. Coaching promotes self-observation and self-correction through a series of conversations and reflections.

Co-instructing. Two or more faculty members/professional development specialists jointly planning, teaching/training, and evaluating courses/inservice activities.

Consistency. The regularity with which a given instructional procedure or intervention practice is used.

Consultative services. A model in which professionals provide training, technical assistance, and/or feedback to those individuals working directly with children (e.g., a consulting physical therapist might work with an early interventionist on issues related to positioning an infant with cerebral palsy).

Contingently. A relationship between two events; if the first occurs, then the second occurs soon thereafter. It usually is associated with adults' responses to children; for example, adults deliver reinforcers contingently, meaning that when the child performs a given behavior, adults quickly respond to that behavior.

Correspondence training. A procedure that reinforces a match (correspondence) between what children say and do. There are several variations of the procedure, including the "plan, do, and review" approach, which involves asking the child what he or she is going to do ("plan"), providing an opportunity for the child to engage in the behaviors listed in the plan ("do"), and after the session asking the child what he or she did ("review"). Reinforcement can be delivered at each step of the procedure.

Curriculum. A planned, sequenced program of study based on knowledge, skills, and disposition standards/competencies.

Curriculum-based (sometimes referred to as curriculum-referenced). A form of criterion-based assessment in which the standards to be achieved are the objectives that comprise the program of instruction or therapy.

Curriculum-compatible norm-referenced scales. Materials used to assess and compare a child's status with a larger peer group and that provide direct linkage with program curricular goals.

Data-based decisions. Decisions that are made based on the results of collecting, summarizing, and analyzing information about children's performance on their goals.

Delivery formats. The means by which the curriculum is delivered (e.g., face-to-face, interactive television, Web-based).

Differential reinforcement. Providing positive consequences (reinforcers) contingent upon a given behavior for the child and not for other behaviors, or delivering a reinforcer for a behavior in one situation but not in other situations.

Disciplines. A branch of knowledge, service, or teaching. In early intervention and early childhood special education, individuals from multiple professional disciplines provide services. Among these are early childhood education, early childhood special education, speech-language pathology, physical therapy, and occupational therapy.

Distance education (also known as **distance learning** or **distributed learning**). A system in which educator and learner are separated by physical distance.

Distributed. Delivering trials (i.e., opportunities for children to respond) on a given behavior over time with opportunities to perform other behaviors between the trials for the target behavior.

Early intervention/early childhood special education (EI/ECSE). Specialized practices, knowledge, and skills needed to meet the individualized needs of young children with special needs and their families.

Embedded. Identifying times and activities when a child's goals *and* the instructional procedures for those goals can be inserted into children's ongoing activities, routines, and transitions in a way that relates to the context. It involves distributing opportunities to learn goals and apply instructional procedures for those goals across different activities, routines, and transitions of the day.

Engagement. In the broad sense, this term refers to children actively manipulating materials, participating in an activity, or interacting with others in appropriate ways that lead to goal achievement.

Expansions. Listening to what a child says, and after the child speaks, repeating what the child has said and adding new words to the child's statement.

Family-centered. A philosophy or way of thinking that leads to a set of practices in which families or parents are considered central and the most important decision maker in a child's life. More specifically it recognizes that the family is the constant in a child's life and that service systems and personnel must support, respect, encourage, and enhance the strengths and competence of the family.

Fidelity. How accurately a person (usually an adult) uses an instructional procedure or other intervention practice.

Field experiences. Application of skills in ECSE settings prior to student teaching or its equivalent.

Fluency. A phase of learning. It refers to learning how to perform acquired behaviors rapidly, smoothly, and at rates needed to be useful in the child's usual environment.

FM system. One of three types of large area assistive listening systems. The FM system is simply a variation on the commercial FM radio. (The other large area assistive listening systems are the induction loop and the infrared [IR] system.)

Formal support. Formal support networks are made up of professionals (e.g., early interventionists, doctors, teachers, social workers) or organizations (e.g., public health clinics, mental health agencies, child welfare agencies) whose responsibility it is to provide needed social support for children and their families.

Frequency. How often an event occurs in reference to a unit of time. For example, how many times per minute a behavior occurs, or how many times per day a given instructional procedure is used.

Function. The effect the behavior has on the environment or the purpose of the behavior as seen from the child's perspective.

Functional analysis of behavior. A method that uses direct observation and recording of behavior to identify circumstances (antecedents) that may trigger and support (reinforce) problem behavior. Functional assessment provides information for conducting functional analysis, in which environmental variables can be manipulated to test findings of the functional assessment.

Generalization. A phase of learning. It refers to learning to use a skill outside of the context in which it was initially acquired. This is often thought of as performing a behavior in another setting, with other people, and/or with materials different from those used in initial instruction.

Graduated guidance. A response prompting procedure used with chained behaviors (a series of behaviors sequenced together to form a more complex skill). It involves prompting the child with the amount and intensity of prompts needed to ensure the behaviors occur and immediately removing those prompts (but reapplying them as needed) to ensure the series of behaviors are done correctly. As the child becomes more proficient the adult "shadows" (follows) the child, ready to immediately apply and remove prompts as necessary.

Group contingencies. Consequences (usually positive reinforcers) that are delivered to a group. The reinforcers can be provided based on the performance of all members of the group, the performance of a subgroup of the members, or the performance of an individual in the group.

Group friendship activities (also known as **affection training activities**). Involves two major components: First, it involves short discussions with children about the value of having friends and what friends are. Second, it involves adapting usual group games and songs to increase the social and physical contact between children when the games are played or the songs are sung. These songs/games are performed with enthusiasm and excitement and with frequent references to the value of having friends.

Helpgiving. The manner or style in which help or assistance is provided to individuals or families with the intent that the help will have positive consequences for individuals or families.

High-probability procedure. This procedure involves providing reinforcement for relatively easy or readily done behaviors (i.e., high-probability behaviors) before asking the child to engage in a behavior that is less likely to occur. Usually, the adult asks the child to do three or four high-probability behaviors in rapid fashion and provides enthusiastic reinforcement for each before quickly asking the child to perform the less likely behavior.

High technology or **high tech.** General terms that are used by researchers and educators. Refers to complex electronic devices such as computers, voice synthesizers, Braille readers, augmentative or adaptive communication (AAC) systems, and environmental control units.

IDEA. The Individuals with Disabilities Education Act. IDEA is the major federal education law providing funding for early intervention and education services and rights and protections for children with disabilities birth to 21 and their families.

Incidental teaching. The environment is structured to increase the probability that a child will initiate to the adult. When the child initiates, the adult requests more elaborate behavior (usually a more elaborate request). If more elaborate behavior is forthcoming from the child, the adult praises the child and responds to the content of the child's initiation. If more elaborate behavior is not forthcoming, the adult prompts the child, allows the child to respond, and then responds to the content of the child's initiation.

Increasing assistance. Another name for the system of least prompts, which involves developing a hierarchy of prompts that are ordered from the least to the most assistance needed to perform a behavior. For each trial, the adult initially gives the child an opportunity to perform the behavior without prompts; if the child does not respond, the adult delivers the least controlling prompt and another opportunity for the child to respond. Again, if the child does not respond or starts to respond incorrectly, the adult delivers the next more controlling prompt. This continues on each trial until the child responds correctly or the most controlling level of prompt is provided.

Indirect services. Services provided to assist the child's learning and development but not provided directly to the child. Consultation or technical assistance provided to the classroom teacher or family member are examples of indirect services.

Individualized Family Services Plan/Individualized Education Program (IFSP/IEP). The written individualized plans for children with disabilities required under IDEA. Individualized Family Services Plans are required for children ages birth to age 3, while Individualized Education Programs (IEPs) are required for children ages three and older.

Informal support. Informal support networks are made up of family, friends, neighbors, church members, association members, coworkers, or others who are not paid to do so but provide social support to children and their families.

Information technology (IT). Includes matters concerned with computer science and technology, and the design, development, installation, and implementation of information systems and applications.

Informed clinical opinion. The use of quantitative and qualitative information to make judgments regarding eligibility or program decisions when child characteristics challenge more direct appraisal. This approach requires some familiarity with the child as well as sufficient professional knowledge for making informed judgments.

Infrastructure. Policies, procedures, and organizational structure that guide all programmatic, fiscal, personnel, and administrative decisions.

Inservice. The process of providing ongoing professional development for professionals and paraeducators in a specific discipline with the outcome being enhanced professional practice.

Instructional strategies. Methods used to facilitate the acquisition of knowledge, skills, and dispositions. Methods are matched to learning outcomes with more passive methods employed to convey knowledge (e.g., lectures, discussions, media) and more interactive methods used to support the acquisition of skills and dispositions (e.g., role plays, simulations, case studies).

Instructional technology. Any item, piece of equipment, or product that is used to increase, maintain, or improve the functional capabilities of a child with a disability.

Intensity. As it relates to instructional procedures or practices, this term refers to how often a given procedure or practice is used (in one setting or in multiple settings). As it relates to the totality of intervention, this term often refers to the number of hours of intervention per week and the number of weeks of intervention.

Interagency collaboration. Cooperative activities between/among agencies or programs.

Interdisciplinary model. An approach in which members of a team employ their own perspectives and materials but who reach decisions collaboratively.

Interrupted chain procedure. A procedure that is implemented during a behavior chain (i.e., a series of behaviors sequenced together to form a more complex skill). The adult interrupts the child's performance of the chain to provide an opportunity for the child to do a target behavior—often a communicative behavior. The adult looks expectantly at the child after interrupting the chain.

Item density. The number of assessment items within an age or developmental range; greater density permits finer detection of change.

Least intensive. A device that requires the least amount of work from the child for the same gain as a device that requires extensive work.

Least intrusive. The arrangement of instructional procedures that provides the minimum amount of assistance required for the child to perform the skill or behavior.

LISTSERV. An automatic mailing list server. When an e-mail is addressed to a LISTSERV, it is automatically broadcast to everyone on the list.

Low technology or low tech. General terms that are used by researchers and educators. Refers to more simple devices, supports, systems, and adaptations such as custom-designed hand tools; positioning devices; and other simple, inexpensive, easy-to-use devices.

Maintenance. A phase of learning. It refers to continuing to perform behaviors that have been acquired after instruction on those behaviors has stopped.

Mand-model procedure. This procedure involves observing the child's focus of attention, asking a non-yes/no question (i.e., a mand) of the child about the focus of his or her attention, and waiting for an answer from the child. If no answer is forthcoming, then a model of the answer is provided. The procedure is embedded into children's play or interactions.

Modeling. An instructional strategy in which skills are demonstrated (e.g., use of prompts, use of reinforcement, storytelling).

Models. This term is used in two distinct ways. First, it refers to the people (adults, other children) who perform behaviors one wants a given child to imitate. Second, it refers to the behavior of another (an adult or peer) that is done with the intention that the child will imitate the behavior. When used in this second way, models often are prompts provided to show children how to do a target behavior.

Natural learning environments. Settings in which children without disabilities spend time. Common places include the home, child care programs, family daycare homes, and in community settings (e.g., stores, barber's shops, doctor's offices, parks, etc.) and programs (e.g., children's hour at the library, gymnastics classes, etc.) available to all children in the society. Activities and routines may need to be adapted to ensure that children with disabilities are able to be integral members of the activity or routine.

Naturalistic time delay. A procedure implemented during children's ongoing interactions with the environment and at a point in which adult assistance or help has been regularly given in the past. It involves the adult waiting (delaying the help) for the child to initiate a target behavior at the point when help has regularly been given. During the delay, the adult looks expectantly at the child. If the child does not initiate during this delay, the adult provides a prompt (i.e., the regularly occurring help) and allow the child to continue the sequence.

Organizational structures. Definable units and/or processes around which personnel and practices are organized. Examples include the configuration of staff into teams, the schedules used to organize the flow of services; the administrative units that comprise an organization (e.g., offices, regions, buildings, programs); and/or an interagency council that provides an organizational structure for multiple agencies and programs to work together.

Participation. Being a part of the activities and routines of any setting in which children spend time. Children's involvement in the activities and routines may need to be adapted to ensure they are able to be an integral member of the activity or routine.

Peer-mediated strategies. A collection of procedures, all of which involve using peers to promote the behavior of a child with disabilities. This may involve having peers model specific behaviors for the child with disabilities to imitate, it may involve teaching the children to initiate social interactions to the child with disabilities, it may involve teaching the children to respond to social initiations by the child with disabilities, it may involve teaching children to tutor the child with disabilities.

Performance competencies. The knowledge, skills, and dispositions that guide the curriculum and identify what program completers must know and be able to do.

Play sequences. Play that involves more than one step (e.g., for a child playing in housekeeping: [1] pick up a doll, [2] feed the doll with a bottle, and [3] burp the doll).

Practitioner-action research. Research conducted by ECSE providers in an applied setting (e.g., home-based early intervention, preschool classroom) for the purpose of answering a question(s) specific to the program.

Preservice. Postsecondary programs at the two-year, four-year, or graduate level that lead to entry-level preparation in the field of study and result in a degree and/or licensure in that field.

Professional associations. Membership organizations on the national and state level that provide various member services and leadership/advocacy for the respective discipline(s) represented by the organization (e.g., Division for Early Childhood of the Council for Exceptional Children, National Association for the Education of Young Children, American Physical Therapy Association).

Prompt fading. The process by which teacher assistance (prompts) is removed when teaching children specific skills. Several systematic procedures exist for delivering and removing prompts, including simultaneous prompting, constant time delay, progressive time delay, system of least prompts (increasing assistance), and graduated guidance.

Prompting/prompt strategies. Any assistance or help given by another person (usually an adult) to assist children in knowing how to do a given behavior or to perform a target behavior in the presence of a target stimulus. Prompts take many forms, including verbal cues or hints, gestures, models of the target behavior, pictures, partial physical prompts, and full physical prompts. Prompts are divided into two broad classes based on their effects on children's behavior: controlling prompts and noncontrolling prompts. Controlling prompts ensure the child will respond correctly when those prompts are delivered, and noncontrolling prompts increase the probability of correct responses but do not ensure correct responding.

Public policy. The rules and standards that are established in order to allocate scarce public resources to meet a particular social need. Policy includes documents, mechanisms, and processes.

Reflection. Systematic and ongoing review, critical analysis, application, and synthesis of knowledge, skills, and dispositions specific to working with children birth through 5 with disabilities/developmental delays and their families.

Reinforcement. A consequence for a behavior that increases the probability that the behavior will occur more frequently, with more intensity, or for longer durations. Positive reinforcement involves adding something to the environment (e.g., praise, access to a toy), and negative reinforcement involves removing something from the environment (e.g., allowing a child to leave an area after putting a toy on the shelf).

Replacement behavior. A behavior that is more adaptive than a regularly occurring behavior yet fulfills the same function (produces the same effect) as the regularly occurring behavior. An adaptive behavior can be taught to replace a problematic or challenging behavior (e.g., teaching a child to say, "my toy" when a peer takes his or her toy rather than biting the peer), and a more complex adaptive behavior can be taught to replace a less complex adaptive behavior (e.g., teaching a child to say, "bye-bye" rather than just waving when the child leaves for the day).

Response shaping. This procedure involves reinforcing successive approximations of a target behavior. Initially, the child's current behavior is reinforced until it occurs consistently, and then a slightly more complex variation of the behavior is reinforced and the original form of the behavior is not reinforced. Over time, progressively more complex forms of the behavior are reinforced and the less complex forms are not reinforced.

Role acceptance. The willingness and ability to learn skills from other members of the team.

Role release. The willingness and ability to share control over a professional/occupational activity in order to facilitate in others the learning of one's knowledge and skills.

Screening. A rapid process for identifying individuals who require closer examination for possible disabilities or special needs. Screening is only used to determine further assessment, and not for diagnosis or placement.

Search engine (Internet). A type of software that creates indexes of databases or Internet sites based on the titles of files, key words, or the full text of files.

Service delivery models. Options for bringing professional assistance, information, or involvement to selected settings or locations (e.g., home- or center-based).

Social support. Information, advice, guidance, and material assistance provided by members of the social network. Social networks are unique from one person to another or one family to another. Members may include other family members, friends, professional helpers, members of one's church or temple, etc.

Stakeholders. People or representatives of groups of people who will be affected by a decision or practice.

Systems change. An approach to both program and system improvement that focuses on: (1) the development and interrelationship of all the main components of the program or system simultaneously, and (2) understanding the culture of the program or system as a basis for changing the system.

Time delay. This term refers to three different strategies. First, it refers to an adult waiting for a child to initiate a behavior, often during interactions or play. Second, constant time delay refers to a procedure in which the adult initially provides sufficient help (a prompt) for a child to perform correctly and then on subsequent trials delays the assistance for a fixed (constant) number of seconds. Third, progressive time delay refers to a procedure in which the adult initially provides sufficient help (a prompt) for a child to perform correctly and then on subsequent trials gradually (progressively) increases the time before giving help. With both constant and progressive time delay procedures, correct responses (prompted or unprompted) are reinforced.

Transdisciplinary model. An approach in which team members share responsibilities and information to the extent that one team member can assume the role of another. Interventions focus on the whole child and family and are provided by a primary service provider. In home-based services, the primary service provider is a home visitor. For classroom-based services, it is the teacher. Children's goals and objectives are integrated in meaningful ways into a single plan. Specialists share their knowledge and skills, especially with the primary service provider and family members. Professionals provide guidance; they trust the regular caregivers to implement the interventions effectively.

Transition-based teaching. A procedure in which a single opportunity to perform a target behavior is delivered to the child at the onset of a transition from one activity or area to another; it can be delivered when the child initiates a transition or when a transition is initiated by an adult. Often, a prompt is needed to get the child to perform the behavior, but the natural consequence is continuing with the transition.

Visual cue systems. The use of stimuli children can see (e.g., objects or pictures) to communicate to children what behaviors are expected or to signal changes in activities and identify the upcoming activity.